DECOLONIZING RESEARCH

DECOLONIZING RESEARCH

INDIGENOUS STORYWORK AS METHODOLOGY

Edited by Jo-ann Archibald Q'um Q'um Xiiem,
Jenny Bol Jun Lee-Morgan and Jason De Santolo

BLOOMSBURY ACADEMIC
LONDON • NEW YORK • OXFORD • NEW DELHI • SYDNEY

BLOOMSBURY ACADEMIC
Bloomsbury Publishing Plc
50 Bedford Square, London, WC1B 3DP, UK
1385 Broadway, New York, NY 10018, USA
29 Earlsfort Terrace, Dublin 2, Ireland

BLOOMSBURY, BLOOMSBURY ACADEMIC and the Diana logo
are trademarks of Bloomsbury Publishing Plc

First published in Great Britain, 2019
Reprinted 2020 (twice), 2021
This edition published by Bloomsbury Academic, 2022
Reprinted 2023

Index by Rohan Bolton
Cover design by Steve Leard
Cover photo © Penny Tweedie/Panos Pictures/Felix Features

A catalogue record for this book is available from the British Library.

A catalog record for this book is available from the Library of Congress.

ISBN: HB: 978-1-7869-9461-5
PB: 978-1-3503-4817-2
ePDF: 978-1-7869-9462-2
eBook: 978-1-7869-9463-9

Typeset in Plantin and Kievit by Swales and Willis Ltd, Exeter, Devon

Printed and bound in Great Britain

To find out more about our authors and books visit
www.bloomsbury.com and sign up for our newsletters.

To Indigenous storytellers of the past, present, and future who have kept and will keep Indigenous stories at the core of the heart, mind, body, and spirit so that Indigenous storywork may flourish.

CONTENTS

ABOUT THE EDITORS

Jo-ann Archibald Q'um Q'um Xiiem is a scholar and educational prac-titioner from the Stó:lō and St'at'imc First Nations in British Columbia, Canada. She is Professor Emeritus in the Educational Studies Department at the University of British Columbia (UBC) Faculty of Education. She was previously the Associate Dean of Indigenous Education, and the Director of NITEP (UBC's Indigenous Teacher Education Program). She is the author of *Indigenous Storywork: Educating the Heart, Mind, Body, and Spirit* (2008). In 2018, she was appointed officer of the Order of Canada for her substantial work in Indigenous education.

Jenny Bol Jun Lee-Morgan is a scholar and researcher of Waikato-Tainui, Ngāti Mahuta Māori descent, Aotearoa New Zealand. She is Professor of Māori Research, Te Wānanga o Wairaka, Unitec. Prior to this she was the Deputy Director of the Te Kotahi Research Institute at the University of Waikato. She previously served as the head of the University of Auckland's School of Māori Education (Te Puna Wānanga). Her previous works include *Mahi te Mahi: Inservice to Homeless Whānau* (Lee-Morgan et al., 2018), co-edited book *Decolonisation in Aotearoa: Education, Research and Practice* (Hutchings and Lee-Morgan, 2016) and *Jade Taniwha: Māori-Chinese Identity and Schooling in Aotearoa* (Lee, 2007).

Jason De Santolo is a researcher and creative producer of Garrwa and Barunggam descent from Australia. He is currently Associate Professor Interdisciplinary Indigenous Design at the University of Technology Sydney (UTS), School of Design. He was previously Senior Researcher and Head of New Media at the Jumbunna Institute for Indigenous Education and Research at UTS.

ACKNOWLEDGEMENTS

A heartfelt thanks to all of the contributing authors, as well as your Elders, families and communities who have been so supportive of this work and collaborative endeavour.

We would like to acknowledge Ngā Pae o te Māramatanga, New Zealand's Māori Centre of Research Excellence and the University of Waikato for funding the *pūrākau* and Indigenous storywork research project that has enabled this wonderful collaboration, and this book to be published.

Many thanks to the super team at Te Kotahi Research Institute for their research and administrative support, including organizing our many symposia so that our communities have direct access to our international Indigenous visiting scholars as well as our own Māori academics and researchers and leaders in Aotearoa New Zealand.

Thanks also to Jumbunna Institute for Indigenous Education and Research University of Technology Sydney for supporting the project collaboration and hosting the storytelling gathering in Sydney, Australia.

Special thanks to Dr Maureen Muller who has assisted in the compilation of chapters from across three countries, and completion of the final manuscript.

FOREWORD

Linda Tuhiwai Smith

This book brings together some of the innovative research of Indigenous scholars across three countries – Australia, Canada, and Aotearoa New Zealand – who use *Indigenous Storywork* as a decolonizing methodology. The right, the space, the voice to "tell our own stories from our own perspectives" has been an important aspect of decolonizing knowledge. This volume presents a powerful collection of Indigenous storyworkers who have thought, not just about the power of stories, but, about the power of working with stories, as a means to draw insights and possibilities to Indigenous experiences and knowledge.

We often hear that telling stories and working with stories is a universal experience across all peoples, cultures, and societies. Unfortunately, we mostly hear that version from a dominant perspective that has assumed the right to tell the stories of the colonized and the oppressed that they have re-interpreted, re-presented, and re-told through their own lens. The storywork in this volume addresses many of the subsequent issues that have emerged from the suppression of stories as a way to colonize Peoples. Much more significantly, however, the chapters begin to lay out the contemporary applications of storywork for working in collaboration with Indigenous communities and Indigenous knowledge to gain new insights and show new directions for knowledge making.

Storywork, a term coined by Professor Jo-ann Archibald, tells us that this is not a book of short stories but a book that works with story making and is as much about the principles of making stories to the art of telling stories and to the cultural understandings for making sense of stories. Many Indigenous stories speak from and to a deep understanding and philosophy about humans and their relations, other entities with whom humans have relationships and responsibilities. Many stories speak from and to places of trauma and injustice. Other stories are more disruptive and show alternative understandings that can guide humans to be better humans. Some of the chapters show how new technologies and contemporary cultural practices can become powerful media for storywork that engages with Indigenous youth. The richness of Indigenous stories is only beginning to be developed as a purposeful and scholarly way to create and share knowledge more broadly.

The chapters in this book cover diverse disciplines from mathematics education to literary studies, film aesthetics to legal practices. The introductory chapter is an excellent introduction to the concept of storywork and decolonizing methodologies and the synthesis of different approaches to storywork across Australia, Canada, and Aotearoa New Zealand. The editors have brought together a significant volume of writings that will have wide appeal to those who work with Indigenous knowledge and Indigenous communities as well as to teachers and students of Indigenous knowledge.

INTRODUCTION

Decolonizing research: Indigenous storywork
as methodology

*Jo-ann Archibald Q'um Q'um Xiiem,
Jenny Bol Jun Lee-Morgan and Jason De Santolo*

Indigenous storywork

Jo-ann Archibald Q'um Q'um Xiiem authored the book, *Indigenous Storywork: Educating the Heart, Mind, Body, and Spirit* (2008) as a result of research with Indigenous Coast *Salish/Stó:lō* Elders, cultural knowledge holders, and educators from Indigenous communities in British Columbia, Canada. During the multi-year research process, she became a beginner storyteller to better understand the process of "meaning-making" using Indigenous traditional and life experience stories for educational purposes at all levels of education. In the role of storyteller, she had to learn more about the nature of and protocols for telling and using Indigenous stories, and had to get herself culturally worthy to work with these precious stories. In Coast *Salish* cultural gatherings, the spokesperson who oversees the event says, "My dear ones, the work is about to begin." When we hear these words, we pay attention to the cultural work that is about to take place because we know that we will either be involved in some way or will be impacted by this work. Archibald coined the term, "Indigenous storywork" so that storytellers, story listeners/learners, researchers, and educators can pay better attention to and engage with Indigenous stories for meaningful education and research. The outcomes of Archibald's story research included the development of an Indigenous theoretical, methodological, and pedagogical framework comprising seven principles: respect, responsibility, reverence, reciprocity, holism, interrelatedness, and synergy. For the purposes of this book, the discussion of Indigenous storywork principles will focus on their methodological application.

In a methodological context, the four principles of respect, responsibility, reverence, and reciprocity act as an ethical guide for the researcher to work with Indigenous people, their Indigenous knowledges, and stories. These ethical principles built upon those of Kirkness and Barnhardt (1991) in their article, "First Nations and Higher Education: The Four R's of Respect, Relevance, Reciprocity,

Responsibility," which focused on transforming higher educational systems to be more responsive to Indigenous learners. Archibald adapted their three principles of respect, responsibility, and reciprocity for Indigenous storywork purposes, and added reverence. These four principles place the emphasis on the researcher to become "story-ready." In this story research process the researcher must listen to Indigenous Peoples' stories with respect, develop story relationships in a responsible manner, treat story knowledge with reverence, and strengthen storied impact through reciprocity. The remaining three principles of holism, interrelatedness, and synergy enhance the meaning-making process about Indigenous traditional and lived experience stories. An Indigenous trickster story will exemplify these principles. Coyote is one of the Indigenous tricksters who has become a critical guide for Archibald and others.

Eber Hampton of the *Chickasaw* Nation told a version of the following story at a research conference. He talked about the issues between motives and methods for research. Hampton eventually gave Archibald permission to use this story and to adapt it to suit her cultural context. The trickster name of Old Man Coyote, often shows up in various Indigenous cultural community stories. Now it is Coyote's turn to tell this story.

Coyote's Story: Searching for the Bone Needle

Old Man Coyote (OMC) decided to go hunting for deer to replenish his food supplies. He packed his bag with his hunting and other gear. After a long, unsuccessful day of walking up hills and down valleys and through thick forest, with no deer in sight, he decided to set up his camp for the night by starting a fire for his meal. After supper, he sat by the cozy warm fire and rubbed his tired feet from the long day's walk. He took his favourite moccasins out of his bag and noticed that there was a hole in the toe of one of them. He looked for his special bone needle to mend the moccasin but couldn't feel it in the bag.

Old Man Coyote started to crawl on his hands and knees around the fire, which was blazing by this time, to see if he could see or feel the needle. He went around and around the fire many times. Just then Owl landed next to OMC because he had watched OMC go around and around the fire. He asked OMC what he was looking for. Old Man Coyote told Owl his problem.

Owl said that he would help his friend look for the bone needle. After he made one swoop around the area of the fire, he told Old Man

Coyote that he didn't see the needle. Owl said that if it were around the fire, then he would have spotted it. He then asked OMC where he last used the needle. Old Man Coyote said that he used it quite far away, in the northern direction, to mend his jacket. Owl then asked OMC why he kept going around and around the campfire when the needle clearly was not there. Old Man Coyote replied, "Well, it's easier to look for the needle here because the fire gives off such good light, and I can see better here." (adapted slightly, Archibald, 2008, pp. 35–36)

Often the Indigenous trickster forgets about or ignores the good teach-ings that come from the land, ancestors, families, and communities. Trickster subsequently gets into trouble when the story stops. It is at this juncture that the story listener or researcher is implicitly invited to work with the story and begin making meaning from and with the story. Old Man Coyote had a bone needle, which could symbolize knowledge of Indigenous stories. He did not treat this bone needle respectfully, responsibly, or reverently and could not use it when it was needed. However, OMC has another chance to find and take care of the bone needle. He was fortunate to have a friend such as the Owl, who may symbolize Elders who provide guidance for helping OMC get ready to work with a bone needle.

First, Old Man Coyote will need to stop going around in circles; a similar action is using research methodologies that are not beneficial for Indigenous people, but continue to be used because they are well known (Smith, 2012). He will need to leave the warmth and light of the fire in order to engage in a decolonizing research approach, which requires that he and we ask critical questions about colonial impact, question what is not working, and understand why (Battiste, 2013; Royal Commission on Aboriginal Peoples, RCAP, 1996). OMC will need to prepare himself for a research journey to find the bone needle. This journey may symbolize developing or finding pathways founded in Indigenous methodologies, such as Indigenous storywork. Old Man Coyote may learn to acknowledge and respect the power and beauty of Indigenous stories, take the necessary time to develop trusting and responsible research relationships, use reverential practices to protect the story's and people's spiritual nature, and strive for a reciprocal ben-eficial outcome for Indigenous people, communities, and researchers.

Let's envision that Old Man Coyote and the Owl find the bone needle. They may try to use the bone needle for various purposes and subsequently take better care of it. Understanding the bone needle's function as a tool may be like trying to understand how Indigenous traditional and life experience stories can help people live better lives. Engaging in holistic meaning-making involves using the heart (emotions), mind (intellect), body (physical actions), and spirit (spirituality), as well as recognizing the relationships of these realms to oneself, family, community, land/environment, and wider society. Telling stories in a research context provides time and space for the research participant to tell the story that is pertinent to the situation. The meaning-making process continues when the researcher searches for ideas, seeking an interrelated understanding of historical, political, cultural, social, or other contextual impacts upon Indigenous Peoples, their stories, and their communities. Developing, sharing, and representing these storied understandings requires a synergistic action on the part of the researcher to use applicable Indigenous storywork principles. This sharing may also spark an idea or understanding for the story listener or reader.

A new spark could be, where the fire symbolizes an Indigenous sacred fire that is used in ceremonies where a fire keeper constantly watches over it until the ceremony has concluded and then carefully puts it out. The embers from the sacred fire could be like Indigenous stories that spark our emotions, make us think more deeply, and help us problem solve and take courageous action to overcome the negative legacy of research in Indigenous communities (Royal Commission on Aboriginal Peoples, 1996). We are fortunate to learn from dear Elders who can help us understand their good teachings, many of which were embedded in their traditional stories. We need to learn to listen holistically to their lived stories of experiencing the trauma of Indian residential schools where they were separated from their families and communities during their childhood (Truth and Reconciliation Commission of Canada, 2015). Their resilience and resistance to this form of colonization continues to be inspirational. We have a responsibility to share these storied understandings with others, to keep these embers alive in our heart, mind, body, and spirit, so that the future generations, especially Indigenous children and youth, have opportunities to learn and live Indigenous storywork. Old Man Coyote interjects with a thought that before he can use Indigenous storywork, he must understand why he keeps going around in needless methodological circles. Decolonizing research and decolonizing methodologies have an important role to play in this Indigenizing research journey.

Decolonizing and Indigenous research methodology

[U]ntil the lions have their storytellers, the story of the hunt will always glorify the hunter. (Ngugi wa Thiong'o, 2017)

Drawing on an African proverb, Ngugi wa Thiong'o points out the power of the storyteller, while drawing attention to the relationship between the colonizer and the colonized. Storywork, in our respective Indigenous traditions, was originally never positioned in this binary. Rather, like all peoples, our stories were part of articulating our world, understanding our knowledge systems, naming our experiences, guiding our relationships, and most importantly, identifying ourselves. Without choice, we became the "hunted" in the story of imperialism that framed the grand narrative of Indigenous Peoples.

Through the multifaceted acts and formations of colonialism, the oppression of Indigenous Peoples is evidenced throughout the world. In Canada, Aotearoa New Zealand, and Australia, historic and continued expressions of colonialism include the imposition of terror and violence on our communities, the removal and schooling of our children, the theft and exploitation of our natural land and natural resources, and the debasement of our intellectual, cultural, and economic systems. A critical tool of colonization was research, of which Indigenous story-taking and story-making was a vital part. Colonial Western research of our traditional stories and research stories of our peoples was used to define, destroy, and deter the valuing of Indigenous knowledge, people, and practices. With an objective façade of research, and an assumed position of racial superiority (sometimes with benevolent intent) on the part of the researcher, the story-takers and story-makers usually misrepresented, misappropriated, and misused our Indigenous stories. More than a theft of cultural property, this "research" was an intellectual, cultural, and spiritual invasion that cast Indigenous characters in particular roles, framed from the vantage point of the "hunter."

"Decolonizing methodologies," as coined by Linda Smith (2012), describes a research approach that recognizes and responds to the historically exclusive and dominant "story" that has emerged from Western "scientific" research, codified within ideologies of imperialism and colonialism. Decolonizing research aspires to re-cover, re-cognize, re-create, re-present, and "re-search back" by using our own ontological and epistemological constructs. However, as Linda Smith points out, such an approach may also use existing research methods, but in ways that attempt to retain the values of the Indigenous communities from which the researchers derive. She states:

> Decolonization ... does not mean and has not meant a total rejection of all theory or research or Western knowledge. Rather, it is about centring our concerns and world views and then coming to know and understand theory and research from our own perspectives and for our own purposes. (2012, p. 39)

Decolonizing research methodologies do not totally dismiss Western methodological approaches; they encourage us as Indigenous researchers to connect research to our own worldviews and to theorize based on our own cultural notions in order to engage in more meaningful and useful research for our people. Indigenous storywork exemplifies this approach by prioritizing the Indigenous principles on which our stories are shared, respected, and treasured.

Given the diversity of Indigenous people and our struggles around the world, decolonizing methodologies and research cannot be reduced to a singular, one-dimensional theory or methodology. Hence, Swadener and Mutua (2008) argue that "decolonizing research does not have a common definition" (p. 33). There is no definitive set of guidelines or methodological practices that researchers can adhere to; rather "scholars engaged in decolonizing research remain constantly mindful of the ways in which the process or outcomes of their research endeavors might reify hegemonic power structures, thereby creating marginality" (2008, p. 33). While decolonizing research must be conducted in a careful, considered, and critical way, Battiste (2000) suggests Indigenous scholarship extends further. She describes:

> the agenda of Indigenous scholarship, which is to transform Eurocentric theory so that it will not only include and properly value Indigenous knowledge, thought, and heritage in all levels of education, curriculum, and professional practice but also develop a cooperative and dignified strategy that will invigorate and animate Indigenous language, cultures, knowledge, and vision in academic structures. (p. xxi)

Indigenous scholarship not only promotes transformative action in pursuit of social justice for Indigenous Peoples in academic settings, but also includes the valuing and validating of our own knowledge systems.

Another critical aspect of Indigenous research that is often beyond the purview of academia is our connection with community. According to Taiaiake Alfred (1999), from the *Rotinohshonni* people of the *Kahnawake Mohawk* Territory, the relationship of the researcher to their community is central to understanding one as Indigenous. He contends, "In fact, it is impossible to understand an indigenous reality by focusing on individuals or discrete aspects of culture outside of a community context" (p. xvi). No matter how much knowledge (or qualification) a person accumulates, if the knowledge, research, or stories do not reach the collective consciousness of the wider group, then the person is failing to act in an Indigenous manner. Decolonizing research is not merely ethical research in terms of the requirements of the academy or institutions; more importantly it meets the criteria set by our own communities, who will often sanction the integrity and credibility of the story using their own measures. Linda Smith reminds us that Indigenous groups will ask critical questions connected to issues of ownership and control of research, particularly stories, to ensure researchers are accountable to the collective. While there is a range of dimensions to decolonizing research, Linda Smith states that they all ultimately centre on "the survival of peoples, cultures and languages; the struggle to become self-determining, the need to take back control of our destinies" (2012, p. 142). In this regard, Linda Smith (2012), identifies 25 decolonizing research projects being undertaken by Indigenous communities, of which storytelling, or what we are refer to as storywork, is one.

Indigenous storywork may be considered a genre of decolonizing methodologies that gives voice to the "lions." In the action of giving voice, Indigenous storywork moves to exemplify an Indigenous methodology. Acutely aware of the way in which research as a tool of colonization has scripted our stories with encryptions of hegemonic oppression, Indigenous storywork seeks to rectify the damage and reclaim our ability to story-talk, story-listen, story-learn and story-teach. As a methodology, Indigenous storywork equips our communities not only to voice, listen to, and understand our stories with "respect, reverence, reciprocity and responsibility" (Archibald, 2008), but collectively to become an Indigenous research community across tribal nations, borders, and countries. In this way, we create what Battiste (2000) refers to above as "a cooperative and dignified strategy" – coming together as Indigenous storyworkers participating in a shared dialogue, writing in ways that resonate with each other, identifying common barriers, and arguing for what Indigenous research ought to be. Indigenous storywork as methodology encompasses powerful forms of academic knowledge creation and production, enabling us to collectively assert a space that contests and challenges colonial research conventions. Furthermore, the chapters in this book illustrate the diversity of Indigenous storywork as it relates to our respective peoples and communities, and the multiple sites in which Indigenous storywork as methodology seeks to intervene, reclaim, develop, and heal.

Collective Indigenous storywork methodology

This book collaboration focuses on sharing methodological applications of Indigenous storywork in Turtle Island Canada, Aotearoa New Zealand, and Australia. Storywork educates and heals the heart, mind, body, and spirit, weaving new synergies of transformational change through deep interrelational understanding of story, people and place (Archibald, 2008). It has been passed down through Coast *Salish/Stó:lō* Elders and cultural knowledge holders, and entrusted to Jo-ann Archibald Q'um Q'um Xiiem to share and enact. The immaculate crafting of Indigenous storywork continues to inspire and mobilize so many of us around the world. This book is a tribute to this vision and the power and beauty of enacting Indigenous storytelling for meaningful education and transformational research.

The book gathers the voices of Indigenous storytellers, scholars, researchers, and community members who are harnessing these methodological principles as a reassertion and enactment of dynamic cultural powers for sustainable living, for social justice, for self-determination. Stories, songs, dances, and languages are integral to the global mobilization and collective survival of Indigenous Peoples and our ways of life. As we journey through Western academic and story institutions it is Indigenous storywork that will hold us in a relational embrace with Indigenous resurgences and worldviews. The book moves into creational realms, engaging with diverse practices, opening up the academic endeavour with art and story technologies that are intergenerational and deeply in the moment.

Indigenous storywork across countries

Canada

The four chapters in this section show how the Indigenous storywork principles of respect, responsibility, reverence, reciprocity, holism, inter-relatedness, and synergy were used as methodology to create an ethical research framework; to shape understandings of Indigenous Peoples' stories about worldview, land, relationships, identities; and to strengthen practices in education, film, and community-based research. Each of these chapters shows how the authors as researchers worked with Indigenous Peoples' stories and perspectives in respectful, responsible, reverent, and reciprocal ways so that Indigenous Peoples' traditional and lived stories retained their power and beauty to help others learn from them.

The chapters also exemplify ways to make holistic story-meaning, through heart, mind, body, and spirit connections or interrelated-ness among these realms. Understanding the impact of colonization on people, their families, and communities is a difficult but important part of the holistic meaning-making process. However, Indigenous values, philosophies, resilience, and resistance that are at the core of Indigenous stories help ease the pain of intergenerational trauma that may surface when sharing lived experience stories, especially those of the Canadian Indian residential schools or those who were taken from families and put into mainly non-Indigenous foster homes or adopted out (Royal Commission on Aboriginal Peoples, 1996; Truth and Reconciliation Commission of Canada, 2015). Indigenous knowl-edge embedded in traditional Indigenous stories has been kept alive in Elders' and cultural knowledge holders' hearts, minds, bodies, and spirits, waiting for the time when these stories could shape ethical, good-quality Indigenous research. That time is now. The authors of these chapters created individual and cooperative synergistic research action through learning, using, and adapting the Indigenous story-work principles for their community and professional sites of practice. Maybe these authors should take Old Man Coyote on exciting research journeys to search for more Indigenous storywork bone needles in places such as Aotearoa New Zealand and Australia.

Aotearoa New Zealand

In Aotearoa New Zealand, a range of highly prized Māori narrative forms serve to protect, preserve, and perpetuate cultural knowledge and wisdom. Each narrative genre, whether it be *waiata* (song), *whakatauki* (proverbs), or *pūrākau* (stories), has its own creative style, complex patterns, and cultural characteristics. Carefully constructed and skilfully delivered, Māori narrative practices were "sophisticated ... and refined through creative, diverse frameworks" (Taylor, 1994, p. 97). In the research context, *pūrākau* are not new but are mostly collections of Māori stories, myths, and legends (Best, 1974; Hiroa, 1982; Orbell, 1992; Reed, 2004).

Jenny Lee-Morgan has argued that as one genre of Māori traditional storytelling narratives, *pūrākau* continues to be relevant to research and indeed critical to our identity as Māori (Lee, 2008). In this book, *pūrākau* as a cross-disciplinary research methodology features topics ranging from Māori law to decolonizing gender violation as part of the Indigenous storywork field that is local to Aotearoa New Zealand, in doing so sharing and supporting many of the Indigenous storywork principles set out by Jo-ann Archibald (2008).

The rising interest by researchers beginning to use *pūrākau* across disciplines, as well the interest in critical Māori storytelling in a wide range of contexts, shows a *pūrākau* approach today to be a growing trend (Dickson, 2010; Hutchings & Lee-Morgan, 2016; Le Grice & Braun, 2016; Mikaere, 1995; Pihama et al., 2016; Te Awekotuku, 2003). However, the theory and methodology of *pūrākau*, which provides a framework for analysis, critique, and practice, has not been extended much beyond *pūrākau* as a performative method, which is sometimes poorly understood and reduced to vignettes or case-studies in research, rather than being applied as a unique methodology and pedagogy grounded within a Māori cultural framework. In response, the Aotearoa section of the book features the way in which *pūrākau* as methodology is being developed by Māori scholars across a range of disciplines.

Australia

The five chapters in this section share powerful reflections on the transformative power and beauty of Indigenous story and storytelling. Together they honour the holistic nature of story and storytelling through place and people and action, as healing, as methodology, as decolonization, as mobilization, and assertive self-determination. What emerges is a deep intent to transform the lives of our families, our communities, and to heal and unite our experiences through story and the profound foundational resonance of Indigenous storywork.

Concluding reflections

Indigenous storywork harmonizes the often fraught and contested experience of operating between the super-privileged spaces of higher education and the fourth world suffering of Indigenous Peoples and our communities. Coming together here in this writing collaboration, we begin this prophetic cultural work, weaving deeper shared under-standings of Indigenous storywork as it resonates across oceans, deeply in tune with the rhythm of our lands and the heartbeat of the peoples. Indigenous knowledge pathways offer hope at a time when environ-mental and social crises threaten all life and ways of being on country. This book evokes a clear challenge – it is time for us to go deeper into our own knowledge systems, deeper into our storyworlds. We must now go beyond what has been "discovered"; we must go beyond the colonizing constraints of Western theories and paradigms. Indigenous storywork is action, it is process, it is the seeking of meaning in commu-nity; as Linda Tuhiwai Smith emphasizes, we can only make meaning within the community and not in the four walls of the tiered lecture theatre (Te Kotahi Research Institute, 2014, August 26). Indigenous storywork traverses new theoretical, methodological, and pedagogical realms where Indigenous stories, experiences, and understandings are the core of the meaning-making process. This book grows collective consciousness and harmonizes the truth and power of our ancestral stories – uniting our resurgences and revealing significant cultural resonances across the oceans (Pihama, 2018; Te Kotahi Research Institute, 2017, March 21).

The decolonizing research movement is bursting with an energy that is hard to describe in words alone. Indigenous storywork is acti-vating decolonizing methodologies as dynamic cultural revitalizing strategies to combat assimilation. Indigenous storywork is also creating space and opportunity to develop specific Indigenous methodologies embedded in Indigenous communities. It is embodied and realized fully through a holistic framework of action – deeply connected to Indigenization, revitalization and a return to reverence for Mother Earth and the ceremony of living relational knowledge (Wilson, 2008). We are once again looking into the branches of Indigenous knowl-edge to maintain vigilance in our role as eternal guardians of lands, waters, and stories. Jenny Lee-Morgan's groundbreaking work leads on from Indigenous storywork, illuminating a pathway to understand-ing *pūrākau* (Māori storytelling) as pedagogy, allowing for an emergent space for "Re-presenting *pūrākau* as pedagogy, Re-portraying *pūrākau*, Re-creating *pūrākau* as political, Re-telling *pūrākau* as provocation, Re-storing *pūrākau* as powerful" (Lee, 2015). Storywork illuminates pathways to liberation, harmonizing story research agendas with Indigenous resurgence movements globally.

Indigenous storywork does not take our Elders' generosity of spirit for granted in this space. As our visionaries, as mediators of the knowledge journey and ceremony, there is reverence for our Elders' relational wisdom. We feel, we experience, we take action. Through intellectual and spiritual journeys into story practices we are drawn deeper into the Indigenous way of being. Our bodies soak up, heal, and transform through the emotional resonance of the knowledge journey in Indigenous storywork. Through the interrelational dimensions of storywork we transcend time and space, connecting on deeper levels of understanding with each other, with all living beings, with the earth and the multiverse.

Indigenous storywork expresses encounters with oppressive systems as storied experiences, speaking back as a way to counter the violence of colonial storytelling (Behrendt, 2016). It is here that the synergetic energies of textual encounter harmonize storyteller, story, and audience. Poetic textual encounters are sensory and emotional – they reach across generations and dimensions. For Indigenous scholars, activists, protectors, and allies, the Indigenous theory of storywork is fluid, organic, and inherently place-based. How else can we transcend the Western educational paradigm and the conditions imposed by neoliberal practices that seek to individualize and commodify knowledge? Indigenous storywork is a global family that is mobilizing for grassroots transformation and social justice at the community level.

Indigenous storywork teaches us to pray again, to meditate, to sit with the land, to commune with each other and our lived spaces. The chapters in this book offer insights into the fluidity and transformative potential of Indigenous storywork. It is diverse and responsive, holding resonance in spaces that decolonize literary theory at one scale. It also builds story project-based ethical research frameworks, while at another level it connects story, film, and musical framework, allowing lyrical wisdoms to emerge as liberational bush reggae rhythms. Storywork is of the moment – it is about freedom of existence through story. It is mindfulness in action; reverence spans all markers of tradition, acknowledging that the cave and rock markings of our ancestors are reframed in youth-driven communication ecologies, where mass consumption models constantly unfold into spaces of the media matrix, or as Pua Case expressed it, within the sacred FB (Te Kotahi Research Institute, 2017, May 21). Indigenous storywork opens up to the world of dream and allows ancestral wisdom and voice to ripple through and take shape in story – it is super "decol" and takes us back into our internal bodies, the gut and the emotional centres of our lived experience (Pihama, 2018).

The collaborators in this book have come together in the spirit of Indigenous unity, harmonizing our own knowledge journeys to heal and protect the people; to heal and protect the land. We are all speaking from our hearts, knowing that our actions today enact the timeless and relational storyworlds of our ancestors of tomorrow. For story is the most powerful intergenerational manifestation of hope. The book aims to rekindle pathways back to our home fires. It disentangles us from our entrapment in knowledge institutions. It breathes life into our process of healing and storying, shifting from a reliance on "dead white man theories" towards a clearer and fiercer reclamation of Indigenous meaning-making and lived experience. Our children will not suffer in the dark; these stories light pathways of liberation and hope. Like the arms of our ancient trees of knowledge, Indigenous storywork energizes us to keep reaching to the horizon. We invite you to sit with Indigenous storywork. It is a knowledge journey that harmonizes heart, mind, body, and spirit. It is the tree of life. Indigenous storywork is eternally in play for it is our moment to shine, remembering that:

"My dear ones, the work is about to begin." (Archibald, 2008, p. 4)

References

Alfred, T. (1999). *Peace, power, righteousness: an Indigenous manifesto.* Don Mills, ON: Oxford University Press.

Archibald, J. (2008). *Indigenous storywork: educating the heart, mind, body and spirit.* Vancouver, BC: UBC Press.

Battiste, M. (2000). Introduction: unfolding the lessons of colonization. In M. Battiste (Ed.), *Reclaiming Indigenous voices and*

vision (pp. xvi–xxx). Vancouver, BC: UBC Press.

Battiste, M. (2013). Decolonizing education: nourishing the learning spirit. Saskatoon, SK: Purich Publishing.

Behrendt, L. (2016). *Finding Eliza: power and colonial storytelling.* St Lucia, QLD: University of Queensland Press.

Best, E. (1974). *The Māori as he was.* Wellington, New Zealand:

A.R. Shearer Government Printer.

Dickson, M. (2010). Te Piringa. *Waikato Law Review 18*, 66–71.

Hiroa, R. (1982). *The coming of the Māori*. Wellington, New Zealand: Māori Purposes Fund Board.

Hutchings, J. & Lee-Morgan, J. (Eds.). (2016). *Decolonisation in Aotearoa: education, research and practice*. Wellington, New Zealand: New Zealand Council for Education Research.

Kirkness, V. & Barnhardt, R. (1991). First Nations and higher education: the four R's – Respect, Relevance, Reciprocity, Responsibility. *Journal of American Indian Education 30*(3), 1–15.

Le Grice, J. & Braun, V. (2016). Mātauranga Māori and reproduction: inscribing connections between the natural environment, kin and the body. *AlterNative 12*(2), 151–164.

Lee, J. (2008). *Ako: pūrākau of Māori teachers' work in secondary schools*. Unpublished EdD thesis. Auckland, New Zealand: The University of Auckland.

Lee, J. (2015). *Ako: pūrākau as pedagogy*. Tuia te Ako Conference Te Kete Ika, Lincoln University, Canterbury.

Mikaere, A. (1995). *The balance destroyed: the consequences for Māori women of the colonisation of tikanga Māori*. Unpublished Master's thesis. Hamilton, New Zealand: University of Waikato.

Orbell, M. (1992). *Traditional Māori stories: he kōrero Māori*. Auckland, New Zealand: Reed.

Pihama, L. (2018). *Transforming lives through research*. Indigenous Feminisms Panel: Decolonizing Emotions, University of Washington.

Pihama, L. E., Te Nana, R., Cameron, N., Smith, C. W., Reid, J. & Southey, K.

(2016). Māori cultural definitions of sexual violence. *Sexual Abuse in Australia and New Zealand: An Interdisciplinary Journal 7*(1), 43–51.

Reed, A. W. (2004). *Reed book of Māori mythology*. Auckland, New Zealand: Reed.

Royal Commission on Aboriginal Peoples. (1996). *Report of the Royal Commission on Aboriginal Peoples*. Volume 3: *Gathering strength*. Ottawa, ON: Canada Communications Group.

Smith, L. T. (2012). *Decolonizing methodologies: research and Indigenous Peoples*. (2nd ed.). New York, NY: Zed Books.

Swadener, B. & Mutua, K. (2008). Decolonizing performances: deconstructing the global postcolonial. In N. Denzin, Y. Lincoln & L. T. Smith (Eds.), *Handbook of critical and Indigenous methodologies* (pp. 31–43). Thousand Oaks, CA: Sage.

Taylor, K. M. (1994). *Conversations with Māori women educators: ngā kupu paake a ngā wāhine Māori*. Unpublished Master's thesis. Auckland, New Zealand: The University of Auckland.

Te Awekotuku, N. (2003). *Ruahine: mythic women*. Wellington, New Zealand: Huia.

Te Kotahi Research Institute. (2014, August 26). *Linda Tuhiwai Smith Keynote: He Manawa Whenua Te Kotahi Research Institute, University of Waikato* [Video File]. Retrieved from www.youtube.com/watch?v=BUm3DVsek-I.

Te Kotahi Research Institute. (2017, March 21). *Moana Jackson Keynote: He Manawa Whenua Te Kotahi Research Institute, University of Waikato* [Video File]. Retrieved from www.youtube.com/watch?v=zV2PoRbBQsM.

Te Kotahi Research Institute. (2017, May 21). *Pua Case Keynote: He Manawa Whenua Te Kotahi Research Institute, University of Waikato* [Video File]. Retrieved from www.youtube.com/watch?v=A-BVnkE9lcM.

The Truth and Reconciliation Commission of Canada. (2015). *Truth and Reconciliation Commission of Canada. Honouring the truth, reconciling for the future: Summary of the final report of the Truth and Reconciliation Commission of Canada.* Retrieved from www.trc.ca/websites/trcinstitution/File/2015/Honouring_the_Truth_Reconciling_for_the_Future_July_23_2015.pdf.

Thiong'o, Ngugi wa. (2017). Foreword. In N. Silva, *The power of the steel-tipped pen: reconstructing native Hawaiian intellectual history* (pp. ix–x). Durham, NC: Duke University Press.

Wilson, S. (2008). *Research is ceremony: Indigenous research methods.* Black Point, NS: Fernwood Publishing.

PART I

INDIGENOUS STORYWORK IN CANADA

Jo-ann Archibald Q'um Q'um Xiiem

In Canada, since contact with non-Indigenous Settlers starting in the late fifteenth century, Indigenous Peoples have resisted subsequent government attempts to colonize and obliterate Indigenous Peoples through laws, policies, and programmes that forbade them practising their Indigenous knowledge systems, values, and beliefs and that had assimilationist goals (Royal Commission on Aboriginal Peoples, 1996). The intergenerational impact of this colonial legacy is a major concern, which has strengthened the self-determination movement of Indigenous Peoples[1] to reclaim, revitalize, and reinforce Indigenous cultures, identity, and knowledge systems, of which Indigenous stories are a core part.

Indigenous Peoples are also reclaiming, recovering, and revitalizing their story-based traditions for individual, family, and community healing, educational, justice, and research purposes. Indigenous story-based or storywork methodologies are also emerging as a result. Indigenous graduate students, at both Master's and doctoral levels, are at the forefront of these new but "old" methodologies. New because the Indigenous methodologies are based on specific Indigenous Nations and communities' stories or used in new disciplinary or transdisciplinary areas. Old because traditional Indigenous stories may be used as a methodological framework and/or as an integral part of the methodological process. Old because ways of making meaning with the stories may reflect traditional epistemological, ontological, or philosophical ways. More Indigenous and non-Indigenous faculty members, school-based educators, and Indigenous community members are forming research relationships for projects that place Indigenous stories at the centre of their inquiry. Indigenous lived experience stories are also gaining prominence within methodology to provide a deeper and more authentic perspective of Indigenous knowledge systems, colonial impact, and sovereignty approaches. Learning from Indigenous Peoples across Canada and internationally is also gaining prominence. The chapters in this section are excellent exemplars of emerging Indigenous storywork methodologies.

Following the song of *k'aad 'aww*: using Indigenous storywork principles to guide ethical practices in research – Sara Florence Davidson

Sara Florence Davidson completed a qualitative case study (Stake, 1995) that was guided by the metaphor and story of the *Haida* dogfish mother of the west coast of British Columbia, Canada to explore how identity texts and narrative writing could strengthen adolescents' writing and support adolescents' identity explorations. Davidson realized that this traditional approach to case study offered her very little ethical research guidance. She subsequently used Archibald's (2008) seven Indigenous storywork principles to create an ethical framework that extended beyond university standards for ethical conduct in research. Davidson's chapter outlines how each of the seven Indigenous storywork principles contributed to the ethical framework of her study and also strengthened the relational accountability (Wilson, 2008) of her research practices to the research participants and to the Indigenous community where the research took place. These descriptions illustrate how these principles were operationalized as an ethical framework while also providing examples of how one might operationalize other Indigenous methodologies proposed by other Indigenous scholars (i.e. Kovach, 2009; Wilson, 2008). The *Haida* dogfish mother story as a metaphor not only describes the way that Davidson engaged with Indigenous storywork as an ethical research framework, but also tells Davidson's research story and how this merging of methodologies invited improvisation, dialogue, and inner reflection to explore the role of stories, ancestry, history, and lived experiences in this research.

Indigenous visual storywork for Indigenous film aesthetics – Dorothy Christian

Dorothy Christian's doctoral research developed a local Indigenous *Secwepemc-Syilx* theory and understandings about visual storytelling, which were related to her production experiences in the film and television industry. This chapter draws upon her doctoral research. Dorothy Christian's chapter lies within an Indigenous research paradigm that privileges Indigenous knowledge(s) through the experiences, expertise, and stories of Indigenous cultural knowledge holders and visual storytellers. A diverse group of 13 knowledge keepers from the *Anishnabe-Cree*, *Cree-Métis*, *Haida*, *Haudenosaunee (Seneca)*, *Hopi*, *Inuit*, and *Secwepemc* First Peoples of Canada and the United States considered differences and commonalities when discussing the relational qualities of land, stories, and cultural protocols. These varied Indigenous worldviews/cosmologies were compared to Archibald's (2008) seven Indigenous storywork principles. Christian's discussions with the Indigenous knowledge keepers shaped her subsequent theoretical and methodological approaches to Indigenous storywork with 17 diverse Indigenous visual filmmakers, which enabled her to extend the film discourse of Indigenous film aesthetics, expand visually sovereign film elements, and to advance the critical role of land, story, and cultural protocols to the place-based political identities of Indigenous visual storytellers. The Indigenous storywork principle of interrelatedness and its relational quality is exemplified in this chapter to show how it guided the analysis and synthesis of the knowledge keepers' and visual filmmakers' stories and knowledges.

Le7 Q'7es te Stsptekwll re Secwépemc: our memories long ago – Georgina Martin and Elder Jean William

Georgina Martin's doctoral research investigated how Canada's colonial control over Indigenous Peoples' individual and collective identities created uncertainty, which was inflicted by legislated interference. The study took place in the *T'exelc* community, which is one of the 17 Indigenous communities of the *Secwepemc* Nation, located in the interior of British Columbia. The collaborative community-based study was led by Georgina Martin and guided by Elder Jean William, both community members. The *Secwepemc* hand drum framed the theoretical and methodological approaches based on Archibald's (2008) Indigenous storywork principles. These principles shaped the cultural protocols necessary to honour and respect story sharing and storytelling. Five of Archibald's (2008) principles – respect, reverence, holism, interrelatedness, and synergy – are addressed in this chapter. Martin and Williams' transformative healing journey and *Secwepemc* epistemic inclusion brought them back to their *Secwepemc* roots to understand how the specificity of their identities, land practices, and stories connected with the wider world of Indigenous knowledges. The cadence of the hand drum and songs drew them inward to experience the memories of their grandparents' teachings, which come alive with the drumming and the singing. The research affirmed how Indigenous Peoples can maintain their cultural identities against the backdrop of government-sanctioned colonial and assimilative practices. Most importantly, the intergenerational process of remembering and telling the stories of long ago is facilitated by cooperative research.

Transformative education for Aboriginal mathematics learning: Indigenous storywork as methodology – Jo-ann Archibald Q'um Q'um Xiiem, Cynthia Nicol, and Joanne Yovanovich

Indigenous storywork, mathematics education, and community-based research provided a rich framework for working with school teachers, Indigenous community leaders and artists, and university professors in the rural and remote community of *Haida Gwaii* along the west coast of British Columbia. Indigenous people constitute 40 per cent of the overall population of this community. The authors, Cynthia Nicol, Joanne Yovanovich, and Jo-ann Archibald, share their methodological reflections, stories, perspectives, and understandings that they gained through this project and their relationships with each other and with community members. Cynthia Nicol, university professor, and Joanne Yovanovich, Indigenous school district/community leader, have worked closely with teachers, community members, and each other on this project for over ten years. Jo-ann Archibald, Indigenous scholar, has continued to work with Cynthia and Joanne on this and related activities.

This research project, known as Transformative Education for Aboriginal Math Learning (TEAM-Learning) had the goal of improving math teaching and learning at kindergarten to grade 12 (K-12) levels in BC, especially for Indigenous students, so that their rates of participation in school math were increased. TEAM-Learning focused on working with K-12 teachers to provide them with professional development opportunities and participatory action research projects, where they learned about culturally responsive approaches to teaching math, became more comfortable with teaching math in general, and learned from Indigenous community members about local Indigenous knowledge. TEAM-Learning grew from a three-year funded research project into an ongoing learning relationship and educational partnership between members of the university and the Indigenous community. Archibald's seven Indigenous storywork principles were used as both a theoretical and a methodological framework for this project. The principles of respect, reverence, responsibility, and reciprocity related to ways of working with people and their Indigenous knowledge (IK). The principles of holism, interrelatedness, and synergy related to how IK and Indigenous stories were used in the research process.

Note

1 The 1.6 million Indigenous Peoples of Canada are very diverse culturally, linguistically, and geographically. The 2016 Canadian Census of Population recorded that approximately 70 Indigenous languages were spoken across Canada, which could be grouped into 12 separate language families (Statistics Canada, 2017). Three major Indigenous groups known as First Nations/Indian, *Métis*, and *Inuit* Peoples constitute "Aboriginal" people as noted in Canada's Constitution Act of 1982 (Section 35). However, Indigenous Peoples prefer to use their own Indigenous names, often written in their Indigenous language. www150.statcan. gc.ca/n1/en/daily-quotidien/171025/ dq171025a-eng.pdf?st=zUdme2XF.

References

Archibald, J. (2008). *Indigenous storywork: educating the heart, mind, body, and spirit.* Vancouver, BC: UBC Press.

Kovach, M. (2009). *Indigenous methodologies: characteristics, conversations, and contexts.* Toronto, ON: University of Toronto Press.

Royal Commission on Aboriginal Peoples. (1996). *Report of the Royal Commission on Aboriginal Peoples.* Volume 3: *Gathering strength.* Ottawa, ON: Canada Communications Group.

Stake, R. (1995). *The art of case study research.* Thousand Oaks, CA: Sage Publications.

Statistics Canada. (2017). *Aboriginal Peoples in Canada: key results from the 2016 Census. Population profile.* The Daily, October 25, 2017. Retrieved from www150.statcan. gc.ca/n1/en/daily-quotidien/171025/ dq171025a-eng.pdf?st=zUdme2XF.

Wilson, S. (2008). *Research is ceremony.* Halifax, NS: Fernwood Publishing.

1 | FOLLOWING THE SONG OF *K'AAD 'AWW*[1]: USING INDIGENOUS STORYWORK PRINCIPLES TO GUIDE ETHICAL PRACTICES IN RESEARCH

Sara Florence Davidson

Introduction

When I began my doctoral programme, I did not intend to use Indigenous methodologies to conduct my research. Because of my mixed Indigenous ancestry and my intention to work with Indigenous students, I believed that I might be challenged in my decision to draw upon a research methodology that could be classified as Western. As a result, I completed coursework that focused on Indigenous perspectives and methodologies in order to be able to fully articulate and defend my decision. My research proposal drew upon the work of Robert Stake (1995) to describe a standard case study that involved interviewing Indigenous and non-Indigenous students from a grade 10 English First Peoples class to explore how identity texts and narrative writing could strengthen adolescents' writing and support adolescents' identity explorations. However, as I conducted this case study, I quickly recognized that the traditional approach to this methodology offered me very little guidance on how to ensure that my research approaches were ethically sound. This resulted in my exploration of the use of the seven Indigenous storywork principles of respect, responsibility, reverence, reciprocity, holism, interrelatedness, and synergy (Archibald, 2008) to create an ethical framework to guide the ethical conduct in my research. I also explored the use of traditional stories to inform my work. When I finally wrote my dissertation (Davidson, 2016), I was guided by our story of the *Haida* dogfish mother of the west coast of British Columbia, Canada.

> There is a story that my father tells when we are about to perform the shark dance. It is about a man who went out to the beach at low tide to "take care of nature," and he heard an unusual sound. When he followed it, he came upon a dogfish mother who had been caught on the outgoing tide. She was in her last throes of life, and her chant was like nothing he had ever heard before. The man memorized her song before returning her to the ocean and it evolved to become the shark dance that we perform today.

When we perform with our *Haida* dance group, the Rainbow Creek Dancers, my father often shares stories about the origin of the songs in the time between the dance performances. This educates the audience about what they are witnessing and gives the dancers time to change into the regalia for the next dance. One of the songs that we perform is called *k'aad 'aww* or the shark dance. When I asked my father for more information about the origin of the song, he told me that in 1980, he hosted a feast, and there he had seen a group of singers from Hydaburg, Alaska, performing the dance. They did not wear masks, but they mimicked the movements of the shark as they danced in a circle. My father was so taken with the performance that he travelled to Hydaburg to ask permission to use the song and to perform the dance. He told me that he asked Helen Sanderson because she was of the *yahgu jaanaas* clan, which owned the song and the dance, and she gave him permission to sing and perform the song and dance (R. Davidson, personal communication, September 29, 2015). According to the *Haida Gwaii* Singers Society (2009), "in 1982, Robert Davidson [my father] traded the Women's Lullaby with the people of Hydaburg at the 'Tribute to the Living Haida' potlatch so that the Massett Haida could use this song once again" (p. 32).

When I was seeking guidance on how to gain permission to use this story in my dissertation, my father told me about the protocols connected with this song. In the story, the man on the beach did not get permission in the same way that my father did. As my father explained, in those days, experiences such as these could be claimed differently. The fact that the man saved the life of the dogfish mother and was inspired by the experience allowed him to claim the right to it. Then later, ownership likely came with an adoption of the experience in a more official capacity. Because this song belongs to my clan, my father felt that I did not need to seek further permission to use it for my research (R. Davidson, personal communication, September 29, 2015).

In her work with Indigenous storywork principles, Jo-ann Archibald (2008) explained:

> There is a "surface story": the text, and the things one has to know about the performance of it for others. The stories are metaphoric, but there are several levels of metaphor involved. The text, combined with the performance, contains a "key" or a "clue" to unlock the metaphor. When a hearer has that story, and knows the narrative sequence of it, there is another story contained within that story, like a completely different embedded or implicit text. (p. 84)

As I sought to find the connection between the various aspects of my study, the story of the dogfish mother returned to me, and I came to recognize that this story could be understood as a surface story. As I worked more closely with the story, I learned how it could be used as a metaphor for the research study. In the same way that the hearer of a story unlocks different levels, I understood the dance and my research more deeply as a result of working with the story. The understanding of each helped me to further understand the other more deeply in a synergistic way.

When I worked with the story as a metaphor, I recognized that, as the researcher, I was the one who was walking on the beach and came upon the dogfish mother. In this interpretation, the dogfish mother represents the participants in this research who must be treated with reverence. This is demonstrated by the fact that the man returned the dogfish mother to the ocean when she had finished teaching him her song. The way the man memorized the chant is the way in which I worked with the participants to understand their perspectives. To continue this metaphor, when the shark dance is performed, the beat of the drum represents the case study research methodology (Stake, 1995) that I used to guide my process and the song represents the Indigenous storywork principles (Archibald, 2008) that I used as an Indigenous ethical framework to guide my conduct.

> When we perform the shark dance, we go out onto the floor and we sway back and forth as the dogfish mother fights the currents above us. We are the foreground, and we complete the illusion that she is travelling through water. Our blankets are her body. When she leaves, we put on our masks and turn around in unison to begin our part of the dance. We separate into individual sharks and dance until the drum beat stops – but the song continues. We turn and then sway to the song as we make our way back off the floor. The drumbeat begins again.

Relational accountability

Shawn Wilson (2008) uses the term *relational accountability* to discuss the topic of ethics in research. I have also chosen to use this term as an overall descriptor for the complete ethical framework that I followed when I conducted this research, because at every stage it was crucial to me to ensure that I maintained respectful relationships. As required by the university, I sought permission from the University of British Columbia's (UBC) Behavioural Research Ethics Board and the school district where the research was conducted. Because I was working with students of Indigenous ancestry, I also sought the permission of the First Nation (Weaver, 1997) to conduct this research. For this community, the role is fulfilled by the Haida Education Council, which was established "to develop a long-term sustained commitment to a partnership between the Haida Communities and the Education Community based on mutual respect and recognition, responsibility, and sharing" (Haida Education Council, n.d.). The Haida Education Council includes *Haida* representatives from the local bands, the Council of the Haida Nation, and the school district and "gives Aboriginal peoples greater influence and control in determining school programs and services for our First Nation students" (Haida Education Council, n.d.).

According to Linda Tuhiwai Smith (2012),

> [F]rom indigenous perspectives, ethical codes of conduct serve partly the same purpose as the protocols which govern our relationships with each other and with the environment. The term "respect" is consistently used by indigenous peoples to underscore the significance of our relationships and humanity. Through respect the place of everyone and everything in the universe is kept in balance and harmony. Respect is a reciprocal, shared, constantly interchanging principle which is expressed through all aspects of social conduct. (p. 125)

Because every aspect of the study was guided by the importance of maintaining strong and respectful relationships, I chose to adopt the perspective that the Indigenous storywork principles contributed to building relationships or developing relational accountability on the part of the researcher. To ensure that this foundational aspect of my research methodology is clearly articulated, I have listed the Indigenous storywork principles of respect, responsibility, reverence, reciprocity, holism, interrelatedness, and synergy and described how each one guided my research practices and enriched my relationships with the participants, the school district, and the community.

Respect

In her description of the Indigenous storywork methodology, Jo-ann Archibald (2008) explained that she began with "the principles of respect for cultural knowledge embedded in the stories and respect for the people who owned or shared stories as an ethical guide"

(p. 36). Though I was not working with traditional stories, I treated the stories that the participants shared with me with the same level of respect that I would use for a traditional story. I recognized that through their stories, the participants were sharing parts of themselves with me. Furthermore, when I was working with the participants, I treated them with the same level of respect as I would an Elder, regardless of their age.

In designing the study, I also incorporated some of the recommendations of Hillary Weaver (1997) for how to engage in respectful research relationships with Indigenous communities, including working with a community that is familiar with me and drawing upon my knowledge of our shared ancestry to ensure that I was respectful throughout both the research process and the dissemination of the findings. She also recommended that researchers have knowledge of the culture of the community, self-awareness, and skills "in determining how to incorporate cultural components into a sound research design" (p. 5).

Responsibility

I recognize that responsibility plays a role at every stage of my research from my first conversation to the last word that I speak about it. I appreciated Jo-ann Archibald's (2008) recognition that she took "responsibility for any mistakes contained in [her] research because those who shared their knowledge with [her] did so with great care and often said that they spoke the truth as they knew it" (p. 24), and I used this as a reminder to remain attentive in my own work. As she later explained, "it is said that you cannot call your words back once they are uttered, and so you are responsible for all which results from your words" (p. 27). Shawn Wilson (2008) also described the importance of responsibility in research:

> As a storyteller, I am responsible for who I share information with, as well as for ensuring that it is shared in an appropriate way, at the right place and time. In receiving the story, you as an active listener are responsible for putting the story into a relational context that makes sense for you and for listening with an open heart and open mind. If you choose to pass along the story or my words, you also take on the responsibilities of the storyteller yourself. (pp. 126–127)

In the story of the dogfish mother, it is not explained how the man gained permission from the dogfish mother to learn her song and share it with others. However, in my own research, I gained permission from the participants to share what they taught me at multiple stages of the study. I recognize that I am sharing their knowledge in another context, in the world of academia, with which they may be unfamiliar. As a result, I have been very vigilant in my work to maintain confidentiality for the participants in the study.

Due to my mixed ancestry, formal education, profession as an educator, and other factors, including the limitations of the term "insider" (Banks, 1998), I do not position myself as such in the context of this research. Nonetheless, because of my familial connections and ongoing visits to the community, I believe that Linda Tuhiwai Smith's (2012) observations about insiders conducting research in their home communities still apply to me. As she noted, "insiders have to live with the consequences of their processes on a day-to-day basis for ever more, and so do their families and communities" (p. 138). She also explained that

> insider research has to be as ethical and respectful, as reflexive and critical, as outsider research. It also needs to be humble. It needs to be humble because the researcher belongs to the community as a member with a different set of roles and relationships, status and position. (p. 140)

A final aspect of responsibility is ensuring that the stories we tell are authentic and accurately reflect the perspectives of the participants in the study (Thomas, 2005) while being entwined with our own perspectives and understandings.

Ensuring authenticity

> In the story of the dogfish mother, the man has a responsibility to do his utmost to ensure that the song he memorizes and teaches others is accurately represented. When I am learning a new *Haida* song, I listen to it and then I practise it and then I sing it with my father. He will often correct me if I am singing it incorrectly. He will continue to practise with me and to correct me until I can sing it properly.

In the story of the dogfish mother, there is no opportunity to check with her to make sure the man has memorized her song correctly – though this would be the best way to ensure we are accurately representing her song. In my study, I was able to check back with the participants to clarify what I understood and thus strengthen the authenticity of my work. In this process, "the [participant] is requested to examine rough drafts of writing where the actions or words of the [participant] are featured, sometimes when first written up but usually when no further data will be collected from him or her" (Stake, 1995, p. 115). Shawn Wilson (2008) also agreed that "authenticity or credibility may be ensured ... through continuous feedback with all the research participants. This allows each person in the research relationship to not only check the accuracy of the analysis but also to elaborate upon ideas" (p. 121). I returned my preliminary understandings to the students, though they did not respond. I also gave all of the participants in the study the opportunity to review the excerpts that I included from their interviews. If they chose, I sent the interview excerpts that I had included in my dissertation to the participants to ensure they were comfortable with how their stories were represented. This was particularly important with the educators who participated, as some of the information they provided in the interviews may have compromised their professional reputations if it was misunderstood. Lastly, I discussed the personal stories and reflections that included historical information with my father to ensure that the information was both accurate and permitted to be shared publicly. Occasionally, I had to rewrite or remove information in these stories based upon his feedback.

Though I was not using storytelling as a methodology, I worked to adopt a similar stance where the participants hold the power and "the 'researcher' becomes the listener or facilitator" (Thomas, 2005, p. 245); this meant that multiple perspectives were represented in my work. In Robert Stake's (1995) view, "most qualitative researchers not only believe that there are multiple perspectives or views of [the case] that need to be represented, but that there is no way to establish, beyond contention, the best view" (p. 108). As a result, he advocated for the presentation of these multiple perspectives for the reader to experience themselves. Despite his assertion that we cannot know the best perspective to share, he still maintained that "we have ethical obligations to minimize misrepresentation and misunderstandings" (pp. 108–109). He further suggested that "the qualitative researcher is interested in diversity of perception, even the multiple realities within which people live" (Stake, 2005, p. 454) and indicated that triangulation could help in identifying these diverse realities. He compared triangulation to navigating a ship and the necessity of using multiple stars to find our way. He completed this analogy with the observation that "our problem in case study is to establish meaning rather than location, but the approach is the same. We assume the meaning of an observation is one thing, but additional observations give us grounds for revising our interpretation" (Stake, 1995, p. 110). In the study, I worked to establish meaning using observations and interviews.

Reverence

In her work with the Elders, Jo-ann Archibald (2008) learned that:

> Storytellers showed reverence through prayer, songs, and the ethical ways that they approached the work with the curriculum staff. Prayer or song helps to create a meeting place for the heart, mind, body, and spirit to interact. Silence creates a respectful space for reverence. (p. 126)

Though Shawn Wilson (2008) worked in a different context, he made a similar observation:

> *Something that has become apparent to me is that for Indigenous people, research is a ceremony.* In our cultures an integral part of any ceremony is setting the stage properly. When ceremonies take place, everyone who is participating needs to be ready to step beyond the everyday and to accept a raised state of consciousness. You could say that the specific rituals that make up the ceremony are designed to get the participants into a state of mind that will allow for the extraordinary to take place. (p. 69; emphasis in original)

Though there were no direct conversations about spirituality, prayer, or ceremony in my study, I brought aspects of reverence to the study through my interactions with the participants. I ensured that I respected their requests and that I honoured their stories and their confidences. As I wrote my dissertation, I continued to hold the highest regard for the people with whom I had worked and did my utmost to ensure that their stories were treated with the reverence that they deserved.

In the fall, following the completion of my dissertation, my father hosted a *gyaa 'isdla*[2] where I gave my research back to the community by gifting framed canvas photographs of the dogfish mother mask to the Council of the *Haida* Nation, band councils, school district, and high schools. I introduced this new research tradition to publicly honour the contributions of the participants and to publicly acknowledge that I do not own this research. I also view this act as an extension of Shawn Wilson's (2008) recognition that research is ceremony.

Reciprocity

In her work with Indigenous storywork, Jo-ann Archibald (2008) emphasized the importance of giving back to the people with whom she was working. This principle of reciprocity, though it was rarely explicitly discussed in her book, was ever-present in all of her interactions with Elders and community members. She explained that one aspect of reciprocity is "sharing this learning with others" (p. 48). Of all of the principles, the commitment to reciprocity was one of the most important for me in my work. The principle of reciprocity closely connects to the notion of contribution – the importance of which was a significant part of my upbringing. Contribution also emerged as a theme in work that I did with my father, learning about traditional *Haida* pedagogical practices (Davidson & Davidson, 2016). Throughout this research, I engaged in reciprocity and made contributions to the community as a researcher, an educator, a facilitator, a presenter, and a community member.

As a researcher

In designing the study, I aligned my questions with both the Aboriginal Education Enhancement Agreement (School District 55 (Pacific Sound[3]), 2012a) and the Achievement Contract (School District 55 (Pacific Sound), 2012b) to ensure that the findings would be useful and relevant to the school district that hosted me. I also committed to sharing the findings with all interested parties, particularly those who were most impacted by the study. Before leaving the community, I attended a meeting to share my findings with the Haida Education Council. The presentation was very well received, and one of the school board trustees expressed appreciation and enthusiasm about using the ethical framework based on Indigenous storywork principles in the policy development for reviewing research proposals for both the school district and local health organizations.

The findings from the study may contribute to improving education for Indigenous and non-Indigenous students who are struggling with print literacy. I also believe that the students in the study may have benefited from the conversations that we had about literacy. As Darryl Bazylak (2002) observed in his study with Indigenous adolescents, it was tremendously beneficial for the students to have the experience of being heard. By participating in the study, I believe the students may have experienced those same benefits and perhaps gained further insights into themselves.

Upon my departure, I donated a class set of novels to the school; these were selected by the principal. I recognize that it may have been more appropriate to share compensation with the individual students who participated in the interviews; however, I was concerned that this might coerce students into participating when they did not wish to do so. Because I was not providing individual compensation to the students, I did not provide individual compensation to the adults who participated in the study.

As an educator

As a certified teacher with nine years of classroom experience, I was able to share ideas with newer educators if it was requested. While I was in the classroom, there were substitute teachers who also covered classes when I was observing, and it was not unusual for them to engage in conversations with me about ways to improve their teaching practices. I would happily have those conversations. I also shared my course units and lesson plans with the two classroom teachers, as neither of them had taught the course prior to that year. I met regularly with the new teacher to discuss planning, classroom management, and assessment strategies – though I was never directly involved with actual student assessment. I also communicated regularly with the Superintendent of Schools and the District Principal of Aboriginal Education to ensure they knew that I was available to help in the district any way that I could.

As a facilitator

While I was doing my research, I was also a teaching assistant for a UBC MOOC (Massive Open Online Course) entitled Reconciliation through Indigenous Education. Because there was an interest at the district administrative level to support educators and other school district employees to complete the course, I worked with the District Principal of Aboriginal Education to facilitate a weekly MOOC working group for school district employees.

Following the first six-week course, the group expressed a continued interest in working with the topics. As a result, I worked with the District Principal of Aboriginal Education to develop and host a series of Tea and Talks. These drop-in sessions were held in communities throughout the district and were open to everyone. They consisted of a presentation by a guest speaker followed by a group discussion period and focused on a range of topics relevant to Indigenous education. The following September, the course was offered again, and I continued my work facilitating a second weekly MOOC working group.

As a presenter

For one of my comprehensive exams, I worked with my father to learn more about traditional *Haida* pedagogical practices. I wrote a paper about what I had learned and also developed a presentation. The District Principal of Aboriginal Education expressed an interest in sharing that presentation with people from the district. At her request, I shared this presentation at one of the Tea and Talks, a principals' meeting, a new teacher orientation, a district math meeting, and a Haida Education Council meeting. We also discussed the possibility of developing the principles from that presentation into a poster that would be available for educators in the district.

As a community member

At the request of the organizers for the Early Learning Forum held in the school district, I opened their event by singing traditional *Haida* songs. Later, I also performed with our *Haida* dance group at a *Haida* chieftainship potlatch on the islands. I share these examples here to demonstrate how reciprocity can look in the context of research. Though I know this was not a requirement for my research, it was an important aspect of my participation in the community. I believe that it influenced my study because it gave the participants and the community the sense that I was not only there to take but also to give.

Holism

According to Jo-ann Archibald (2008),

An Indigenous philosophical concept of holism refers to the interrelatedness between the intellectual, spiritual (metaphysical values and beliefs and the Creator), emotional, and physical (body and behaviour/action) realms to form a whole healthy person. The development of holism extends to and is mutually influenced by one's family, community, band, and nation. (p. 11)

Dwayne Donald (2009) also contended that "we must look at the world holistically and search for regular observable patterns in nature as a way to make sense of the world and our place in it" (p. 13). Though he is referring to a connection with nature, I believe that this connection extends to understanding the wider environment people inhabit in order to understand more about them. In his work with case study, Robert Stake (1995) also emphasized the importance of the context of the case. Further understanding of this context can be achieved through communication with those around the people included in the case; therefore, I talked to others who were familiar with and/or supported the students in the study. This allowed me to gain a more holistic perspective and insights on the students and their literacy experiences.

My commitment to understanding the context by talking to others outside the case was emphasized when I was working through my research proposal for UBC's Behavioural Research Ethics Board approval process. When I had to complete the section that described who would be excluded from my study, I realized very clearly that I did not want to exclude anyone. I believed that if anyone wanted to contribute, I would find a way to honour their contribution. I am grateful that I made that decision, as some unexpected individuals came forward to share with me, and each person provided valuable information with regard to the students in the case study. Listening to the stories of the people who surrounded the students in the case allowed me to understand the students in a more holistic way and provided much of the information about the context of the study. Because I had adopted a more holistic perspective early on in the research, I was better able to anticipate and respond to these contributions.

Interrelatedness

While I was working with the students, particularly during the interviews, I understood that the participants were telling me a story and I was the listener. This experience resonated with Jo-ann Archibald's (2008) observation that "an interrelationship between the story, storytelling, and listener is another critical principle of storywork" (p. 32).

I was incredibly aware of the connection between how the students were telling the story and what lessons I was learning from them. This interrelatedness continued as I worked to transcribe the interviews and new understandings emerged. As I sat with the stories longer, I became increasingly aware of how my own life and experiences shaped my understandings of their stories. The sense of interrelatedness contributed to the reverence and appreciation I had for the participants and their willingness to teach me with their stories.

This notion of interrelatedness continued as I endeavoured to clearly articulate my understandings for the readers of this work. Robert Stake (2005) also explored the significance of the connection between the researcher and the reader in his description of the importance of providing vivid descriptions or naturalistic generalizations in our writing to allow for this to occur.

> Experiential descriptions and assertions are relatively easily assimilated by readers into memory and use. When the researcher's narrative provides opportunity for *vicarious experience*, readers extend their perceptions of happenings. Naturalistic, ethnographic case materials, at least to some extent, parallel actual experience, feeding into the most fundamental processes of awareness and understanding. (p. 454; emphasis in the original)

It was therefore important for me to provide sufficient contextual information in my dissertation, so the reader would "make some generalizations entirely from personal or vicarious experience" (Stake, 2005, p. 454).

Synergy

Jo-ann Archibald's (2008) final Indigenous storywork principle is synergy. As she explained,

> the power created during the storytelling session seemed interrelational as it moved among the storyteller and the story listeners in the storytelling situation. This interaction created a synergistic story power that had emotional, healing, and spiritual aspects. The synergistic story power also brought the story "to life." (p. 100)

Initially, I struggled to understand how synergy impacted my own study until I began working with the story of the dogfish mother to understand the role of my ethical framework in my research decisions. Later, after reflecting upon the experience, I was excited to learn that my understanding of the shark dance had been enhanced through my work with the metaphor. Furthermore, my understanding of the importance of my ethical framework became clearer as a result of working with the metaphor. I was amazed that the story had been able to contribute so much to my understanding of the case study methodology after years of working with textbooks and trying to make sense of it in more conventional ways. I have come to believe that this is the power of synergy in my work, and I view it as an example of the synergistic connections between the story and my life experience (Archibald, 2008).

The use of the Indigenous storywork principles as an ethical framework in research

Prior to beginning the study, I did not realize the extent of my own commitment to ethics while doing research. One of the first steps in this realization happened long before I entered the classroom. Working through the task of completing the application for the UBC Behavioural Research Ethics Board was an intensive yet informative process, as it allowed me to fully reflect on how I intended to conduct the study from the beginning to the end. As a result of the process, I realized I was committed to holding myself accountable to a much more rigorous level of ethical conduct than was being asked of me in the online submission forms. Throughout the study, I worked to achieve this higher standard by ensuring that I followed the requirements set out by the UBC Behavioural Ethics Board and then enriched them using the Indigenous storywork principles.

The decision to use the Indigenous storywork principles began as an exploration, as I wondered how they might connect to the ethics of my research. Because *Indigenous Storywork* is written as a holistic narrative that embeds the principles and their descriptions throughout, I initially found it challenging to confirm my interpretation of each Indigenous storywork principle. Therefore, to deepen my understanding, I created a table of the seven principles and carefully re-read the book noting all the descriptions that were provided regarding each principle. This was a lengthy and sometimes frustrating process as I struggled to make meaning. However, as I continued to work to understand these principles, I came to appreciate that this struggle contributed to my greater understanding.

I am aware that adhering to these more stringent ethical protocols was, at times, restrictive and compromised my ability to share some of the more salient aspects of my research. This was particularly evident in my decision to provide very little information about the participants and to mask or omit some aspects of conversations that had the potential to harm them. I do not regret this decision because my strongest commitment was to ensuring that I was respecting the confidentiality and protecting the well-being of the participants in the study.

As I completed this research, my focus was on how it would contribute to the lives of the people in the local community; however, I recognize that it also made contributions to the research community. The study provided a model of ethical research practices with an Indigenous community and illustrated ways in which Indigenous and non-Indigenous research methodologies can be used together to strengthen a research study. The study also operationalized some of the theoretical ideas that have been touched on by Indigenous scholars (i.e. Kovach, 2009; Wilson, 2008). My decision to draw upon Indigenous and non-Indigenous methodologies was rooted in a desire to explore the strengths of both methodologies. This research became an illustration of how they can be used together synergistically to conduct research that is respectful and responsive. This is particularly useful for newer researchers wishing to learn more about how Indigenous methodologies and perspectives may be taken up in research.

The use of the Indigenous storywork principles provided a solid foundation for my research. By operationalizing them here, I was able to provide examples of ways to take them up as guidelines for conducting ethical research with Indigenous and non-Indigenous communities. The conversations I had at the Haida Education Council meeting demonstrated for me the promise of using these principles to guide policy for future research in education and health in the community. I modelled respectful research practices – particularly those that made contributions to the lives of the residents of the local community – in the hope that future research partnerships will be held to a high standard before being considered.

The significance of research methodologies

Through this research, I have come to understand that the kind of methodology we practise does not protect us against our mistakes. We need to find a methodology that allows us to be our authentic selves – that is, an extension of who we are as researchers and human beings so that we can "always think the highest thought" (Cajete, as cited in Archibald, 2008, p. 12) and conduct ourselves accordingly. We can continue to measure our decisions against the various ethical checklists, but in the end we are truly accountable to ourselves and only we know whether we have behaved in a way that honours our history and our upbringing.

> My uncle taught me how to do the shark dance properly, but ultimately when I am dancing at a feast or a potlatch, it is up to me to ensure that I am doing it correctly – that I am honouring the dance and the song that emerged from that dogfish mother on the beach so long ago. And as I move through the water, I am guided by the drumbeat but not defined by it. I follow the song, but it is up to me to fully understand the practices that I choose to draw upon, so that when it comes time to improvise, I can do so from a place of knowledge and understanding and respect. (Davidson, 2016, pp. 225–226)

Acknowledgement

This research was supported by the Social Sciences and Humanities Research Council of Canada.

Notes

1 *k'aad 'aww* is the *Haida* word for shark or dogfish mother. Both of these terms are used in this chapter.

2 The *Haida* word for "give away." This was a potlatch.

3 This is a pseudonym used for the school district where the research took place. It is also used in the references where any information identifying the school and district has been masked.

References

Archibald, J. (2008). *Indigenous storywork: educating the heart, mind, body, and spirit.* Vancouver, BC: UBC Press.

Banks, J. A. (1998) The lives and values of researchers: implications for educating citizens in a multicultural society. *Educational Researcher* 27(7), 4–17.

Bazylak, D. (2002). Journeys to success: perceptions of five female Aboriginal high school graduates. *Canadian Journal of Native Education* 26(2), 134–151.

Davidson, S. F. (2016). Following the song of *k'aad 'aww:* adolescent perspectives on English 10 First Peoples, writing, and identity. Unpublished doctoral dissertation. University of British Columbia, Vancouver, Canada. Retrieved from https://open.library.ubc.ca/cIRcle/collections/ubctheses/24/items/1.0319062.

Davidson, S. F. & Davidson, R. (2016). Make your mind strong: my father's insights into academic success. *Canadian Journal of Education 39*(2), 1–21.

Donald, D. T. (2009). Forts, curriculum, and Indigenous Métissage: imagining decolonization of Aboriginal-Canadian relations in educational contexts. *First Nations Perspectives 2*(1), 1–24.

Haida Education Council (n.d.). District committees: Haida Education Council. *Last* retrieved July 21, 2016, from [website masked to maintain confidentiality of participants].

Haida Gwaii Singers Society (2009). *Songs of Haida Gwaii: Haida Gwaii singers anthology.* Surrey, BC: Haida Gwaii Singers Society.

Kovach, M. (2009). *Indigenous methodologies: characteristics, conversations, and contexts.* Toronto, ON: University of Toronto Press.

School District 55 (Pacific Sound) (2012a). *Aboriginal Education Enhancement Agreement 2012–2016.* Last retrieved July 21, 2016 from www.bced.gov.bc.ca/abed/agreements/.

School District 55 (Pacific Sound) (2012b). *Achievement contract School District 55 (Pacific Sound).* Last retrieved July 21, 2016 from [link masked].

Smith, L.T. (2012). *Decolonizing methodologies: research and Indigenous Peoples.* (2nd ed.). London, UK: Zed Books.

Stake, R. (1995). *The art of case study research.* Thousand Oaks, CA: Sage Publications.

Stake, R. (2005). Qualitative case studies. In N. K. Lincoln & Y. S. Denzin (Eds.), *Handbook of qualitative research* (pp. 443–466). Thousand Oaks, CA: Sage Publications.

Thomas, R. A. (2005). Honouring the oral traditions of my ancestors through storytelling. In L. Brown & S. Strega (Eds.), *Research as resistance* (pp. 237–254). Toronto, ON: Canadian Scholars' Press.

Weaver, H. N. (1997). The challenges of research in Native American communities. *Journal of Social Service Research 23*(2), 1–15.

Wilson, S. (2008). *Research is ceremony.* Halifax, NS: Fernwood Publishing.

2 | INDIGENOUS VISUAL STORYWORK FOR INDIGENOUS FILM AESTHETICS

Dorothy Christian

The backstory

When directing, segment producing, and writing documentaries for the national broadcaster VISION TV from 1995 to 2003, I was privileged to carry Indigenous stories to the national screen culture in Canada. I visited many Indigenous territories throughout Turtle Island (North America) and into Mexico. This was a very rich personal, cultural, and professional experience where I encountered a number of queries that prompted me to enrol in graduate studies to explore these questions. The prevailing one that underlay all the others was, "What is the role of culture in Indigenous production practices?" My MA thesis, *A "Cinema of Sovereignty": Working in the Cultural Interface to Create a Model for Fourth World Film Pre-production and Aesthetics*[1] (Christian, 2010) partially answered the central question. The natural next step was to delve deeper into how cultural knowledge informs our ways of doing, acting, listening, and being when constructing our films/videos as visual narratives.

Visualizing Indigenous storywork

My doctoral work is titled *Gathering Knowledge: Indigenous Methodologies of Land/Place-Based Visual Storytelling/Filmmaking and Visual Sovereignty* (Christian, 2017) and is a part of "Critical Indigenous Inquiry" (Denzin, Lincoln & Smith, 2008, p. ix). It is an Indigenous-to-Indigenous dialogue steeped in Indigenous systems of knowledge. This research is a critical qualitative study that centres Indigenous knowledge(s), is firmly grounded in an Indigenous research paradigm, and uses Indigenous methodologies and methods in the gathering of knowledge (Kovach, 2009; Wilson, 2008). It is a part of decolonizing the literature in Indigenous film/Fourth World cinema and intervenes in the globalization discourse by creating an Indigenous place-based identity.

In social and political discourse, George Manuel (*Secwepemc*) named the Indigenous reality in colonizer nation-states as "the Fourth World" (1974). In Indigenous film discourse, Māori filmmaker Barry Barclay coined the term Fourth Cinema (2003a, 2003b) when he placed the camera in the hands of Indigenous directors "on the shore" (p. 8) watching the Settlers arrive on our lands. By changing who controlled the camera lens, Barclay created an Indigenous gaze. I bring the two terms together and speak from a Fourth World Cinema space. I affirm the Indigenous gaze of visual storytellers/ filmmakers[2] and address concerns discussed in the film discourse. Specifically, I examine the relational qualities of land, story, and cultural protocols and how this shapes our Indigenous place-based identities, which in turn inform how visual storytellers construct the aesthetics for their visually sovereign films and videos. I join numerous global Indigenous scholars working in this fourth space as I theorize a "localized critical theory" based in *Secwepemc* and *Syilx* knowledges (Christian, 2017, p. 9).

The main objective of my research was to answer a titillating question that Archibald (2008) asks:

> Even though the latter [television, video, and digital technology] may allow for use of visual images and the sounds of the storyteller, the same questions that confront the relationship between orality and literacy apply. How can the story be portrayed so that its power to make one think, feel, and reflect on one's actions is not lost? Can the cultural context be sufficiently developed so that the listener/viewer can make story meaning? (p. 81)

This question was central to my exploration of whether or not visual storytellers could maintain the "power" and the cultural context of the oral story. I wanted to see if our stories maintain their cultural meanings even though we are using state-of-the-art technology and living in a society where the colonial Settler narrative dominates.

To begin, I established whether or not the seven operating principles of Archibald's (2008) Indigenous storywork (ISW) process: respect, responsibility, reciprocity, reverence, holism, interrelatedness, and synergy (p. 33) were a part of the conversations I had with knowledge keepers and visual storytellers. By doing this I extended Archibald's ISW process to an Indigenous visual storywork process guided by the same principles. This is a purposeful "talking in" (Barclay, 1990,

p. 76) dialogue that may provide insights to non-Indigenous film theorists when discussing Indigenous film practices.

The knowledge keepers: the principle of interrelatedness

This work is unique because it is a layered Indigenous-to-Indigenous discussion – Indigenous knowledge keepers speaking with an Indigenous visual storyteller about how their cosmologies and worldviews situate their cultures in the universe. The diverse group of Indigenous knowledge keepers are from the *Anishnabe-Cree, Cree-Métis, Haida, Haudenosaunee (Seneca), Hopi, Inuit, Métis,* and *Secwepemc* Nations. Some of them are oral storytellers, others are filmmakers, and some have worked in the film industry.

In the stories and conversations with the knowledge keepers, we discussed cultural stories from our respective lands outside the dominating colonial narrative and certainly beyond the Euro-Western understanding of positioning them as mere myths or legends. Some elaborate their worldviews that situate their people and their stories in relation to the cosmos, outside the physical realm of the earth. In addition, it is important to know that a fundamental assumption held by the knowledge keepers and me is that the spiritual energies (life force) of the seen and unseen entities infuse all the cultural stories. The scope of this chapter does not allow for each storywork principle to be examined; therefore, the focus is on the concept of *interrelatedness*. I used this particular principle to guide the analysis and synthesis of the knowledge gathered from both the knowledge keepers and the visual storytellers to examine how we make meaning through stories in our contemporary lives as Indigenous Peoples. I focus on the principle of *interrelatedness* because of its relational qualities and because in many ways it incorporates all the other principles.

Mike Myers, *Seneca* knowledge keeper, brings a deeper understanding to a term that is frequently used in Indigenous settings, which is the words "All My Relations," which most Indigenous people summarize as meaning that we are related to all things, not just human beings. Myers speaks of a specificity of relationship from his knowledge base that expands this clichéd way of explaining this concept. He brings a much more profound meaning to Archibald's principle of *interrelatedness* as he explains how his worldview situates him in the universe and who his relatives are in the unseen universe. To be congruent with my Indigenous paradigm and methodologies, I choose to use lengthy quotes so as not to de-contextualize the stories/information shared. Further, this approach maintains a semblance of orality with the conversational method of Indigenous inquiry.

> [I]n terms of our family tree then, on our mother's side, *Etinoha*, the earth itself is our mother, our *Aksodaha*, our grandmother on our mother's side is Sky Woman, … she became moon. Our grandfather on our mother's side is still back in the Sky World and is still the Caretaker of the Tree of Life. Now, on our father's side our grandmother on our father's side is Ocean. Our grandfather on our father's side is Thunder. That's why we call them our grandfathers. And our three uncles are the other three winds, south, east and north winds are our uncles, but our father is west wind. But interestingly enough our cousins on that side are tornado and cyclone and dust devils and hurricanes, those are all our relatives, those are our cousins. And so when we look at this powerful family that we come from it tells us that we were sent here to be powerful people because we come from this powerful lineage. We were sent here and with the expectation of doing great things because everybody in our family has done great things. We may never ever do things as great as creating a world, but the expectation is that we're to do great things, good things, positive things that are going to contribute to the sustenance of life forever in this place.
>
> …
>
> what was [going on] at the time before she [Sky Woman] fell from the Sky World to here, what was going on up there, and the creation of the universe, the coming of the universe, this being, this entity that exist[s] at the centre of the universe as the first creative force. And I think one of the important differences in our spiritual understanding is that there is not a singular creative force. There are several creative forces. And for us humans the most powerful creative forces starts with the Sky Woman and her daughter so it is the start of the matriarchy – the female origins of who we are as a people. When we look at her transformation, when she fell from the Sky World, they say that in the course of her transformation from spirit to physical is mapped in what is called the Milky Way. Now, we call that the Sky Road. That when our time here in the physical realm is over that's the road we travel on back to our Grandmother's Land where she came from. (Myers, M., personal communications, February 2014)

Beyond the connections to the universe, there is another aspect of *interrelatedness* that Mona Jules, highly respected *Secwepemc* knowledge keeper, speaks of in terms of how we see our human relationships. At age 75 and the mother of eight children, she is a grandmother to many and a great, great, great grandmother to some. She is a language teacher from *Simpcw*, one of the 17 communities of the *Secwepemc* Nation. Her explanation of the complexity of our *interrelationships* in our extended families provides some understanding of why the sense of community is so strong. She states:

> Because of our customs in our family, we have extended family and the *Secwepemc* are very fortunate, we were surrounded by [our] grandmothers because your grandmother is different than other cultures' grandmothers. In *Secwepemc* culture, your grandmother's sisters and also her first cousins are also your grandmothers, all of them. So we knew that in the community. (Jules, M., personal communication, April 2014)

Kukpi (Chief), Dr Ron Ignace (*Secwepemc*) affirms Mike Myer's *Seneca* way of knowing when he says, "our knowledge was of the universe … If you look at our stories, there are different worlds, different universes that our people talked about" (Ignace, R., personal communication, May 2014). In shifting from the cosmos to the physical reality, *Kukpi* Ignace addresses our physical relationship to our ancestral homelands in his 2008 PhD dissertation. He shows how the cultural stories are embedded and written into the land by braiding together the language, the oral stories, and geographical locations on the land. Ignace brilliantly interfaces Euro-Western scientific knowledge from the archaeology, geology, and paleo-ecology[3] disciplines to confirm facts in *Secwepemc* oral stories. He did this "to cross check and triangulate evidence" that he received from oral stories he heard during his upbringing (Ignace, 2008, p. 31).[4] I believe the knowledge transmitted through the stories reveals the interrelatedness principle through the layers of relationship that the people have with the land. These are the personal, embodied, reciprocal, interdependent, and spiritual relationships.

Clearly, the Indigenous philosophies of the *Secwepemc* and *Seneca* point to differences between their Indigenous perspectives and some Euro-Western understandings of temporal space and *interrelatedness*. However, the knowledge keepers convey an expansive, in-depth, and complex meaning of the concept of *interrelatedness* on a macrocosmic level. I see Archibald's (2008) storywork principle of *interrelatedness* as the microcosmic level, as she is discussing the relationship between the storyteller, the story, and the listener/reader in a physical encounter (Christian, 2017, pp. 32–33). Both the microcosmic and macrocosmic levels of interrelating around land and story are influenced by how the principle is enacted and acknowledged as viable.

Land, story, and cultural protocols

In formulating a *Secwepemc-Syilx* perspective of how we self-identify on our ancestral lands, I put forward a counter-narrative to the deeply entrenched colonial story of the Settler population that denies Indigenous people's long relationship with the lands. What is critical to how I formulate a culturally specific Indigenous identity is that I move away from the pan-Indigenous approach of policy makers and affirm the unique cultural specificity of each Nation. In my doctoral dissertation, I had permission to use the full text of a *Secwepemc Sek'lep/Coyote* story that was told in *Secwepemcstin* (the *Secwepemc* language), with English translation[5] (Christian, 2017, pp. 118–124). I used this story as a "theoretical anchor" (Simpson, 2014) because it embeds teachings about "not copying others," which I interpreted as not copying white people but also not copying other Indigenous Peoples. It is with this understanding that I discuss the relational qualities of Indigenous land, story, and cultural protocols.

That said, I turn to Maria Campbell to underscore some of the shared values of Indigenous Peoples. Campbell, 78 at the time of our conversation, speaks four languages: *Cree*, *Michif*, *Saulteaux*, and English. She is a renowned author, activist, storyteller, television series producer, and knowledge keeper. She explains from her *Cree-Métis* point of view what I believe is a level of relationship to land that most Indigenous Peoples feel but have difficulty articulating. She says,

> [T]he land doesn't speak out loud … the environment doesn't speak out loud. It talks to you in other kinds of ways. And that's what's important … so there's a whole other language that sometimes isn't spoken that you have between you and the connection to the land … you don't have to own the land. You don't even have to speak the language to have that connection with the land. (Campbell, M., personal communication, September 2013)

What Campbell is pointing to is very important because she is talking about a state of being that is beyond the physical relationship; that is, the spiritual relationship that Indigenous Peoples have to the land.

Further, she opens the conversation about the role of ceremonies in strengthening and deepening that connection to the land (Campbell, M., personal communication, September 2013; Young Leon, 2015). The land speaks a whole other language that we can access if we are mindful of the energies that reach out to us.

To explain, affirm, and extend the understanding of the spiritual connection to the land through cultural stories that shape the specific way *Secwepemc* and *Syilx* peoples (Armstrong, 2009; Ignace, 2008; Sam, 2013) enact and embody their way of being Indigenous on the land, I go to Jeannette Armstrong's (2009) concept of Indigeneity as a social paradigm. She says this is not an identity but that her paradigm recognizes how localized *Syilx* peoples interact with the land to gain wisdom and knowledge so that life may continue to perpetuate itself in a continuous cycle of regeneration on the land for all life forms, not just humans (Armstrong, 2009, p. 1). Armstrong's social paradigm is in essence the cornerstone of a *Syilx* place-based identity.

Armstrong (2009) provides a full explanation of the depth and breadth of how *Syilx* oral stories relate to the people and the territories. She is a *suxʷqʷaqʷalulaxʷ* "speaker for the land" and "hold[s] the highest qualification within the knowledge structure of the *Syilx Okanagan*" (p. 6). A highly respected writer, philosopher, activist, and scholar whose PhD dissertation, *Constructing Indigeneity: Syilx Okanagan Oraliture and _tmixʷcentrism*, in part explains that the *Syilx Okanagan* stories in *Nsyilxcen* (the language) are a system of documentation and preservation of the social experience on the land, which explains the interrelatedness of the people with each other, the land, and all the other seen and unseen beings on the land. Armstrong elaborates that, "The *Syilx* protocols for storytelling are practiced as custom to observe the purpose of (a) formal or public gatherings; (b) informal social occasions; (c) informal family-centred gatherings; and (d) for individuals or select audience situations" (2009, pp. 91–92).

To fully understand how story knowledge is transmitted in these settings and how to make meaning with stories, it is vital to understand that the concepts are embedded in the language. The first concept, central to *Syilx Okanagan* ways of knowing and seeing, is what Armstrong (2009) calls *"tmixw"* (pp. 148–149), which translates to "life force,"[6] and can be understood as the spirit or essence central to each life form on the land. This essence for human beings is named *"tmx w ulax w"* (life-force-place) (pp. 149–150), which reinforces a sense of belonging to the land and affirms a place-based identity. Further, this gives insight into why Indigenous Peoples are so strongly related to their ancestral lands. Armstrong explains that from a *Syilx* point of view, each life form has a right to be regenerated to continue to bring new life.

For many Indigenous Peoples it is this depth of connection to the land that also ties the people to the place-based landmarks on our territories. They signify how our stories are physical manifestations and viable proof of the content of our stories.[7] Many Indigenous Nations consider these landmarks as substantial expressions of our connections to the land and they are considered sacred. For some non-Indigenous peoples, it seems that these significant markers are only tourist attractions to photograph or to deface. These features on our ancestral territories are our oral stories physically written into the land. Language speakers have the benefit of the embedded knowledge, which describe what our old people wanted us to remember and learn about our place on the land. As *Kukpi* Ignace explains:

My ancestors called rock-paintings or pictographs *stsq'ey* – saying, "*yiri7 re stsq'eys*" – "it's written." "*Yiri7 restsq'eyems le q'7es te kw'seltktens*" – "this is the writing/how it was marked by our long ago relatives." Thus, "*tsq'iyulecw*" means to "mark the land" in the way our ancestors marked the landscape with their deeds, gave names to places, and thus claimed the land as *Secwepemculecw*. (Ignace, 2008, pp. 91–92)

Secwepemc knowledge keeper and language teacher, Mona Jules, aged 75, remembers a story from her childhood. She says:

I heard that story from my grandmother, years and years ago. It was a Medicine man who could make stone people and there are markers all over *Secwepemculuw*, the *Secwepemc* land ... And a lot of it has been blasted away by highways over in Cache Creek there was some highway marker that was like a stone head. You see those all along, towards Jasper but these were right down close to the land. These big rocks, where they were in the forms of heads ... There were 3 women and a head of a guy who had a contest and he pushed his head through a rock to show that he was the most powerful Medicine man and so, storytelling really is telling stories about the culture ... They knew exactly where these rocks were – where they left the stories behind.
Up in Dog Creek, there is a big Coyote that is up in the side of the road, it's like a clay bank but it's in the shape of Coyote that never

ever goes away. It may be rock but somebody was saying it's been there forever, Coyote howling. (Jules, M., personal communication, April 2014)

Coyote howls to the spirits of *Secwepemc* and *Syilx* peoples when we are away from our homelands. I believe this strong internal pull is what we feel when we are away from our land for too long. It is difficult to describe this heartfelt, spirit-felt connection to the land. When our spirit is called we just have to go home. On other Indigenous lands, it is *Wesakechak* for the *Crees*, *Raven* for West Coast *Salish* Nations, Nanabush for the *Anishinabes* or *Glooskap* for the *Mik'maq* on the East Coast that call out to the spirits of their peoples.

From my lived experience, I know that my identity as a *Secwepemc* and *Syilx* woman is strong because my connection to the territories is irrefutable. The concept of a collective memory still exists within our genetics[8] and is what Hawaiian scholar Lelani Holmes calls heart knowledge and blood memory (2000, pp. 44–47). I strongly believe that no matter how long we have been away from the culture or how the continuity of our knowledge transmission process has been disrupted, we are still connected to the collective memory of our people. We connect to our ancestors when we participate in ceremony where we enter a sacred space, which often triggers collective/genetic memories. I maintain that Indigenous visual storytellers still have that connection with their collective memories whether they/we live in their/our home territories or in urban centres (Campbell, M., personal communication, September 2013). It is within this framework and knowledge base that I turn to having conversations and sharing stories with Indigenous visual storytellers to elicit their production experiences.

The visual storytellers/filmmakers

I had conversations with a multi-generational group of Indigenous visual storytellers, ranging in age from early 20s to mid-80s, to see how the Indigenous storywork principles are used in the construction of their visual narratives. The visual storytellers also represent a diverse spectrum of Indigenous Nations. In this work I was fortunate to have many of the movers and shakers of the Indigenous film world respond favourably to my request. They are from the following Indigenous Nations: *Abenaki/Odanak*, three *Cree-Métis*, *Métis*, *Inuit*, *Hopi*, *Swampy Cree*, two *Kahnawake Mohawks*, *Heiltsuk*/Six Nations

Mohawk, Anishinabe, Ktun'axa/Secwepemc, Six Nations *Mohawk, Anishinabe/Cree, Cree/Saulteaux,* and Plains *Cree.* All of these visual storytellers work in the industry with the exception of the youngest, who is a film student, and three women who are community-based visual storytellers and do not make films commercially. I identify the specific location of some of the filmmakers who come from the same Nation because the place-based aspect of their identity is important. Central to the examination are the relational qualities of land, story, and the implicit cultural protocols.

Indigenous film aesthetics: cultural congruency and visual sovereignty

While working in production, I did not have the luxury of time to ponder conceptual terms for the visual stories I was creating, much less articulate the film language of aesthetics. However, since doing this research for both my MA and my PhD, I have concluded that visual storytelling is a form of contemporary knowledge production. By weaving together Indigenous sounds and images of the communities we film, we present culturally congruent stories of the Indigenous Peoples we are representing.

In the shared stories and conversations with the visual storytellers, we discussed many aspects of our filmmaking practices; however, for the scope of this chapter I focus on the importance of the interrelatedness of language and our connection to land, thus shaping our place-based identities. In addition, our spiritual connection to our homelands is central to the stated fact that our aesthetics begin in the sacred (Masayesva, V. Jr. cited in Leuthold, 1998, p. 1).

With the skills of the film and video technology mastered, I truly believe that even though many of us do not speak our Indigenous language, we innately understand the story and structure our visual narratives with layers of soundscapes and visualscapes that give us the deeper meaning of the story. When our stories have purposefully selected sounds and visuals that speak to the genetic memories we carry in our blood, then our ability to make meaning of the story is not lost.[9] One visual storyteller, who is a language speaker, shared a fascinating experience that gives insight into how we make meaning with our visual stories.

Kevin Burton is a Swampy *Cree* from Devil's Lake in northern Manitoba. He is a language speaker. In 2007, he made a short documentary,

Writing the Land, in which he asked the Elder for some of the place-names in the hən'q̓əmin'əm' language of the *Musqueam* people and then he translated those place-names to his *Cree* language. Kevin told me he had a huge light bulb moment when he completed this production because he realized that the language is tied to the place where it originated. When he translated the place-names in Coast *Salish* territories of the *Musqueam/Tsleil-wau-tuth/Squamish*, to his *Cree* language, he said it felt very disembodied and displaced. Kevin said, "I felt displaced in Vancouver." Following this west coast production, he made *Nikamowin* (2007), which was based in his *Cree* home territory. He decisively deconstructed and reconstructed his language, which provided the melodies of his soundscape. In other words, Kevin was bringing the sounds of his language and the images of his land to the aesthetics of this production (Burton, K., personal communication, February 2014). This is a profound realization in terms of how language is absolutely a foundation of Indigenous aesthetics.

Visual storyteller Zoe Leigh Hopkins (*Heiltsuk/Mohawk*) speaks to another aspect of Indigenous aesthetics, which is her connection to land. In discussing how her relationship to land informs the scripts of her stories, she says:

> First of all, having that connection to both a place and a people makes it almost impossible to write about anything else. My characters are always set in one of those places, or the story is set in one of those places. Having the deep knowledge of what that place is and who those people are, I am tied to those things. (Hopkins, Zoe L., personal communication, November 14, 2013)

And Zoe provides some insights about cultural protocols when she says,

> [W]orking on a film that is set in my community – production and pre-production are very different than if I was working somewhere where I didn't know anybody … it takes longer but it is just different. There's so much more to do … There are community and cultural protocols that you have to follow – making sure you don't step on any toes and this real strong desire to do it right and to please people and to make people happy.
>
> …
>
> [Y]ou can't just do whatever the hell you want on somebody's territory. Everybody has to know; everybody has to say it's okay.

There's this whole thing of getting permission for everything …
and that's a multi-level permission. You need to get band council
permission, and hereditary council permission and then depending
on where you are shooting, permission of the people who live there
and the families around them and stuff. Probably, a 3-or 4-tiered
levels of permissions to go and do something. Then, like just being
respectful, there's this concept of being respectful of where you are
like – unlike shooting somewhere else, like in the city, you might not
worry so much if it got dirty, or there's garbage or whatever … But
when you are shooting in someone's home, in their territory, it's like
extra special care … in every aspect of it. And, making sure, for me,
there's more attention, in the pre-production phase of making sure
that you have crossed all your t's and dotted all your i's; making
sure that everybody is okay with what you are doing. Because the
last thing you want to do is piss people off. (Hopkins, Zoe L.,
personal communication, November 2013)

Another filmmaker/visual storyteller, Danis Goulet's, (*Cree-Métis*)
film *Wakening* (2013) was selected to be the opening film for the 2013
Toronto International Film Festival. She had a political struggle in
the cultural interface with this major venue in that she had to fight
with one of the executives so that her *Weetigo* character could speak
her *Cree* language with English subtitles. Her resolve was solid. She
told me,

I was really fully willing to walk away at that point. I felt that strongly
about it and also like that person was participating in the silencing of
Indigenous language. No, no, no. This will not fly. If Jabba the Hutt
in *Star Wars* can speak in subtitles, my *Weetigo* is going to speak in
subtitles too! (Goulet, D., personal communication, November 2013)

Each one speaks to the critical interrelatedness of land, language, story,
and cultural protocols that relate to the aesthetics of their films. These
aspects overlap and interrelate in complex ways for visual story construction. These facets of contemporary knowledge production also
inform how an Indigenous place-based identity is formed.

I am certain that each visual storyteller has their own unique story of
a dis-connection to land/place, culture, and language even though they
may not describe it as that. I believe every Indigenous person across
the territories in what is known as Canada feels the loss or disconnect
from our homelands because the intergenerational transmission of

story knowledge has been interrupted by residential schools, the 1960s scoop, forced dislocation, and other traumatic experiences.

It is within this context that I turn to the revitalization of *Secwepemc-Syilx* systems of knowledge to illustrate a culturally specific way that the principle of interrelatedness weaves together the land, language, and cultural stories. I bring together Armstrong's (2009) *Syilx* notion of Indigeneity as a social paradigm and use Sam's (2013) *Syilx/* Indigenous analysis of the globalization phenomenon. I assert that with the coupling of their formulations, they provide an intellectual intervention in the regularly used terms of Indigeneity and deterritorialization in the globalization discourse. By developing a localized *Secwepemc-Syilx* theory, I refine a nuanced application of *Secwepemc* and *Syilx* concepts (Armstrong, 2009; Ignace, 2008; Michel, 2012; Sam, 2013) to expand and strengthen the intellectual intervention to formulate our Indigenous identity. I put forward a localized *Secwepemc-Syilx* theory as a theoretical framework of a place-based identity.

The localized *Secwepemc-Syilx* theory and place-based identity

In the articulation of a critical localized theory from a *Secwepemc-Syilx* perspective, I present a specific bioregional point of view that is located within and from the ancestral lands that my family and two Nations have lived on for generations. Visually I see the representation of the theory like a strand of DNA, a spiral that is often referred to as the building block of life. It is also reflected in the meaning in the language for the *Syilx* people. "The word for our people or ourselves is *Sqilxw*, which in a literal translation means the dream in a spiral. We recognize our individual lives as the continuance of human dreams, coming to reality in a spiraling way" (Cohen, 2010, p. 4). *Secwepemc* storyteller and scholar Ignace sees our Indigenous history and knowledge as a spiral, which he says is different from a circle because it is always moving, developing, and changing (Personal communication, May 2014). With that archetype held deeply in my collective ancestral memories, I put forward my critical localized *Secwepemc-Syilx* theory as a way of self-identifying on the land and being a part of perpetuating life on the land.

The continuous spiral frame has two outer strands. One is the *Secwepemc reciprocal accountability* principle (Ignace, personal communication, August 25, 2014) and the other is the *Syilx regenerative principle* (Armstrong, 2009). The linking threads that hold the two strands together are the *Secwepemc* concepts of *k'weltktnéws* (interrelatedness) and *knucwestsut.s* (personal responsibility) (Michel, 2012, p. 48). These principles that link the two fundamental concepts of the outer strands are only two of many *Secwepemc* concepts in the way of knowing the world. When I internalize these principles and enact them on the land with the people, then my *Secwepemc-Syilx* identity is reinforced and affirmed.

This localized *Secwepemc-Syilx* theory can be a guide for visual storytellers because I believe the language of every Indigenous Nation has words that express the same concepts. These principles speak to taking personal responsibility in how you give back to your family/community/Nation through your individual actions, to become a part of the collective. Within this way of knowing and doing, we as visual storytellers become valued members who interrelate in healthy ways on all levels when we take personal responsibility for how we interpret our cultural stories when making contemporary knowledge as visual narratives. By participating in this way we honour storywork principles, become a part of regenerating life on the land (Armstrong, 2009), and we attend to the layers of multiple accountabilities in our communities. Most importantly, we are accountable to our personal integrity as artists.

Conclusion: interrelatedness principle and the methodology of visual storywork

Clearly, the interrelatedness principle permeates both the worldviews of the knowledge keepers and the creative processes of the visual storytellers/filmmakers. The knowledge keepers show this principle is fundamental to Indigenous ways of knowing on a macro level by locating their stories as Indigenous Peoples beyond the physical reality of earth. Also, on a micro level the interrelatedness principle embedded within the cultural knowledge(s) is integral with the way the weaving together of land, story, and cultural protocols shapes a culturally specific place-based identity on particular lands. The visual storytellers confirm this principle is an important factor in the doing – that is, in the actions they take throughout their creative process.

For me as an Indigenous researcher and visual storyteller, it is necessary to tease out the complexity of the relational qualities of Indigenous concepts when using the interrelatedness principle as a tool for methodological analysis and synthesis. What helps greatly is the opportunity to engage in storied experiences and write within an Indigenous research paradigm, which provides a theoretical framework where Indigenous methodologies are automatically applied.

Notes

1 Full text available at: http:// summit.sfu.ca/item/11842.

2 Throughout this chapter I use the term "visual storytellers" to describe people that the film discourse identifies as filmmakers.

3 Defined as a noun, the branch of ecology dealing with the relations and interactions between ancient life forms and their environment, retrieved from http://dictionary.reference.com/browse/ paleoecology retrieved June 11, 2015.

4 Ron Ignace is a scholar and the *Kukpi* (Chief) of his *Skeetchestn* community. He comes from a long line of leaders who have been a part of the resistance of the imposition of colonial powers on *Secwepemc* lands. He was fortunate to be raised by grandparents and great grandparents. He is a language speaker and a keeper of cultural knowledge.

5 In the Preface of my PhD dissertation, I included "A Note on Copyright and Intellectual Property Rights," which essentially says the *Secwepemc* Nation collectively owns the copyright of the Coyote story I used and that I do not as a Secwepemc individual claim ownership of this story.

6 Ignace refers to life force as *soomik* in the *Secwepemc* language.

7 Ajax Mine is proposing an open pit mine at the site where one of the *Secwepemc* oral stories (the Trout Children) occurred. The *Secwepemc* Nation, local Settler communities, and environmentalists are opposed to this development. Information at: http://sierraclub.bc.ca/residential-neighbourhood-no-place-open-pit-mine retrieved May 5, 2016.

8 In Chapter 1 of my PhD dissertation, I share an experience of one of my ancestors, my great Uncle Joe coming to visit me in a dream and he transmitted specific instructions on my writing.

9 One audience member at one of the screenings of my work said to me, "I always cry when I watch films you have produced." To me, that indicated that I was giving meaning to other Indigenous Peoples with my stories

References

Archibald, J. (2008). *Indigenous storywork: educating the heart, mind, body, and spirit.* Vancouver, BC: UBC Press.

Armstrong, J. C. (2009). *Constructing indigeneity: Syilx Okanagan oraliture and _tmix^wcentrism.* Unpublished doctoral dissertation. University of Greifswald, Germany.

Barclay, B. (1990). *Our own image.* Auckland, New Zealand: Longman Paul.

Barclay, B. (2003a, July). Celebrating Fourth Cinema. Lecture presented September 17, 2002, at the Film and Media Studies Department, Auckland University, Auckland, New Zealand. *Illusions Magazine*, 1–11. Retrieved from www.maoricinema. com/wp-content/uploads/2014/02/ BarclayCelebratingFourthCinema. pdf retrieved July 14, 2016.

Barclay, B. (2003b, July). Exploring Fourth Cinema. Lecture presented at *Re-imagining Indigenous Cultures: The Pacific Islands*, Summer Institute, the National Endowment for the Humanities, University of Hawai'i, Honolulu, HI.

Christian, D. (2010) *A "cinema of sovereignty": working in the cultural interface to create a model for Fourth World film pre-production and aesthetics.* Unpublished Masters thesis. Simon Fraser University, Burnaby, BC.

Christian, D. (2017). *Gathering knowledge: Indigenous methodologies of land/place-based visual storytelling/filmmaking and visual sovereignty.* Unpublished doctoral dissertation. University of British Columbia, Vancouver, BC.

Cohen, W. A. (2010). *School failed coyote, so fox made a new school: Indigenous Okanagan knowledge transforms educational pedagogy.* Unpublished doctoral dissertation. University of British Columbia, Vancouver, BC.

Denzin, N. K., Lincoln, Y. S. & Tuhiwai Smith, L. (Eds.). (2008). *Handbook of critical and Indigenous methodologies.* Los Angeles, CA: Sage Publications.

Holmes, L. (2000). Heart knowledge, blood memory, and the voice of the land: implications of research among Hawaiian Elders. In G. J. Sefa Dei, B. L. Hall, & D.G. Rosenberg (Eds.), *Indigenous knowledges in global contexts* (pp. 37–53) Toronto, ON: University of Toronto Press.

Ignace, R. E. (2008). *Our oral histories are our iron posts: Secwepemc stories and historical consciousness.* Unpublished doctoral dissertation. Simon Fraser University, Burnaby, BC. Retrieved from http://shuswapnation.org/wordpress/wp-content/uploads/2016/01/Ron-Ignace-PhD-Thesis.pdf.

Kovach, M. (2009). *Indigenous methodologies: characteristics, conversations and contexts.* Toronto, ON: University of Toronto Press.

Leuthold, S. (1998). *Indigenous aesthetics: Native art media and identity.* Austin, TX: University of Texas Press.

Manuel, G., & Posluns, M. (1974). *The fourth world: an Indian reality.* Don Mills, ON: Collier-Macmillan Canada.

Michel, K. A. (2012). *Trickster's path to language transformation: stories of Secwepemc immersion from Chief Atahm School.* Unpublished doctoral dissertation. University of British Columbia, Vancouver, BC.

Sam, M. (2013). *Oral narratives, customary laws and Indigenous water rights in Canada.* PhD dissertation. University of British Columbia (Okanagan), Kelowna, BC.

Simpson, L. (2014). Land as pedagogy: Nishnaabeg intelligence and rebellious transformation. *Decolonization: Indigeneity, Education & Society 3*(3), 1–25.

Wilson, S. (2008). *Research is ceremony: Indigenous research methods.* Black Point, NS: Fernwood Publishing.

Young Leon, A. (2015). *Indigenous Elders' pedagogy for land-based health education programs: Gee-zhee-kan'-dug cedar pedagogical pathways.* Unpublished doctoral dissertation. University of British Columbia, Vancouver, BC.

3 | *LE7 Q'7ES TE STSPTEKWLL RE SECWÉPEMC*: OUR MEMORIES LONG AGO

Georgina Martin and Elder Jean William

Introduction

When I (Georgina Martin) asked Elder Jean William if she would co-author this chapter with me, after the completion of my PhD thesis in 2014, she supported me and wanted to know what would be involved. The title of the chapter, *Le7 Q'7es te Stsptekwll re Secwépemc* does not have a literal English interpretation. In our *Secwepemctsin* (meaning *Shuswap* language) it means the stories are passed on through the generations from the memories of long ago. I explained that this chapter is an opportunity for us, as Indigenous people, to tell our stories and show the world that some Indigenous people have thrived and that Indigenous people are not invisible. This explanation stirred her emotions, given that in 2017, Canada celebrated its 150th birthday. She responded that here we are in Canada and only celebrating 150, so what about celebrating Indigenous *Secwepemc* people at 10,000 years plus? She further stated that since we were on the brink of these celebrations, this chapter intensified the importance of educating others about our history through the strength and memories of the Elders and ancestors. The original peoples of this land were present long before 1867, so it would be an insult to think that this country's Indigenous Peoples have existed for only a short time. Archaeologists' reports have provided evidence of the *Secwepemc* people's early existence, which the *Secwepemc* Elders term the time of creation (Billy, 2017). Elder Jean learned our history through her communal creation stories. She voiced her disdain about the lack of First Peoples' presence in Canada's 150th anniversary of Confederation, given that the *Secwepemc* existed well before then. Because of the blatant silence and our non-inclusion in these celebrations, our ire was raised and we became more determined to tell the *Secwepemc* stories and memories of long ago.

Background

The partnership between Jean and I evolved from the reciprocal relationships that matured during my doctoral research about

Secwepemc identities. My doctoral project is titled *Drumming My Way Home: An Intergenerational Narrative Inquiry about Secwepemc Identities*, and was completed in 2014. The study took place in the *T'exelc* community (also known as Sugar Cane). The *T'exelc* community is the homeland of both co-authors and it is situated 11 kilometres south of the city of Williams Lake in the interior of British Columbia. This community lies within the territories of the 17 nations that constitute the *Secwepemc* peoples.

Since we are immersed in the sharing of our personal and ancestral stories, first names will be used frequently and when "I" is used it represents Georgina's voice as the co-ordinating author. I am the daughter of Tommy Wycotte II and Suzie Wycotte. My maternal grandparents are Ned and Nancy Moiese. Jean is the daughter of Frank and Anastasia Sandy. Her maternal grandparents are Tommy Wycotte I and Felicia Wycotte. A common thread between us is that we were both raised around and influenced by our grandparents. I spent my formative years with my maternal grandparents as they raised me; Jean lived with her maternal grandparents as well. From these experiences, we were both gifted with teachings from our grandparents and value the rich stories about our heritage. Jean has a *Secwepemc* name *Mumt re Nunxenxw te Nek'westsut* while I do not. There was a break in the tradition of ancestral naming, for reasons unknown.

During my doctoral study, I worked on retrieving some of my history in order to recognize how certain lived experiences contributed to my fragmented sense of identity and shaped my lost sense of belonging. I described these influences as legislated interference based on policies enforced by the federal government, namely Indian hospitals and residential schools. Both Indian hospitals and residential schools were federal government-sanctioned institutions established to segregate Indigenous Peoples from their families and homelands. Indian hospitals were set up to house Indigenous people who were quarantined with tuberculosis (TB) while residential schools functioned under the guise of education with the sole intent of assimilating Indigenous children (Truth and Reconciliation Commission of Canada, 2015). I was affected by both entities and I continue on my healing journey. Consequently, these complex manifestations were disorientating. On the one hand I experienced a happy childhood growing up alongside my grandparents, but I later felt rejection, which was very confusing. The feeling of rejection was associated with the fact that I did not have a relationship with my birth mother. I saw my PhD research as an opportunity to investigate the dichotomy between a happy childhood and feelings of loss later in life. I knew that the process would be challenging and painful but necessary. It was essential to shape the stories with Elder Jean as she provided the details to unpack these mysteries. Jean holds celebrated wisdom from her traditional teachings that illuminate the importance of *Secwepemc* child rearing. A particular story she shared was that when she was a child her grandparents took an interest in her. A cultural practice by grandparents was to keep an eye on their grandchildren for the purpose of choosing a grandchild that they would raise as their own. That child would be taught ancestral knowledge and they would also become caregivers for their grandparents later on. This practice protected the Elders because there were no long-term care facilities in earlier days so the *Secwepemc* maintained a familial system to look after their people when they aged. Jean's explanation helped me understand the important bonds between grandparents and their grandchildren. The children were seen as gifts so her story helped me revere my time with my grandparents even more.

I appreciate the way stories teach about the significant roles of Elders and grandparents in *Secwepemc* society. To further signify Elders' positions, I observed an Elder's reaction in a First Nations course I co-teach at Vancouver Island University in British Columbia. Recently, I gave a class presentation about my doctoral study and I highlighted my three research questions. One of them asks, "How do Elders shape cultural identity?" (Martin, 2014, p. 3). When I read it, I saw our Elder co-instructor Delores Louie's face light up. She was thrilled to hear about how we pay attention to Elders and she reaffirmed her feelings through her stories. She explained how Elders treated her kindly and they offered her a very traditional upbringing. The strength of Elders is widespread among Indigenous Nations. Jean and I felt their presence too. Below, I describe how personal and physical spaces are parts of storytelling.

Positionality

In our "*Le7 Q'7es te Stsptekwll re Secwépemc*: Our Memories Long Ago" book chapter, I position myself as a *Secwepemc* person, Indigenous scholar, and community member. Jean is *Secwepemc*, a cultural advisor, community member, mentor, language speaker, and traditional knowledge holder. My point of reference in this story is to provide insights from my journey through academia by sharing the application of *Secwepemc* "ways of knowing" and "ways of being" through the embodiment of the *Secwepemc* hand drum. Jean takes the role of transmitting, guiding, and telling the stories passed on to her from her Elder teachers that represent ancestral knowledge gained by living alongside grandparents. The synergistic liaison between Jean as the storyteller and me as the listener grew and strengthened. The synergy is vital to correctly deliver the meaning of the stories. Storytelling is crucial; as Archibald (2008) outlined, we need to "examine Indigenous knowledges and Indigenous ways of knowing within academe" (p. 5) without feeling that Indigenous epistemological approaches will be treated as trivial within these institutions. Resuming with the Indigenous storywork theme, Elder Jean and I maintain an ongoing symbiotic alliance in a learner–teacher–storyteller relationship involving story sharing of the long-ago ancestral memories of the *Secwepemc* people. Much like Archibald's (2008) storywork approach, Jean's stories show the meaning of our *Secwepemc* stories in "teaching, learning and healing" (p. 85). To maintain the honour and respect involved in sharing and interpreting stories, five of Archibald's (2008) principles – respect, reverence, holism, interrelatedness, and synergy – are our focus. Sharing the memories and voices of the *Secwepemc* through story is our shared way of understanding the world.

Story is Indigenous theory

Here I reflect on orality as the process for resilience. Resilience comes to mind because when I first set foot in an academic institution, I did not know exactly where my research would take me, nor did I know what epistemic and methodological approaches I would find. There were two things I did know. First, my priority was to continue to examine my identities and second, I needed to ensure that I did not leave myself outside the door of the academy. Far too often Indigenous people, and probably other ethnicities, are forced to leave a good part of who they are behind when they enter academia. Battiste (2000) explains that Aboriginal people have been subjugated by the military, political, and economic systems, but the most effective oppressive attack on First Nations cultures has been the educational system. She further states that "the subtle influence of cognitive imperialism, modern educational theory and practice … destroyed or distorted the ways of life, histories, identities, cultures, and languages of Aboriginal people" (p. 193). To be true to myself and especially my grandparents, who supported me throughout life, I had to embody the vision expressed in the words of my grandfather, that I should "know who I am and where I come from." His words became the impetus to question why I had developed notions of a lost sense of belonging along the way. I felt that while these feelings developed from somewhere it was likely that other Indigenous people felt the same and this is why studying disrupted identities is important.

I knew that the topic and process would be personal and sensitive. In anticipation of the discomfort and internal challenges I expected to face, I needed a theoretical and methodological approach that would not be harmful and would also be conducive to story sharing. Accordingly, Archibald (2008) outlines how we acquire knowledge and codes of behaviour that are embedded in our cultural practices, and notes that a key role of oral tradition is storytelling. I needed to augment my study with a theory and methodology that would honour our ways of being, so I chose Indigenous storywork, which anchored my place in the academic world. To be true to my roots, I dispelled the notion that storytelling and story sharing are not validated in academic approaches. Six years after *Indigenous Storywork* was published, Million (2014) explains how "American Indian, First Nations, and Indigenous scholars recognize orally based communal knowledges as organized epistemic systems that do exist ... though they may not be legitimized by academia" (p. 35). She further asserts that story is Indigenous theory. Through this theory, "narratives seek inclusion" as "Indigenous narratives are emotionally empowered" (p. 35). I found my inclusion through personal narratives as I examined the feelings of losing some of my identities and as I dug deep into my soul, I felt emotionally charged responses. Thankfully, Archibald's (2008) seven principles of respect, responsibility, reciprocity, reverence, holism, interrelatedness, and synergy created the space to support balance and harmony between my community, my study participants, and the academy. Jean and I took up where Archibald left off. Through storytelling, I shared my lived experiences to sort through the misgivings I had about my identities. Elder Jean's "give-away" was extending her "personal life experiences as teaching stories in a manner similar to how [storytellers] use traditional stories" (Archibald, 2008, p. 112). Jean's expression of a "give-away" relates to *Secwepemc* practices. The *Secwepemc* people pride themselves on being a giving people. Long ago, the people gave gifts every day; it did not require a special day. When the Christians came, the annual Christmas gift-giving ritual was adopted. Jean carries on her traditional knowledge and language speaking and offers these gifts to the *Secwepemc* community as her give-away to support the retention of culture and language. She guided us through the process of making meaning of the stories as they correlated to relational connections with grandparents.

We experienced our Indigenous ways of understanding the world through our teachings. A vivid example was when visitors arrived from neighbouring communities; their meals and accommodation were organized and the length of their stay was never a concern. To teach us respect for the travellers, my grandfather told stories about how many days it would take people to travel by horse and wagon to reach our village and that they were tired. It was our job to ensure their comfort. He framed his teaching in the context that we are to treat others as we would like to be treated. He explained that the children had a place to sit while the guests were fed. When the meal was finished, the children cleared the dishes while the adults visited. Without being direct, he taught me what my role was as a host. I learned from that example that whenever we visited other communities they would reciprocate. His lessons were conveyed in a gentle and caring way through a story approach and I gained a wealth of knowledge from my grandfather by observing and following his directions. While her grandparents also groomed Jean, she valued their *Secwepemc* teachings. In turn, she passes this knowledge on to members of the community who are willing to learn. The youth participant, Colten Wycotte, and I were fortunate to learn from Jean's teachings during my research project. In the next section, segments of Jean's stories are featured to explain how the teaching relationships and meaning-making unfolded.

Grandparents' teachings

Jean's stories

Jean shared the strength of her relationships with her grandparents and the manner in which they taught her, which was by communicating in a good way, not with authority or discipline. The following six vignettes are her narratives, taken from my study. These memories feature the horses and wagon, caring for grandparents, grandpa as advisor, sharing chores, spirituality, and cultural/traditional practices.

1. *Horses and wagon*: The memories Jean displayed about the horses and wagon involved the connection she shared with her grandfather. She said he used to travel with his horses and wagon.

She remembered the times she reined in the horses. Her grandpa would sing to her when he needed the horses, and that was her cue. This was a special time and she always had a horse to ride.

2. *Caring for grandparents*: Jean remembered when she cared for her grandparents but it was never explained to her why they took her in. Through inquiry, she found out later in her adult years. She thought she was given away, but in fact her grandparents wanted her. They knew that when they got older she would look after them like an old age home. Her grandpa never went to the hospital when he got sick in his elder years; Jean looked after him at home. These were her best memories. She enjoyed her grandpa.

3. *Grandpa as advisor*: Jean says that her grandpa had an advisory role, which is interesting because she has the same role now. She is the cultural advisor. She recalled how the hereditary Chiefs would drop by and visit her grandpa. Often, they asked for his advice and input before they made decisions. His children and the community respected him. He was a leader and treated everyone well. A childhood memory was when he brought her popcorn from his trips into town. Out of nostalgia, Jean still buys the same popcorn.

4. *Sharing chores*: Jean says she was never really disciplined. She wasn't given orders; when chores needed to be done, they were done without question. When a sweat lodge was needed, all granny had to do was say "we need to get the water ready" and the sweat would be prepared. On Sundays when the church bell rang everyone knew it was time to go to church; no one had to be told. It was the same with everything else. Packing wood, picking berries, collecting water; through a few words or actions everything fell into place.

5. *Spirituality*: In terms of spirituality, Jean says, "While I was growing up we always thanked the Creator. We took time to be thankful for what we had, especially our health" (Martin, 2014, p. 140). Spirituality was practised on the land and it continues to be very important. She stated, "I am experiencing my own healing so I try to forgive people … That's my own belief" (Martin, 2014, p. 140).

6. *Cultural and traditional practices*: Some of the cultural and traditional activities practised by Jean's grandmother involved picking plants in the spring. Her grandmother made powder for poultices from the plants. The medicine was used for colds. Other examples of traditional methods were drying meat and fish, preparing jams,

and picking berries. She remembers that her grandma couldn't read or write but she says "man could she make jams" (Martin, 2014, p. 142). Jean practised the sweats. The sweats are a highly regarded part of the *Secwepemc* culture. The *Secwepemc* people use the sweat lodge for many reasons, including cleansing, preparing for hunting, and other wellness needs. The sweat lodge is a domed structure made from willow branches, covered with blankets to capture the heat. The people inside form a circle around a pit filled with red-hot rocks. A variety of medicines such as sage, tobacco, or cedar are placed on the rocks before they are splashed with cold water to create steam. In the long ago days, Jean says, "sometimes the men would drum and the women danced." Her son is carrying on the traditions now and they are passing them down to her grandson. This is proof that the traditions were shared and they survived through the use of oral teachings and practice. Thankfully, through her guidance, this knowledge is being passed to the fourth generation in her family.

Jean continues to preserve the *Secwepemc* culture that was transmitted through the solid traditional teachings of her Elders and grandparents. It is evident that the time she spent with them is how she acquired the important ancestral knowledges that she values so highly. It was easy for her to learn because of her respectful relationships with her teachers. There is a strong indication that the *Secwepemc* people in her era were willing learners. Currently, the Elder–youth relationships are not as strong. Passing on the knowledge is imperative to keep the teachings and memories of the *Secwepemc* people active.

Georgina's stories

As I slide back in time, I admire my grandparents as my teachers and caregivers too. My situation evolved out of circumstance. When I was born, my mother was in the Coqualeetza Indian hospital located in Sardis, which borders Sardis and Chilliwack, BC. The hospital was 448 kilometres south of my home community of T'exelc. Coqualeetza was called a hospital but it was really a sanatorium that quarantined Aboriginal people with tuberculosis (TB). My mom had TB, so upon my birth I was taken from her. My grandmother (her mom) took me from the sanatorium and my grandparents raised me as their own. It was this disconnect that constituted the breakdown in my being, which bred my lost sense of belonging. It was not until my PhD study that I gathered up the courage to examine why I felt this way. The confusion appeared between the dichotomy of my loving and nurturing grandparents and the absence of my mother during the important years of my development. I did not understand why this was so; I just felt unwanted. I did not understand the forced separation from my mother until I shared the purpose of my study with a University of British Columbia professor when I told him I was looking into the reality of not having a relationship with my mother, which has affected me. I explained that when I was born, I was taken from her because she had TB and she was deemed contagious. In an astonished voice that startled me, he said, can you imagine what that must have felt like for your mother? Honestly, until he said that, I had only focused on how I felt without the closeness of a mother.

Through this conversation, I started to turn my pain into understanding. I realized that it was not her fault. She did not decide that she did not want me; she was not allowed to have me. Through my story search, I have no recollection of when she returned to the community, I just knew that I remained with my grandparents throughout life. While I was collecting, and organizing the stories, working with Jean, I understood and I cherished even more the importance of grandparents and I knew that I was in good hands.

Later, I learned that my grandparents wanted to keep me even when my mom was out of the sanatorium. In retrospect, I see how much my grandparents positively influenced me. Their teachings held steadfast in my character and work ethic. They reared me in the same non-disciplinary fashion as Jean was raised; Jean and I both learned how to work very hard. My grandfather rewarded me with fruit and sometimes a piece of candy for finishing my jobs. The system worked because I got the job done without any prodding and I did my best to satisfy my grandparents. It was important for me to know that they were happy. I enjoyed the time I lived alongside them.

As my grandparents grew more elderly, they enrolled me in the residential school around the age of 12 because they could no longer take care of me. The residential school was the second disruption that resulted from circumstance. The residential school was certainly another level of violence but it will not be discussed in detail in this article. Jean confirmed that my dad had been placed in the same residential school during his childhood. He had major difficulties there and the most prominent was that he was not raised in a nurturing environment; therefore, he did not develop the capacity to nurture his children. Finding this out elevated my awareness of the breakdown bred by residential schools. Through this discovery, I realized that my father's attendance at the school, combined with mine, are contributing factors in the collapse of identities and resulting intergenerational trauma. The trauma is described by Duran (2006) as cumulative. He contends that when trauma is passed through generations it becomes more severe as each generation compounds it. Since many generations are not conscious of and responsive to the effects of trauma, it passes through to the next. I estimate that the setback caused by residential school may begin to improve in my family by the fifth generation. My father was the first generation, which passed negative behaviours to me. I, in turn, unintentionally passed them on to my children, who still feel the consequences. My children's children have been exposed to and influenced by residential school as well. I anticipate change will occur when my great-grandchildren overcome the breakdown in their identities and become enlightened.

Thankfully, Jean's and my collective strengths were engrained in us through our relationships with our grandparents, who were our teachers and guides. In similar fashion to Archibald (2008), I felt that it was necessary to return to the Elders for answers. I understood how Indigenous storywork adhered to and respected cultural protocols, especially in terms of the intensity and sacredness of the subject matter. In order to correctly make meaning of stories, Jean's strength of Indigenous knowledge was a perfect guide. As we collectively embarked on our journeys to share stories, we were guided by our grandparents' teachings, which motivated our approach to research, writing, and teaching. The synergistic relationship we shared was born from the trust that was extended between us to know that the stories would be told in a meaningful way. The ancestral knowledges we acquired are juxtaposed against the clashes forced upon us by government legislation, policies, and programmes. Fortunately, we managed to retain our grandparents' transformative teachings and we are encouraged that we can share these stories from our combined lived experiences to celebrate our culture, traditions, and ancestral knowledges. The retention of these teachings and the deep connections are what Holmes (2000) describes as "heart knowledge" (p. 46). She characterizes these knowledges passed down in her Hawaiian culture as the source that unites generations and she calls these relationships "blood memory" (p. 46). The stories that we hang on to are our blood memory and the new stories we can tell are our ceremonies.

Ceremonies in story

Our stories are drawn from the teachings gained from our grandparents and they will come alive now in the retelling. I will describe how I incorporated our *Secwepemc* hand drum in my identity inquiry as my epistemic and theoretical framework, in order to remain true to my heritage. The cadence of the hand drum drew me closer to the teachings of my grandparents. Jean further demonstrates the broadening of her knowledge through her relationship with pictographs as a way to show how the practice of her experience and knowledge preserves the integrity of the *Secwepemc* peoples that connects to her memories of long ago. I begin by narrating how the hand drum became the heart of my theory and methodology to guide my delicate inquiry into *Secwepemc* identities, ensuring that the people and the stories were honoured and respected.

The Secwepemc *hand drum as my theory and methodology*

To protect the stories and how they are told, my *Secwepemc* hand drum framework channelled my epistemic and theoretical approaches and it became my trusted guide while privileging our ancestral knowledges. In the spirit of Indigenous storywork, the hand drum epitomizes respect, reverence, holism, interrelatedness, and synergy. The first three principles are embraced through the hand drum's connection to the spirit, earth, and the circle of life. The finished hand drum is a sphere, similar to Atleo's (2004) concept of *heshook-ish-tsawalk* in the *Nuu-chah-nulth* language, which means mind, body, and spirit are connected. These ideals coalesce with Archibald's concept of holism. The circle frame means there is no beginning or ending and all the parts are interconnected and equally important. I did not stand on my own; through my heritage, I was connected to my participants and my community. The wooden frame of the drum derives from the tree, which is born from the land; this reminds the *Secwepemc* of their responsibilities to both land and community. When the *Secwepemc* people are gifted with an animal's life, they make an offering to the Creator for the spirit of the animal that gifts its life to feed the people and support our cultural practice. The people respect all things and they believe that all animate and inanimate beings have spirits that must be revered. Another level of reverence is the drummer's respect for the drum. The hand drum in my study was gifted to me by my friend Lena Paul and I took up the responsibility to care for it and use it in a good way.

The passing of the hand drum follows a code of cultural respect, and the drum comes to life. It is not merely the giving and receiving of an object. Jean adds that the hand drum is like the teachings. There is protocol around how both are handled. She says that this is where our traditional and natural laws evolved. The way we prepared the drum, and how, when, and where it is used are all part of protocol. These are all important teachings and we must respect them before we proceed.

The cultural ethics surrounding the hand drum became my research ethics for conducting research in an Aboriginal community. I remembered that in order to work with Indigenous people, I needed to foster reciprocal relationships. The cadence of the hand drum was a constant reminder to bring me back to the necessary protocols and safety around community-based interaction. The hand drum–community–researcher relationship epitomizes the principles described by Archibald (2008) as interrelatedness and synergy. These principled practices were crucial. Therefore to ground me, I learned and practised drumming and singing one song during my time at the University of British Columbia. Singing and drumming requires intimate synergy with the drum. It took an entire year to learn how to drum the one song I can lead with comfort. Each time I took up the practice of hand drumming, I was reminded of its important values, which guided my methodology. The antler handle of my drum represented my grandparents; I clung to them and the vivid memories of their teachings. The four sinew straps that attach the hide to the frame represented the following ideas in my study:

1. Indigenous knowledge is the culturally relevant framework that uses Indigenous methodologies to privilege the voices of the participants and promote safety.
2. Experiences represent the depth of our culture and our connection with it.
3. Stories are the traditional knowledge gained by living alongside grandparents, which shaped our successes and who we have become.
4. Teachings moved me from my head to my heart, which reflected a process of reconciliation and the inner struggles to integrate the teachings of our Elders.

In order to examine disrupted identities, it was important to include the *Secwepemc* people; therefore I engaged with community members, education staff, Elders, and leaders. Various methods of engagement were established for two-way communication about the processes of my educational study. When the dissertation was accepted by the university, I was invited home to celebrate with my community.

Jean's living memories of petroglyphs and pictographs

Jean began by explaining the meaning of a rock formation in the *Secwepemc* culture. According to the Elders, rock is our paper. In the *Secwepemc* language, it is *Stsq'ey'ulecw ne tmicws – kucw* and there is no way to describe it in English. The land is marked because our markings are on the land. It must have been there all the time. In legal terms, *Stsq'eys – kucw* are our rights written in stone or rock.

As Jean explains, there were no written systems long ago so the origin stories are etched in petroglyphs and pictographs; these are our manuscripts. During our planning phase in August 2017, Jean explained:

> As *Secwepemc* we have a very distinctive role. We see ourselves as caretakers. Stewards of our *Secwepemcul'ecw*. We have a strong spiritual connection to our land. All of its resources have nurtured us. We have always lived in harmony with all living things that has met all our personal needs. Food, shelter, medicine. We always believe for instance that water is good medicine, it is the best.

The importance of animals is shown in the *Secwepemc* stories through the markings of animals seen in rock art. The landform also features petroglyphs, known as coyote rocks. Jean asks: Do they define our territory? We know the symbols. Does this mean we are connected to or own the land? It strengthens our identities; these are our boundaries. Due to the difficulty in translation between the *Secwepemc* language and English, Jean explained further. When granny went to tell a story she always referred to the old people before her who told the stories. Granny would explain the meaning and emphasize how important it is to pass them on orally. She always stressed where the stories originated and how the *Secwepemc* are an oral society. This is the way culture is preserved; it is the ancient way of passing on knowledge and cultural teachings. There was nothing written that would be more important than the ancient rock etchings. The etchings tell the stories of what someone dreamt or what a guest saw. Only the person who saw it could pass it on.

Jean has difficulty explaining in words what the paintings and markings mean. She describes a few of the etchings, which are birds and other animals, the sun or lightning flashes. She asks: What would the spiritual leaders see? A cultural person like her may see or interpret for a young person going into adulthood. What is his dream? The dream might be an experience linked to a vision quest. The story would show the young person moving into adulthood what their purpose would be later in life. This is our spiritual time, our sacred journey to find strength to deal with health issues, connecting with the Creator for deeper spirituality, asking for help, and connecting to the land. She states, "We are searching, it is so hard to talk about." The difficulty expressed by Jean is not uncommon among knowledge holders of creation stories. The stories are told in ways that the local people understand them. If they are not orated correctly, the meaning loses its source. Many of these stories only remain with the Secwepemc storytellers. They can only be shared through oral practice, otherwise they are lost. Jean's recollections are the memories brought forward from the Elders of long ago. She was born into and practised the traditional lifestyle, which transfers a huge responsibility to pass this knowledge on. This is known as *Yecw meń ul e cwem*, which means taking care of the land. It is the *Secwepemc* way of life, but now many people struggle to understand the concept of the sacredness, spiritual connection, and thankfulness. The *Secwepemc* are stewards of the land and they must take care of it. The sacred sites are our creation stories that are preserved in petroglyphs and pictographs.

One example is the legend called *pellsqwyets* in the Snow Mountains. It describes how we must darken our faces before we gather berries and medicines. This is the way our ancestors will recognize us. *Stsq'eylecw* are the markings on the rock that tell *Secwepemc* stories. It is difficult to describe this in English, as there is no literal meaning. Many of the *Secwepemc* stories of long ago can only be passed on orally and they are hard to describe if one does not know the language. There is no equivalent in the writing otherwise the meaning changes. Jean explains that when we work together it builds up who we are and enhances our learning journey. From the learning, we have the capacity to pass on our own descriptions of how we see the world. We are encouraged to think hard and the outcome is developing better judgement. In her case, she adds more to her stories to bring joy and laughter, which is good for the soul. The *Secwepemc* still practise this; we are humorous, full of fun and laughter.

On June 13, 2012 a ceremony was held on the *Secwepemc* traditional territory to repatriate a rock that was taken by the Vancouver Parks Board in 1926. The rock was taken without the *Secwepemc* peoples' consent, relocated to Stanley Park in Vancouver, BC and set up outdoors as an Aboriginal artefact. In 1992, it was relocated to the courtyard of the Museum of Vancouver where it remained until 2012. The repatriation and return of the rock to the *Secwepemc* territory was a joyous occasion because the spirit of the ancestors contained in the rock moved home and they could rest. These stories are ones that the general public do not understand. The sacredness and vibrancy of the culture and traditions are enclosed in the *Secwepemc* paper (rock) and story forms that only the *Secwepemc* can read. The remnants of these drawings are found scattered throughout the *Secwepemc* territory.

Jean recognizes the importance of her Eldership in passing on the cultural teachings. It is crucial because she is one of the few fluent, knowledgeable speakers of the language left. She says that we need to encourage storytellers to continue telling the stories because without the stories, we lose our language, our identity, and our culture.

Conclusion

It is understandable that dismay about Canada's 150th celebration arose in us, given that the country's colonial policies and practices almost destroyed the language and lives of the *Secwepemc* people. The lack of agency by the developers of Canada 150 displays an intolerance toward all Indigenous Peoples in Canada. The country retains a burdened conscience.

Therefore, it is important that the *Secwepemc* and all Indigenous Peoples around the globe continue to tell their stories to preserve their cultures, especially in oral societies. Indigenous storywork principles offer critical, ethical, and methodological guidelines that become seamlessly linked to Indigenous traditional and lived stories. Such stories must be told through storywork; not doing so undervalues the stories' meanings. Elders must be recognized for their storytelling wisdom, or the intent and content of the stories change. By remembering the lessons learned from our grandparents and through Jean's ongoing traditional practices, there is hope that our ancestral knowledge will be transformative throughout the generations, using our timeless practice of telling the stories of long ago.

References

Archibald, J. (2008). *Indigenous storywork: educating the heart, mind, body, and spirit.* Vancouver, BC: UBC Press.

Atleo, R. E. (2004). *Tsawalk: a Nuu-chah-nulth worldview.* Vancouver, BC: UBC Press.

Battiste, M. (2000). Maintaining Aboriginal identity, language, and culture in modern society. In M. Battiste (Ed.), *Reclaiming Indigenous voice and vision* (pp. 192–208). Vancouver, BC: UBC Press.

Billy, J. (2017, November 20). *The Secwepemc: the people, land of the Shuswap [Website].* Retrieved from www.landoftheshuswap.com/people.html.

Duran, E. (2006). *Healing the soul wound: counseling with American Indians and other Native Peoples.* New York, NY: Teachers College Press.

Holmes, L. (2000). Heart knowledge, blood memory, and the voice of the land: implications of research among Hawaiian elders. In G. B. S. Dei, B. Hall & D. Goldin Rosenberg (Eds.), *Indigenous knowledges in global contexts: multiple readings of our world* (pp. 37–53). Toronto, ON: University of Toronto Press.

Martin, G. (2014). *Drumming my way home: an intergenerational narrative inquiry about Secwepemc identities.* Doctoral dissertation, University of British Columbia, Vancouver, BC.

Million, D. (2014). There is a river in me: theory from life. In A. Smith & A. Simpson (Eds.), *Theorizing Native studies* (pp. 31–42). Durham, NC: Duke University Press, 2014.

Truth and Reconciliation Canada. (2015). *Honouring the truth, reconciling for the future: summary of the final report of the Truth and Reconciliation Commission of Canada.* Winnipeg, MB: Truth and Reconciliation Commission of Canada.

4 | TRANSFORMATIVE EDUCATION FOR ABORIGINAL MATHEMATICS LEARNING: INDIGENOUS STORYWORK AS METHODOLOGY[1]

Jo-ann Archibald Q'um Q'um Xiiem, Cynthia Nicol, and Joanne Yovanovich

Introduction

This chapter focuses on a long-term research project (2005–2017), exploring the development of culturally responsive education in a rural Indigenous community, which we call *Transformative Education for Aboriginal*[2] *Mathematics – Learning (TEAM-Learning)*. We focus on our research methodology in one rural community where we describe our efforts to develop relationships, working together as Indigenous and non-Indigenous scholars for culturally responsive consciousness and practices. We highlight a participatory process that has required a long-term commitment toward learning about self and self in relation to others, culture, and community, as well as academic and everyday mathematics. This project shares the goal of Marshall, Williams, and Stewart (2008) that "building curriculum and teaching it in Indigenous communities should be to empower, listen, communicate, and connect with students" (p. 168). This goal presents a challenge for both Aboriginal and non-Aboriginal educators. For Aboriginal educators, Castellano (2000) notes the challenge is to go beyond the critique of colonial institutions and to "give expression to [A]boriginal philosophies, world views, and social relations" (p. 23). For non-Aboriginal educators the challenge is to recognize the cultural resilience of Aboriginal students (Battiste, 2000) and to create educative spaces for the inclusion and serious intellectual consideration of Indigenous values and worldviews.

Our methodological framework for TEAM-Learning and its focus on culturally responsive pedagogy includes the intersection and interconnectivity of: (1) students and their learning experiences; (2) community values, culture, and Indigenous knowledges; and (3) mathematics. This framework guides our work with teachers and community members to explore and articulate what a culturally responsive pedagogy for mathematics teaching and learning might look like within the semi-isolated Indigenous community, *Haida Gwaii*, in British Columbia. We address the following research question in the study:

> How can Indigenous storywork as a methodology help researchers and teachers develop and sustain their roles and relationships to each other; to students, families and community; to Indigenous knowledge; and to mathematics?

Indigenous storywork methodology

The TEAM-Learning project uses Indigenous storywork for its methodology (Archibald, 2008). In Archibald's methodological framework the 4Rs of respect, responsibility, reverence, and reciprocity relate to ways of working with people and with Indigenous knowledges. The remaining principles of holism, interrelatedness, and synergy relate to how Indigenous knowledge and Indigenous stories are used in the research process. This chapter will focus on how Indigenous storywork as methodology helped TEAM-Learning researchers from the University of British Columbia and the *Haida Gwaii* School District develop and maintain positive and mutually beneficial research relationships with teachers and Indigenous community members in one semi-isolated community site, *Haida Gwaii*, in British Columbia's Pacific Northwest over a 12-year period. However, the early years of this research project are emphasized in this chapter to illustrate relationship-building processes.

Archibald's methodology (2008) was adapted to the purposes of the TEAM-Learning project because her storywork and our project included learning from and working with the traditional and life experience stories of Indigenous Elders, cultural knowledge holders, storytellers, and educators. In TEAM-Learning, *respect* was demonstrated by building upon the knowledges and experiences of Indigenous community members, including students, and teachers throughout the research process. Multiple layers of accountability helped researchers carry out their *responsibilities* to the people they were researching with, to Indigenous knowledges, to quality math education, and to themselves. *Reverence* involved sensitivity to the ways in which we respectfully honoured our relationships and interactions with participants, their knowledges, and with the land/nature in a spiritual manner. *Reciprocity* included ways that this research contributes to the sustainability of Indigenous knowledge, and bringing math, culture, and community together for educational and community-oriented purposes.

The principles of *holism*, *interrelatedness*, and *synergy* created space for meaningful interaction among research participants, researchers, and community members to share and listen to life experience and traditional stories (gather data), to make meaning from them through critical reflection and discussion (analysis), and to develop new knowledge and understandings based upon their learning experiences and interactions (identify findings). TEAM-Learning approaches, experiences, and issues in using Indigenous storywork methodology are exemplified in this paper.

The research context

Haida Gwaii, meaning People of the Islands, is on the northwest coast of British Columbia. It is a semi-isolated First Nations community, accessible via two-hour air travel one way throughout the year or a six-hour ferry ride from the mainland. Following European contact and the spread of disease and epidemics in the mid-1800s the *Haida* population was reduced to less than 1,000 people living in two major *Haida* communities, Old Masset in the north and Skidegate in the south. Currently the Islands have a population of less than 5,000 people, with about 40 per cent identifying as being of *Haida* or First Nations ancestry. The one public school district that services all of *Haida Gwaii* has less than 500 students, of whom 70 per cent are Indigenous, while most of the teachers are non-Indigenous. There is also one school (kindergarten to Grade 5) located in Old Masset that is not part of the public school district and one school (kindergarten to Grade 7) in Skidegate, located within the reserve, which is a public school. Despite a declining non-Indigenous student population, the Indigenous student population is expected to increase steadily over the next few years. The public school district has one district-wide principal of Aboriginal education. Over the years, the district has focused attention on improving students' performance in provincial assessments of writing and reading, and on working with teachers to understand and appreciate *Haida* culture and values.

Our community-oriented research project emphasizes developing relationships with Elders, community members, and teachers. We have asked about and listened to their desires, hopes, problems, and possibilities for mathematics teaching and learning as well as strategies to build upon *Haida* cultural knowledge, place-based knowing, and community resources. On *Haida Gwaii* we have had multiple meetings and conversations with community Elders, community artists, Indigenous knowledge holders, the *Haida* Education Council, the *Haida Gwaii* School District, and teachers.

Since 2006, two very supportive school district Aboriginal education directors/principals[3] have provided valuable support to the project. The first director facilitated discussions with the community *Haida* Education Council to gain approval for conducting this study on *Haida* lands and with communities, provided communications liaison with school district teachers, and facilitated two Elders meetings held in both the communities. Since 2008, the second school district principal has continued to participate as a project co-researcher and facilitator, providing significant liaison between the district, community, schools, and university researchers.

Over the years, project university researchers, the district principal of Aboriginal education, teachers, and community members have met to discuss strategies, ideas, challenges, and possibilities of connecting *Haida* culture, community, mathematics, and school both within and beyond school contexts. Since the project began more than 20 teachers and administrators and ten community members have participated. During the early years of the project we met as a group every six to eight weeks as funding allowed. Now, with less funding to support transportation and teacher release time, we meet once every three months.

Data collection has included field notes, teacher journal writing, digital photos, individual interviews, group discussions, video data of project meetings, and classroom episodes. Another key component of the methodology included teachers' participation in full-day group meetings about every four to eight weeks throughout the school year. Community members often attended these meetings as guests and participants. Field trips took us to local artists who invited us to their carving sheds. Many land/ocean-based experiences inspired us to explore an openness toward connecting mathematics, Indigenous ways of knowing, students' thinking and emotions, and community.

The focus of the meetings was determined by the interests and questions of those attending, and the interests and needs of the community. Some meetings were focused on collectively solving mathematics problems that might inspire and engage students. Other meetings focused on learning more about *Haida* ways of knowing. Still others focused on learning more about the changes to the revised school mathematics curriculum. Some meeting topics included: (1) exploring students' mathematical thinking to learn more about students' strengths and interests; (2) understanding student emotions, identity, and agency to consider how we might teach mathematics lessons that are emotionally engaging; (3) investigating mapping and *Haida* oral stories to examine the interrelatedness of mathematics education and cultural, social, political, and historical issues; (4) exploring digital images of the place of *Haida Gwaii* to inspire mathematical problem solving in the culture and community; and (5) exploring the processes of canoe building, weaving, and carving and the mathematics involved in collaboration with museum curators. The meetings were organized by the university team with input from teacher participants. Between meetings teachers worked on various tasks, piloted projects, developed math problems in their classes, and collected digital images of the land and culture of *Haida* as sources of potential problem-solving contexts.

The next part of our chapter discusses three major understandings about Indigenous storywork methodology that we have acquired from interviews with community members and teachers and from our reflections: (1) establishing relationships through protocol, visiting, listening, and "being there"; (2) learning from each other through sharing personal teaching stories and mentoring; and (3) learning about Indigenous knowledges through experiencing Indigenous stories.

Establishing relationships through protocol, visiting, listening, and "being there"

In June 2005, Cynthia Nicol and Jo-ann Archibald made their first visit to the community site to meet with the school district superintendent, school district principal of Aboriginal education, community education council, and teachers. Cynthia, a non-Indigenous scholar, had taught high school math in this school district for eight years before leaving to pursue graduate education and subsequently a faculty position. She knew the schooling context and knew what it was like to live in a semi-isolated community. Jo-ann, an Indigenous scholar, had been to this school district once as a conference speaker and also knew First Nations community members from this community who became educators. She has worked in Indigenous education for 36 years. During this visit, they received a strong indication of interest from the school district to participate in this study due to the district's concerns about making math more successful for Aboriginal learners. In 2006–07, the school district data show that 56 per cent of *Haida* students did not meet expectations in grade 4 provincial mathematics assessments compared to 38 per cent of non-*Haida* students. The grade seven assessments indicate that 53 per cent of the *Haida* students did not meet grade level expectations compared to 44 per cent of non-*Haida* students. Local Aboriginal students' mathematics assessments were relatively lower than Aboriginal student data collected at a provincial level (British Columbia Ministry of Education, 2007). Joanne Yovanovich, co-researcher, joined the project in 2006, first as principal of one of the district schools and then as principal of Aboriginal education for the school district.

The school district leaders and *Haida* Education Council voiced their support and approval for the project in a letter from the school district and verbal agreement at a council meeting attended by the researchers. At first, the researchers discussed the possibility of having a research agreement between the community and university. However, as the project proceeded, the *Haida* Education Council requested that project updates be presented at their council meetings on a fairly regular basis. Cynthia and the school district Aboriginal education director met with the council about twice a year. The *Haida* Education Council continues to be very interested in and supportive of the research project.

In January 2006, Cynthia and Jo-ann visited the schools to give more teachers information about the project and to see if anyone was interested in being a participant. The teachers had received information about TEAM-Learning prior to their visit as described earlier. The *Haida* education director arranged for Cynthia and Jo-ann to meet with two Elders' groups from the two communities. At these sessions we explained the study and had engaging discussions about how they had used math in their everyday lives while growing up and earning a living. Some at first did not think that they had used math in their daily lives, but as the discussion began, and members shared their ways of using math, those who doubted the use of math began to recount experiences that included aspects of math. They were enthused about the study because they had a positive attitude to and experience of math. To them, they used math for a reason. Many of their stories centred on the numerical characteristics of math, and other concepts were illustrated, including proportion, estimating, and problem-solving.

The Elders also talked about their concerns and perspectives relating to their grandchildren's and great-grandchildren's educational experience. One Elder remembered what he called "zeal" for learning in his family and wondered "how much zeal teachers have" for teaching math. They were very concerned to hear that First Nations children in their communities were experiencing such difficulty with math. Many recalled that math was an integral part of their lives and recounted how important it was to their everyday life, as indicated in the following quotes:

> [M]ath is the most important thing in life. The [fisher] figures out the tides, financial settlements for the men working on the fish boats, figures out how much fuel to buy, how much food to get for fishing trips.
>
> [W]e never used to measure anything ... we used our hands and our bodies to figure out measurement.
>
> [O]ur bent wood boxes were always straight and perfectly square, without using measuring tapes ... our tall totem poles were straight.

Cynthia felt that she needed to spend more time on *Haida Gwaii* in order to continue developing relationships with the teachers and facilitate the group discussion sessions, which have become a very important part of the methodology. Since January 2007, the teachers and Cynthia have met every two to three months.

We are reminded of Linda Smith's (1999) notion of the "seen face," where researchers need to be seen as active participants in the community in order to gain credibility and to build relationships. It took about a year to get school district and community approvals and to secure teacher participants. We were mindful and respectful of the heavy responsibilities that both Indigenous community members and teachers have in their daily lives and tried not to rush our project. Teacher participants were involved in the project for varying lengths of time. Some committed to the project for three consecutive years, others moved off the Islands and continued to be involved although at a distance, and teachers new to the *Haida Gwaii* School District have become involved. District teacher turnover is typically high so it was expected that teacher involvement in the project would fluctuate over the years. However, both mathematics and non-mathematics teachers are participants, providing thought-provoking and enriching contributions to the group and project meetings.

Learning from each other by sharing personal teaching stories and mentoring

As noted above, each teacher shared her/his TEAM-Learning experiences by telling their stories, showing samples of student work, showing photographs, and presenting video teaching episodes. A trust and willingness to talk about problems and successes in conceptualizing and designing culturally responsive mathematics lessons and then trying them out with students developed as the project continued. We noticed that as each person shared her and his experiences, a space was created to listen to each other, and to engage in a dialogic action where participants respond to each other's questions and concerns. A synergistic action occurs, where new understandings are created. The following quotes show the benefits of the discussion sessions in response to the question about what has stood out so far about the project:

> sharing of information and the sharing of experiences that people have had within our little group. (Teacher 8, interview)
>
> The most beneficial thing? … there are so many things. To brainstorm ideas in terms of somebody will say something and that spurs a thought that I wouldn't have had on my own, or that kind of thing. As well as just to go away and try something and come back and see how different people approached it and what that looked like in different scenarios. And just meeting to discuss lessons and kids and math. (Teacher 5, interview)
>
> The neat thing I found was getting together with the colleagues at different grade levels or different teaching and seeing what they deal with because sometimes any teacher can get in their own [self-contained classroom]. I mean you talk to someone who teaches your same grade level, but to deal with what … their issues are in mathematics and we try to take the same thing and take it back to our classroom and have our students do it, but we have to adapt to the different age level, so that is really fascinating to see that how it's done at different grade levels and show share how we adapt it. (Teacher 2, interview)

The group's diversity of different grade level teachers, non-Aboriginal and Aboriginal teachers, new and seasoned teachers, and different schools is beneficial in a number of ways. Teacher participants gain an understanding of students' math learning that happens before and after their particular teaching level. They either gain cultural understandings from those who shared it or have the importance of cultural knowledge reinforced by group members who have experienced positive results from using Indigenous knowledge (IK) in their math lessons. Joanne, principal of Aboriginal education, noted the positive effect of the group sessions: "When I was working in the school a couple of my teachers were involved in the project. They would come back to work as if they'd been off on a holiday, and yet it wasn't a holiday. I knew they were working" (interview, 2008).

Teachers emphasized the importance of Cynthia's mentoring role. She helped them think about math in many different ways and by using various approaches such as taking photos of the community/environment, taking nature walks, visiting the local First Nations museum, watching Indigenous artists at work, meeting in a community longhouse, and as mentioned, listening and interacting with community people. Study participants also mentioned their appreciation of her giving them structured activities to complete such as interviewing their students "one on one, so that we could see where their understanding is with the [math] problem-solving" (Teacher 5, interview).

A concern and challenge of the project team is how to continue the momentum – the synergy that participants experience in the group sessions – after the research project is finished. Participating teachers note a heavy reliance upon Cynthia to keep the "project" going, as noted by one teacher who stated: "I think we're becoming somewhat dependent on her being there, for her expertise, for her making us do tasks and keeping us motivated." Participants acknowledge the important mentoring and coordinating roles she has played. At the same time, they also acknowledge their appreciation of school district support for teacher release time to attend the group meetings and their appreciation of Indigenous community support for sharing their cultural knowledge and for using their on-site facilities for group meetings. As we reflect upon this concern, we believe that providing teachers with learning opportunities about IK and the teaching/learning role of Indigenous stories may encourage teachers to use their pedagogical agency in this area.

Learning about Indigenous knowledges (IK) by experiencing Indigenous stories

Over the years Cynthia worked closely with the teacher participants through many site visits, email, and a graduate course offered on

Haida Gwaii. She also involved community knowledge holders such as well-known artists, storytellers, Elders, and community organizations, such as a local museum, in the research process. The teachers learned about the IK of the *Haida* by hearing traditional and life experience stories told to them in the one-day meetings and via visits to cultural sites. This section focuses on the influence of Indigenous stories because through storywork teachers began to appreciate the value of building upon the knowledges of the local culture and community. Indigenous stories were recorded by a community member who works on heritage language and culture, and the TEAM-Learning group was given permission to use them. One particular Raven story became a catalyst to bring the concepts of culture/community, students' learning, and math together. By engaging in and working with this traditional story teachers began to learn more about *Haida* knowledge such as values, teachings, art, history, and place-based education. They also examined math concepts such as surface area, volume, and geometry through a class project where students made nested boxes from paper.[4] The cedar boxes mentioned in the story are still used by the community today, so students are very familiar with them. Community artists visited and talked about Haida knowledge, culture, and values.

During the talks, the community knowledge holders reminded the teachers to appreciate the knowledge expertise of Indigenous people, and to think of math in a very different way, as shown in this quote from *Haida* artist Robert Davidson, known internationally for his pole and mask design carvings as well as his printmaking and jewellery.

Last night someone asked if these images tell a story. Franz Boas, [an anthropologist] showed a beautiful box that was probably made around 1890, to Charles Edenshaw who was a master artist who lived the culture, knew the stories, and Boas asked him what does this [design] mean? So Edenshaw recited a Raven story from the box and Boas in his brilliance found the story a bit fanciful. Here is this outsider from New York doubting the Haida master who is also one of the leaders of the culture that breathed and lived culture. So the meaning part? What is math? Like meaning could be made to make math interesting … It is up to us to tell our story, to give it our meaning. For example, when we are fishing, I am cleaning fish and I am putting fish on the rack any old way. My Dad said to put the salmon heading up stream because that ensures the spirit to always come back. So if there is some kind of spirit in math, math is a spiritual being that helps to develop your mind. (Robert Davidson)

Teachers who were at first hesitant and anxious about including IK in their math lessons gradually became more comfortable using this pedagogy through guided group activities led by Cynthia and by hearing stories told by many other Indigenous community members. The following two quotes show one teacher's anxiety and then her openness to a culturally responsive pedagogy after two years of being involved in the project.

Teacher A2:

I have no problem bringing in examples from my past – like the number of dogs and horses – but I feel really awkward saying the number of Indigenous whatevers – like differentiating between Indigenous and non-Indigenous. Or talking about something that I feel I have no right to talk about. If we are talking about Indigenous art shapes that's different. I'm uncomfortable. Some of the kids look at you – and no one has even said anything to me – but I think in the back of my mind they look at you and think, "Who is she to be talking about this?" I look at Indigenous culture as a belief system – like a religion. You don't want to offend anyone so you just don't touch it. (Teacher project meeting, 2007)

Teacher A2 two years later:

In response to the question, "I used to think … and now I think …" The first thing that popped into my head was I used to think Indigenous culture was scary and something I couldn't touch and wasn't allowed to talk about … now I think … I can talk about [it] as long as I'm respectful. [Before] I was afraid of offending somebody … now I realize that it is something that you can talk about and you can learn from the students because they want to tell you about it, they want to tell you what they know, and they want to share it with you, and it's OK if you make a mistake, they will correct you and laugh at you [in a good way]. That's OK. So, I'm not afraid of talking about [Indigenous culture], of bringing it into the classroom anymore. (Teacher interview, 2009)

The TEAM-Learning methodology of having teachers meet with Cynthia every two or three months to discuss aspects of math that are found in the everyday lives of the students and their families, and in Indigenous cultural knowledge, seems to have contributed to the development of teachers' understandings and appreciation of a culturally responsive educational approach. The Raven story was the first major project that became a catalyst to bring culture/IK, math, and students' thinking together in a non-threatening way for teachers. The value of working with Indigenous stories is reinforced by this teacher's reflection: "[The group sharing] has taught me so much. It has taught me about the legends, I keep harping on that, it has opened my eyes to another way of thinking" (teacher interview, 2009). In the group sessions they agreed upon a math project that they would adapt to their particular grade level and complete before they met next. In the subsequent meeting they "talked story" by sharing their experiences – challenges and successes. Cynthia took on the role of math mentor and also connected the teachers to many Indigenous community members who talked to the teacher group. Our research project contributed various resources to the school and community such as digital and video cameras and a computer so that students and teachers could take pictures of community and cultural life for the math projects. Community resource people agreed to speak to the teachers because the principal researcher either knew them or asked them. The teachers appreciated learning from community knowledge holders as indicated in the following quote:

> … if it wasn't for … this programme about culturally relevant math, I wouldn't know what I do know [now] because she brought in so many people for us to talk with … for an hour or two at a time. They are artists, they are business owners, they are people who are extremely busy. (Teacher 1 interview, 2009)

From January to May 2010, a graduate education course was offered on site to TEAM-Learning participants and interested community members on *Haida Gwaii*, focusing on culturally responsive education for mathematics learning. The study participants had indicated interest in having this type of course offered within their school district. Cynthia negotiated having this course offered through the UBC Faculty of Education's external learning programmes and agreed to teach it. Readings for the course included Archibald's (2008) *Indigenous Storywork: Educating the Heart, Mind, Body, and Spirit* as well as interviews with *Haida* Elders conducted for the book: *Gina 'Waadluxan Tluu: The Everything Canoe* (Ramsay & Jones, 2010). Course members read these interviews, spoke with community Elders, studied *Haida* stories and explored ways of designing a curriculum that could be "more responsive to community hopes and desires, relevant to students' lives and needs, reciprocal in how it gives back to communities, and respectful in ways that open up possibilities for multiple ways of experiencing the world" (Nicol & Yovanovich, 2011, p. 12). A significant outcome of the course was the collaborative development of *Tluuwaay 'Waadluxan: Mathematical Adventures* (Nicol & Yovanovich, 2011) a collection of mathematical adventures created by teachers, inspired by Elder stories.

During project meetings we worked together to listen to community stories and explore opportunities within the stories for mathematical engagement. One story, mentioned earlier, was *Raven Brings the Light*. It involved a series of nested bentwood boxes and became an agreed-upon context for an engaging mathematics problem. We listened to a version of the story told by *Haida* community Elders and knowledge holders (CBC Radio, *Legends of the Old Massett Haida: Gaaw Xaadee Gyaahlaangaay*, 2007). The teachers explored both the content of the story and the characters for their potential to inspire mathematical inquiry (Nicol, Archibald & Baker, 2013). Teachers brainstormed the following mathematical ideas after listening to the *Raven Brings the Light* at one of the project meetings.

- Students could calculate the volume of the sun, the light.
- They could explore what is meant by infinity. All the light in the world. What would that be?
- Compare surface areas and volume of the nested boxes.
- Transformation – the idea of shape shifter as changing. So this could carry over to concepts of mathematical transformations: rotations, tessellations, symmetry …
- Comparing the sizes of boxes. How big or small do they need to be so that they can be nested … How could a lid be made for the box?
- The ball of light becoming the sun, moon, and stars. Could explore size – how big is that? How many stars? How big is a million?
- How does paper size and shape affect the box shape?

They also wondered about their own understandings of the story and discussed how the story could be a place to explore both mathematical ideas and *Haida* culture:

- What about Raven? Raven as problem solver, trickster … what would Raven do if he were stuck and couldn't figure out how to solve a [math] problem? How would he creatively solve it?

- Transformation ... we could build on transforming ... the idea of getting unstuck. Transforming the problem into something that can be done. How to change the situation, as Raven did, so that it can be solved. Using what we know to solve something we don't know.
- Seeing or bringing the light as understanding math – that "Aha!" moment.

With permission to share the story with students in classrooms, project teachers from kindergarten to Grade 10 classrooms examined students' responses and were excited by the interest students demonstrated both in the mathematics of building nested boxes and in the connections to *Haida* culture (Nicol, Archibald & Baker, 2013; Nicol, Yovanovich & Gear, 2016; Nicol & Yovanovich, 2017).

Discussion

The methodological use of Indigenous storywork principles of respect, responsibility, reverence, and reciprocity created a shared space for bringing together teachers' thinking/learning, students' and community members' Indigenous culture/IK and community, and mathematics. The research team demonstrated *respect* toward Indigenous Peoples, Indigenous knowledges, and non-Indigenous peoples at the research site by first taking the time necessary to develop positive interpersonal relationships with teachers, school administrators, and community members and second, exercising care in learning about the cultural and community context for each site. It took at least one year to develop trust and working relationships with teachers at the sites. When possible, researchers attended community cultural events and meetings. Twelve years later, although many people have changed roles, the research and educational relationship continues, involving teachers, school district, community, and university. *Responsibility* was demonstrated by acquiring ethical approval from the community-based Indigenous educational council, the public school district, and the university to conduct the research. *Reverence* was practised by learning about how to understand and use Indigenous knowledge in a way that did not disrespect cultural protocols or community ethics and that did not essentialize or appropriate IK. For example, local Indigenous stories were used with permission by the applicable community member/organization. Community cultural knowledge holders shared their holistic IK with teachers and researchers to help them better understand cultural knowledge, their stories, and local values/ teachings and Aboriginal languages. TEAM-Learning projects, which became a form of *reciprocity*, were cooperatively agreed upon by the participating teachers and researchers. They included curriculum units and multi-media learning resources. These learning materials are now available for use in the schools and the school district so that other teachers can use them in the future.

Teachers' knowledge and understanding of culturally responsive pedagogy improved through their TEAM-Learning experiences. The storywork principles of *holism, interrelatedness*, and *synergy* helped them explore and share their evolving understandings in the regularly scheduled group meetings. During the research process teachers gathered to share their classroom experiences, to talk about their anxieties about teaching math or using Indigenous culture, to cooperatively plan their projects, and to discuss what they learned about bringing together students' math learning, their community context, and their culture. The researchers and teachers listened, asked questions, and gave suggestions. Storywork encourages participants to engage holistically – addressing the intellectual, emotional, spiritual, and physical realms of our humanness. Often, teachers do not get the chance to talk with their school colleagues in a manner that is holistic; nor do they talk across grade levels. TEAM-Learning sessions brought primary grade and high school teachers together to create a shared knowledge about the interrelated connections between math, community, and culture. Teachers' enthusiasm and feelings of frustration created a synergistic action that brought culturally responsive pedagogy to life for them, their students, and the community.

The success of the project continues, despite various challenges (Nicol & Yovanovich, 2017). Participating teachers have presented aspects of their experiences and learning in district professional learning workshops, provincial professional development conferences, as well as national conferences. These presentations helped them to articulate the relationship between culturally responsive educational principles and the applied nature of their math projects. A course assignment in the aforementioned education course held on *Haida Gwaii* had a service learning and reciprocity component, where the learners developed a culturally responsive education and math project that was useful to a school or community group. The study participants who were enrolled in this course had another opportunity to deepen their understandings of IKs in relation to culturally responsive education. Through these types of presentations, the teachers receive positive reinforcement about their culturally responsive pedagogy and most importantly, they re-imagine their role and relationship to mathematics, to their students, and to themselves.

The TEAM-Learning university researchers will need to address concerns about how to lessen the mentoring dependence on the principal researcher and transfer that role to the participating teachers. The various presentations and new projects as noted above, and the group meetings, help the teacher participants re-imagine their role and/or look at their culturally responsive approaches from new perspectives. The Indigenous story of Raven, a trickster figure, started a synergistic storywork action that has transformative possibilities for improving Aboriginal math teaching and learning. We look forward to encountering the next story on our journey.

Acknowledgements

We are grateful to the Elders, community, teachers, and students, and their families, as well as the place of *Haida Gwaii*, for their contributions to this work.

Notes

1 Funding for this project is supported through grants from the Social Sciences and Humanities Research Council of Canada, the Vancouver Foundation, and the Canadian Council on Learning.

2 Both terms, Aboriginal and Indigenous, will be used interchangeably throughout this chapter. In Canada, the term, Aboriginal includes First Nations, Metis, and Inuit people. The term Indigenous, is used more often today when a collective term is needed.

3 The title changed from district director to district principal.

4 See TEAM-Learning paper "Living Culturally Responsive Approaches to Mathematics Education."

References

Archibald, Jo-ann (2008). *Indigenous storywork: educating the heart, mind, body and spirit.* Vancouver, BC: UBC Press.

Battiste, M. (2000). *Reclaiming Indigenous voice and vision.* Vancouver, BC: UBC Press.

British Columbia Ministry of Education. (2007). *How are we doing? Demographics and performance of aboriginal students in BC public schools.* British Columbia Ministry of Education Foundation Skills Assessment Results. Available at www.bced.gov.bc.ca/abed/performance.htm.

Canadian Broadcast Company, CBC. (2007). *Legends of the Old Massett Haida: Gaaw Xaadee Gyaahlaangaay* [DVD].

Castellano, M. B. (2000). Updating Aboriginal traditions of

knowledge. In G. Dei, B. Hall & D. Rosenberg (Eds.), *Indigenous knowledges in global contexts: multiple readings of our world* (pp. 21–36). Toronto, ON: University of Toronto Press.

Marshall, A., Williams, L. & Stewart, S. (2008). Indigenizing education: principles and practice. In R. Wesley Heber (Ed.), *Indigenous education Asia/Pacific* (pp. 167–177). Regina, SK: Indigenous Studies Research Centre, First Nations University of Canada.

Nicol, C., Archibald, J. & Baker, J. (2013). Designing a model of culturally responsive mathematics education: place, relationships and storywork. *Mathematics Education Research Journal 25*(1), 73–89.

Nicol, C. & Yovanovich, J. (2011). *Tluuwaay 'Waadluxan: mathematical adventures.* Skidegate, BC: Haida Gwaii School District 50.

Nicol, C. & Yovanovich, C. (2017). Sustaining living and learning culturally responsive pedagogy. In J. Archibald & J. Hare (Eds.), *Learning, knowing, sharing: celebrating Aboriginal education K-12 success* (pp. 83–100). Vancouver, BC: BC Principals' and Vice-Principals' Association (BCPVPA).

Nicol, C., Yovanovich, J. & Gear, A. (2016). Considering place for connecting mathematics, community and culture. In A. Anderson, J. Anderson, J. Hare & M. McTavish (Eds.), *Language, learning and culture in early childhood: home, school and community contexts* (pp. 123–141). New York, NY: Routledge.

Ramsay, H. & Jones, K. (2010). *Gina 'Waadluxan Tluu: The everything canoe.* Skidegate, Haida Gwaii: Haida Gwaii Museum Press.

Smith, L. T. (1999). *Decolonizing methodologies: research and Indigenous Peoples.* London: Zed Books.

PART II

INDIGENOUS STORYWORK IN AOTEAROA NEW ZEALAND

Jenny Bol Jun Lee-Morgan

In Aotearoa New Zealand, *pūrākau* was one Māori narrative form. Traditionally, the multiplicity of *pūrākau* covered ranged from explanations of the origins of the universe to specific historic tribal events or particular incidents (Orbell, 1992; Walker, 1990). Some *pūrākau* contained volumes of detailed information, including genealogical names and tribal places, whereas others had more gripping storylines and pertinent as well as complex teachings, although these were not necessarily exclusive of each other (Biggs, 1997). Some *pūrākau* were responsible for maintaining absolute accuracy and knowledge, and others were embellished to invoke "the *wairua* (spirituality) and the *mauri* (life force) of the story" (Bishop, 1997, p. 25). The presentation of *pūrākau* varied in style, which was highly dependent on the narrator, the context and purpose (Metge, 1998). However, the general pedagogical practice and function of *pūrākau* remained the same, predetermined by the need to consolidate and construct contextual knowledge in an orally based culture.

As part of the development of *kaupapa* Māori theory (Pihama, 2001; Smith, 1997) and decolonizing methodologies local to Aotearoa New Zealand, Jenny Lee-Morgan's methodological development of *pūrākau* as narrative inquiry was inspired by Jo-ann Archibald's (1997) lead in creating scholarship space for Indigenous storywork. Like Archibald, Lee-Morgan's interest in *pūrākau* stemmed from her work in the education field, but began with the investigation of contemporary Māori narratives. Her doctoral thesis started out as a study of *ako* (Māori pedagogy) of Māori teachers. Not about all Māori teachers (an impossibility anyway), but a group who considered that being a Māori teacher is not just a matter of ethnicity, but also involves a reclamation of culture, politics, and identity. Beyond classroom practice, she was interested in, to use Durie's (2001) phrase, the ways Māori teachers fulfil Māori aspirations to "live as Māori." Once understanding that *ako* simultaneously shaped Māori teachers' work, and was shaped by Māori teachers' work, the challenge was not so much to analyse what teachers did, but how they thought about what they did – the challenge became methodological. The development of *pūrākau* as methodology also needed to respond to the orthodoxy of "evidence-based" research in education developed at that time in Aotearoa New Zealand (Alton-Lee, 2004). Subsequently, *pūrākau* was purposefully chosen and developed as a culturally appropriate methodology because it was, she argued, our "evidence."

The popularity of *pūrākau* also aligns with the growth in *kaupapa Māori* research and the articulation by senior Māori scholars of the need to undertake more in-depth exploration of specific *mātauranga Māori*-based methodologies and methods (Pihama, 2001; Smith. 1997; Smith, 2012). The chapters in this section exemplify the ways in which *pūrākau* is being progressed across different disciplines, topics, and contexts, and sometimes with different and specific purposes. A glossary of Māori words used across the following chapters is located at the end of this section.

"He would not listen to a woman": decolonizing gender through the power of *pūrākau* – Hayley Marama Cavino

In Chapter 5, Hayley Cavino explores a personal *pūrākau* that was recently used as part of her embodied doctoral research project oriented to decolonizing gender violation. This chapter speaks to the relational imbalance between Māori men and women occurring in the context of colonization and played out in the Māori Land Court at the turn of the nineteenth century. Moreover, Cavino demonstrates the way *pūrākau* also serves as expression of agency – especially for women. Cavino shows that the struggles of her grandmother, spoken through this *pūrākau*, to which she contributes, also shape our multiple social relations and belongings. She argues that when used as a cultural analytic, *pūrākau* can provide a way to better understand and place contemporary events within their historical and colonial contexts. Furthermore, described as a discursive geography, Cavino asserts that *pūrākau* can accommodate a multiplicity of stories, including targeted ways to write alongside dominant heteronormative narratives that can heal our stories.

Naming our names and telling our stories – Joeliee Seed-Pihama

Joeliee Seed-Pihama's chapter draws on her doctoral research, which investigated Māori names as signifiers of stories. She explores *pūrākau* as a contemporary and creative storytelling research method that she calls "story building." Tracing traditional stories embedded in the names of our ancestor Māui-tikitiki-a-Taranga, through to name-gifting her own children, she illustrates the way in which *kōrero ingoa* (naming stories) both "story our names," and "name our stories." In doing so, *kōrero ingoa*, in particular, work to reassert and reclaim our Māori names, while becoming a tool for conscientization and decolonization. Finally, Seed-Pihama shares a personal *pūrākau* of practice that demonstrates the power of story to "speak back" and "speak forward" in order not only to understand, but to transform our colonial reality as Māori.

Indigenous law/stories: an approach to working with Māori law – Carwyn Jones

In Chapter 7, Carwyn Jones discusses the ways in which Māori law requires practitioners to look for legal principles in cultural expressions of Māori knowledge, such as *pūrākau*, rather than statutes and court reports. This chapter explores the use of Indigenous storywork to articulate an internal perspective of Māori law, building on the cultural and experiential groundings of Māori communities. Jones argues that adopting this approach, which he refers to as the "*Kōrero* Analysis Framework," reveals particular patterns of authority and decision-making (and constraints on legal authority), particular forms of legal communication, argumentation, and reasoning, and distinctive mechanisms for enforcement and remedy – the hallmarks of a well-developed legal system. Using a *pūrākau* from his own tribal group, "*Kahungunu and Rongomaiwahine*," Jones demonstrates the way key Māori principles of *whanaungatanga, manaakitanga, mana, tapu/noa*, and *utu* form the basis of the *Kōrero* Analysis Framework and can be applied to understand Māori law and legal processes. Ultimately, Jones shows how an Indigenous storywork approach can contribute to Māori communities seeing Māori law as dynamic, relevant, and applicable to a full range of legal issues we face as Indigenous Peoples.

Whānau storytelling as Indigenous pedagogy: *tiakina te pā harakeke* – Leonie Pihama, Donna Campbell, and Hineitimoana Greensill

In Chapter 8, Leonie Pihama, Donna Campbell, and Hineitimoana Greensill discuss a research project centred on *whānau* wellbeing that involved inviting the participants to share *pūrākau* related to raising children and grandchildren in accordance with our cultural values, practices, and beliefs. *Pūrākau*, in this chapter, feature as a life-long (including pre-natal) and inclusive pedagogy that provides children as well as adults with guidance about how to live, as well as their roles as part of a *whānau*, *hapū*, and/or *iwi*. As part of the research findings, *pūrākau* arising from *whānau* interviews became a critical part of the knowledge base for the research, as well as a key tool for teaching and learning at community-based project gatherings. Pihama, Campbell, and Greensill argue that *pūrākau*, like Indigenous storywork, is an Indigenous pedagogy that recognizes the sacred position of children within our communities, both in the stories themselves and in the way in which we continue to tell them. In doing so, they hope our stories will replenish our connections with each other, our lands, our past, and our children and grandchildren.

Pūrākau from the inside-out: regenerating stories for cultural sustainability – Jenny Bol Jun Lee-Morgan

The last chapter in this section, written by me, is inspired by the conceptual understanding of *pūrākau* as *"te pū o te rākau"* (the core of the tree). This chapter explores the cultural clues that point to the significance of narratives in our lives as trees. Distinguishing the inside from the outside is not straightforward or necessarily easy. Rather, the directive to storywork from the inside-out not only reinforces the significance of stories to our cultural sustainability as Indigenous Peoples, but like the other chapters in this section, provides some guidelines for *pūrākau* as methodology. Often antithetical to Western conventional research approaches, *pūrākau* encourages a return to Indigenous ways of relating, reviewing, researching, and regenerating our traditional and contemporary knowledge, practices, and beliefs to provide nourishment to our cultural selves now and far into the future.

References

Alton-Lee, A. (2004). *Guidelines for generating a best evidence synthesis iteration.* Wellington, New Zealand: Ministry of Education.

Archibald, J. (1997). Coyote learns to make a storybasket: the place of First Nations stories in education. Doctoral dissertation. *Burnaby, BC:*

Simon Fraser University. Retrieved from www.collectionscanada.gc.ca.

Biggs, B. (1997). *He Whiriwhiringa: selected readings in Maori.* Auckland, New Zealand: Auckland University Press.

Bishop, R. (1997). Māori people's concerns about research into their lives. *History of Education Review 26*(1), 25–40.

Durie, M. (2001). *A framework for considering Māori educational advancement.* Paper presented at the Hui Taumata Matauranga. Turangi and Taupo, New Zealand. Retrieved from www.literacyandnumeracyforadults. com/public/files/13093955/ Duriemaorieducationalachievement. pdf.

Metge, J. (1998). Time and the art of Māori storytelling. *New Zealand Studies 8*(1), 3–9.

Orbell, M. (1992). *Traditional Māori stories: he kōrero Māori.* Auckland, New Zealand: Reed.

Pihama, L. (2001). *Tīhei mauri ora: honouring our voices: mana wahine as Kaupapa Māori theoretical framework.* Unpublished PhD thesis. Auckland, New Zealand: The University of Auckland.

Smith, G. H. (1997). *The development of Kaupapa Māori: theory and praxis.* Unpublished PhD thesis. Auckland, New Zealand: The University of Auckland.

Smith, L. T. (2012). *Decolonizing methodologies: research and indigenous peoples.* (2nd ed.). New York, NY: Zed Books.

Walker, R. (1990). *Ka whawhai tonu mātou: struggle without end.* Auckland, New Zealand: Penguin.

5 | "HE WOULD NOT LISTEN TO A WOMAN": DECOLONIZING GENDER THROUGH THE POWER OF *PŪRĀKAU*

Hayley Marama Cavino

Introduction: why *pūrākau*?

In this chapter I engage a *pūrākau* that was told in the Māori Land Court by one of my maternal ancestors at the close of the nineteenth century. My engagement with this *pūrākau* lets me examine how the stories told by our people, especially our female ancestors, illustrate their knowledge and experience of the ways gender worked in their lives, in their relationships, and on their territories. The title "He would not listen to a woman" comes directly from a *pūrākau* my ancestor shared in court. It is a story about the relational shifts occurring between Māori men and women. It is especially about the deterioration of Māori women's authority and status under conditions of land confiscation.

Pūrākau[1] is a Māori narrative process which links, contextualizes, and politicizes stories and draws on Māori oral literature tradition, knowledges, philosophies, histories, experiences, dreams, and aspirations (Lee, 2008; Metge, 1998). *Pūrākau* is pedagogy (Lee-Morgan, 2017); it is a *kaupapa Māori* research praxis grounded in Indigenous rights to claim and share knowledge in meaningful ways (Pihama, 2017; Smith, 1999) and is thus an expression of our agency (Smith, 2017). This chapter explores the use of *pūrākau* to tell stories that consider the salience of gender, and is based in part on recent work I undertook as part of a research project oriented to decolonizing rape and other forms of gender violation. *Pūrākau* is especially appropriate for this task because it enables us to produce narrative that is not only descriptive, but also woven through with analysis. In this chapter I aim to demonstrate how *pūrākau* can be particularly useful for *wāhine* (women) engaged in writing alongside dominant narratives, especially those produced by men (both our own and Settler men). I share an example drawn from a larger dissertation project to illustrate the potential of *pūrākau* as gendered counter-narrative.[2]

Pūrākau is our word for story and although there are many interpretations of the deeper meaning of the word, I draw particular inspiration from the translation that focuses on the concepts of *te pū* (the origin or foundation, the roots) and *rākau* (the wood, branches, and leaves). This is because my work is particularly concerned with the use of *whakapapa* (how we use it, who we claim, and why) to engage gender politics in Māori worlds (Graham, 2005; Holmes, 2012; Lee-Morgan, 2017; Osorio, 2004; Whiteduck, 2013; Wihongi, 2002). *Whakapapa* (genealogy work) is a kind of tree. My work asks how we might use *pūrākau* as a story form that can allow that relationship tree, and us, to grow. I'm interested in how *pūrākau* can heal our *whakapapa*, our histories, and our present.

As this book indicates, Indigenous storywork (including *pūrākau*) is alive and is constantly being (re)theorized (Thomas, 2005; Wilson, 2008). *Pūrākau* is fluid, modern, and can change according to our needs. We adapt our stories to suit our purpose (Archibald, 2008). *Pūrākau* is a narrative form that not only shares knowledge but also pays attention to how we speak, listen to, and think about stories. We can take up the *pūrākau* of our ancestors in new ways; we can examine their words and add our analysis to draw out meaning, to reframe history, and to reconsider how to tell the story. These new and/or recovered versions and interpretations can become a kind of contemporary *pūrākau*; a modern version that we can use to recreate, retell, and restore our narratives and knowledge. In this regard *pūrākau* is a praxis that is political, provocative, and powerful (Lee-Morgan, 2017). I argue that one of the places where this becomes most important is in the use of *pūrākau* to purposefully gender a story.

Pūrākau are told in specific ways to suit different purposes relevant to the context in which they are told. *Pūrākau* were shared in legal domains such as the Land Court in order to make claim to territory (Parsonson, 2001). For this purpose particular versions of *pūrākau* were told, in which some information was amplified while other information was left out. In other places *pūrākau* are told in particular ways to emphasize a specific point of view (for example in Ngahuia Te Awekotuku's *Ruahine* (2003) and in Robyn Kahukiwa and Patricia Grace's *Wahine Toa* (1984), which both shared *pūrākau* that emphasized *wāhine*). These adaptations, and the ways they often also shine a spotlight on the partiality and limits of dominant colonial versions of stories, pose important questions about how we tell a story and also how we listen to it. They also provide us with opportunities to think about how we work with existing stories and how we might add to *pūrākau* to share new understandings and insights (Lee-Morgan, 2017).

Contemporary *pūrākau* also emerge out of our need to do decolonization work around the methodologies we use for research and knowledge-sharing purposes (Archibald, 2008). Contemporary *pūrākau* work is particularly useful for interrupting stories that we understand to be "traditional" in the colonial sense. By this, I mean static and unchanging (Barker, 2011; Lee-Morgan, 2017). In the early colonial period Settlers (often ethnographers) collected our *pūrākau* and produced hybrid stories about us. These were stories that were often commodified for white consumption (Lee-Morgan, 2017; Mikaere, 2011) and over time became "set in stone"; they became the authoritative and hegemonic version of our story. These stories (stories *about us*) often perpetuated a single truth (Adichie, 2009); there was little or no room for disruption, nuance, or unanswered questions. They were also sanitized (for example, there was usually no reference to sex) and frequently romanticized (Lee-Morgan, 2017; McFadden, 2014). These colonial versions of our stories disrupted our way of seeing the world; for example, Māori women were often excluded from the narrative while men were re-cast as the primary agentic subjects and protagonists. When *wāhine* reclaim and reauthor our *pūrākau* we can reinstate our women as holders of knowledge and concurrently disrupt the dominance of male-focused stories (Anderson, 2016; Te Kawehau Hoskins, 1997). This is the decolonizing potential of contemporary *pūrākau* work. Contemporary *pūrākau* recognize and name the ways our stories have been transformed.

In the example following I use a historic *pūrākau* shared by one of my grandmothers to weave a new contemporary *pūrākau*. In this reconsideration of the story she told in court I explore "what we can claim to know" about gender politics and power, paying particular attention to the ways our knowledge is shaped and transformed across pre-colonial, contact, and colonial time/space. This undertaking (the examination of "what we can know") becomes a "what we can do" when we share the insights we have gained and tell the story anew.

"He would not listen to a woman": *pūrākau* as gendered narrative

In this section I share a brief *pūrākau* in which I am in conversation with the historical record (in this instance Native Land Court documents).

It is important to know that the Land Court files I reference here are currently incorrectly indexed, leading to an obscuring of the voices of female ancestors and the critical role they played in court and in their communities. This indexing of only male names in the record recasts our male relatives and their (male) Settler counterparts as the primary agents in the unfolding drama.[3] In considering the original *pūrākau* my three-times great-grandmother shared, and in weaving my own contemporary interpretation of the meaning of her words, she and I engage in a conversation across time and space. This "collaboration" reinstates her experiences and the way that she critically engaged them at the time, providing an additional layer of analytical engagement in light of contemporary theorizing around colonization and gender, and interrupts and rights the historical record about the substantive nature of our women's lives and their agentic resistance to the oppressions they encountered. *Pūrākau* is uniquely capable of allowing us to work within and across time and place in this way.

My engagement with this *pūrākau* originally took place within the context of broader work that traced the *whakapapa* (genealogy) of violence impacting women and children in our *whānau* (extended family) in the contemporary moment. As part of that contextual-ization I examined the history of my grandfather's tribal territory in *Tauranga Moana*. This was the *Ngapeke* Block, a small tract of land left to the *iwi* after *raupatu* (confiscation) (Waitangi Tribunal, 2010). My brief examination here of a portion of the *Ngapeke* Block land partition case is followed by a consideration of the significance of *pūrākau* as a decolonizing methodological praxis that specifically addresses gender.[4]

Confiscation of land and its subsequent partitioning into small sole-family blocks occurred within the context of the Māori Land Wars and the need to individualize land title in order to secure it for *Pākehā* settlement.[5] The *kāinga* (home) *Ngapeke* Block was first partitioned in 1896 by the Native Land Court against the wishes of the major-ity of the *hapū*. This occurred as a result of application by eight of the Māori owners (lodged in the name of my *tipuna wāhine* Katerina Te Atirau), on the basis of *whakapapa* to the original "owners."[6] My ancestors David Asher, Katerina Te Atirau, and Rahera Te Kahuhiapo were amongst those who benefited from the terms of partition. They were assigned parts of the land that were considered some of the most fertile and thus desirable.

On September 27, 1897, one year after the original partition of the block, the *Ngapeke* Partition case is opened again on appeal. The case is brought by our men. Hirama Mokopapaki[7] is one of our relatives who speaks for the appeal applicants, and his testimony (as well as that of other men who corroborate it) is clearly oriented to addressing the disproportionate terms of the earlier partition. The strategy employed is to disinherit some of the women who are living on the more desirable coastal sections of the block and in this they pay particular attention to my three-times great-grandmother Rahera. The way they do this is by claiming that she is only entitled to *Ngapeke* through "*aroha*," an act of love/generosity based on her marriage to a man who is characterized here as a "true" descendant (rather than being entitled through her own *whakapapa* (genealogy)). It is a particular irony that *aroha* (love) is used here to denote the limits of belonging. Also significant, it is the *whakapapa* of Rahera's *maternal line* that is held in doubt. One of our men testifies as follows:

> These are the only people who I know of who had any right through "*aroha*." They came to live at *Ngapeke* through Rahera's marriage with Te Atirau ... The term "*aroha*" applies only to the three persons first named (Rahera ... [and two others]). They had no right in *Ngapeke* through their mother.

Our men also give testimony as to the close proximity with which the *hapū* lived at *Ngapeke* at that time – a situation greatly exacerbated by the colonial confiscation of most of the land and the inequitable nature of the individualized disbursement of what remained:

> Our principal objection to last court decision is that by it we have lost 12 houses and our *kāinga*. I ask that our houses and *kāinga* should be left to us and also our cultivations. I am willing to give Katerina two acres where she has a house.

Within the climate of land scarcity prompted by settlement, proximity becomes a source of conflict for Māori, rather than cohesion. The disastrous relational fractures illustrated by this testimony come to be managed and mediated through the same Settler legal systems that caused them.[8] Rahera's testimony, which follows that of the men, is key in providing nuance here. It is through her words that we come to understand further the deeply gendered nature of this conflict:

In somewhat recent times I had a ditch and bank fence … [A male relative] came and took up residence at *Ngapeke*.[9] He simply came and located on my cultivations. He first went to live at Hirama's place and then he thought he would start a *kāinga* for himself – separate from Hirama. I had cultivated kumara etc. there. I objected as I did not wish all of the place to be taken. He persisted. *He would not listen to a woman* … I recollect Mr Asher going last year to stop Ruka from ploughing our subdivision until the Appeals Court had decided matter. He would not desist. (pp. 60–62; emphasis mine)[10]

When I encountered this recovered testimony for the first time I was struck by the power of those seven simple words: "He would not listen to a woman." I felt a visceral sense of their importance and significance to the broader story I was attempting to tell. Rahera's statement invokes Jamaica Kincaid's (1998) exclamation that there is a "world" in the supposed banality of everyday observations – a painful world that we frequently cannot or will not fully engage with. Similarly, in her recent conversation with Jenny Lee-Morgan (2017), Jill Tipene spoke on the importance of seeking out "narrative fragments" in order that we might disentangle our stories from the underlying patriarchy of dominant colonial interpretations. I am reminded also of the words Mereana Pitman shared with me during the course of my broader research (Cavino, 2017). Mereana asserted that colonization was a seduction of our men; a process through which they were encouraged to take up power *over* women (rather than power alongside us). In recounting her version of the on-the-ground contestations happening at *Ngapeke*, Rahera works to gender the conflict in precisely this way, by pointing out what that "power over" looks like from her standpoint.

Rahera's testimony also spoke to the issue of her belonging. She gave her *whakapapa* from the eponymous ancestor Pūkenga and linked this to both her paternal grandmother Hinemarama, and to her mother Rangiawhao's mother Te Amomate. In the recitation of her *whakapapa* Rahera specifically worked to rehabilitate her female relatives – it is a clear statement not only of her being of *Ngāti Pūkenga*, but of the inherently female way she belongs. Rahera also points out that the condition of multiple belongings (to diffuse tribes and territory) adheres as much to the men as it does the women. With regard to her facility with the *whakapapa* and the history of the *iwi*, Rahera uses *pūrākau* in her testimony to demonstrate knowledge.[11]

Pūrākau as decolonizing praxis

Pūrākau is a discursive geography that can accommodate a multiplicity of stories – it can therefore be used in targeted ways to write alongside dominant patriarchal narratives. In her claim that the objecting Māori male witnesses would not listen to a woman asserting her rights during confrontations occurring on the land, Rahera's testimony gives us a window on the state of gendered relations *within* as well as *between* peoples. It is not insignificant that Rahera needed to seek the authority of white men to buttress her claim to the land in the wake of the refusal of *her men* to recognize her authority at home. It is clear from her testimony that Rahera understands her femaleness as the condition that precipitates refusal on the part of our men to hear her. No matter that she is by this time an Elder in a system of social organization and control that purportedly privileges age. By speaking of her circumstances in open court Rahera offers us the opportunity to analyse the ways femaleness becomes a kind of pollutant under conditions of colonization (see Ngahuia Murphy (2013), who tracks the colonial ethnographic history of *wāhine* framed as pollutants in her work on menstruation in the pre-colonial Māori world[12]). For me, Rahera's testimony is particularly revelatory in that it is, in fact, a *mana wāhine* (Indigenous feminist) analysis of her circumstances: here is someone who clearly understood the significance of gender in her life. The broader *pūrākau* represented in the court testimony also paints a vivid picture of differential power relations between Settler and Māori men. Significantly, siding with the women (as in this case) allows Settler men to publicly exercise power over Māori men. Our women's stories thus also help illuminate the experience of our men under colonization.[13]

This brief *pūrākau* also shows how Māori men and women were induced to work within the Native Land Court system to consolidate their belonging through negation of the belonging of their relatives. In this case the dispossession is clearly drawn along gendered lines. But in a broader sense, through sharing selective and partial stories of belonging in court, both our male and female ancestors take on the bulk of the dispossessing labour of the new Settler state. This is the common ground that binds their stories together – our fates are so clearly intertwined. When we (their descendants) take up their stories, it is thus critical that we do so with attention to the deeply coercive context in which they were originally shared. Because of this context, our *tipuna* often needed to encode their understanding of events in the words they chose in ways that were not always obvious; a lot went unsaid or unelaborated (Lee-Morgan, 2017). So, part of the work of contemporary *pūrākau* is to use the words of ancestors and tease out the deeper meaning, bringing them to life and making us consider more deeply their circumstances and our connections to them.

In the remainder of this section I consider how engagement with the story shared by my grandmother Rahera produced a contemporary *pūrākau* that is an example of decolonial praxis. *Pūrākau* enable us to examine our current experience of violence within the context of scarcity (of land, resources, *aroha*) that colonization so frequently invokes. The *pūrākau* shared by my *tipuna* Rahera and further engaged by me ties contemporary cycles of violence to the threat and actualization of alienation from places we call home. Rahera's story is one of substantive and relational displacement and disconnection – conditions that are the precursor for growing rape and gendered abuses in contemporary *whānau* life. As evidenced in Rahera's testimony, *pūrākau* can also be a guide to how we ought not to behave (Pihama & Cameron, 2012); they are an enduring mechanism through which to learn how to better manage our relationships, responsibilities, and belongings. Using *pūrākau* in this way is thus concurrently knowledge *and* pedagogy.

I return here to my earlier framing of *pūrākau* as "what we can do." As praxis, *pūrākau* is always gendered work, regardless of whether this is openly acknowledged (or not). It is work that is not static; when we interpret stories we are always also asking and answering questions about what stories we are choosing to tell, how we are telling them, and what meaning we are making of them. *Pūrākau*, like tradition, is an active, negotiated, relational, and political process (Barker, 2011). Gendering *pūrākau* may require us to reframe our thinking and understandings of our relationships, histories, and identities. Reflecting on her recent memoir about intergenerational trauma, Native American author Terese Marie Mailhot (see Seghal, 2018) said "In my culture, I believe we carry pain until we can reconcile with it through ceremony." I would like us to think about *pūrākau* as a kind of ceremony (Wilson, 2008). *Pūrākau* is a way to reconcile the past's ever-present presence.

In her recent (2017) work on *loea mele*,[14] *Kanaka Maoli* scholar Kahikina de Silva recentres an Indigenous intellectual tradition of interpretative analysis to interrupt the ways we are positioned as only useful to Settlers insofar as we provide raw material for stories. In the colonial imagination it is the work of non-Indigenous scholars to engage with and critique the story; this is work done by them because we are thought incapable of producing such critiques on our own. *Pūrākau* can and should be used by us as an analytical technique. As we refuse the racist praxis of Settler authorship and return to taking up our stories in creative and intellectually rigorous ways what, then, are the main tasks of *pūrākau* for us? And given the impact of colonization on our relationships with each other, how might it be especially important to use *pūrākau* as a way to decolonize gender? Recentring *tipuna wāhine* testimony/stories, highlighting the critical analysis they provided at the time, and adding our own additional Indigenous feminist analysis not only allows for proper nuanced analysis of our experiences under colonization but also puts us back into conversation with those same *tipuna* (Allen, 1988; Anderson, 2016; Clothier, 1993; Deer, 2015; Dominy, 1990; Goeman & Denetdale, 2009; Gray-Sharpe, 2007; Hall, 2009; Irwin, 1992; Million, 2009; Tuck & Yang, 2012).

My work with *pūrākau* as a culturally grounded method is motivated by a desire to heal our stories. One of the ways we do this is by privileging the voices of our *wāhine*. In her testimony, my grandmother Rahera Te Kahuhiapo exclaimed "He would not listen to a woman." In making her statement, she not only demanded an audience in the (then) present time and space of the Land Court – she also made space for us, her descendants, to speak to and of our contemporary experiences as *wāhine*. When we take up this challenge and do work to repair our stories, we enter a space of powerful and creative decolonizing praxis. By explicitly gendering *pūrākau* we not only claim a fuller, more complex past, we also weave a new sense of belonging to the people and places we have lost.

Notes

1 I am indebted to the work of Jenny Lee-Morgan, not only for her written work on *pūrākau*, but her guiding role as a member of my dissertation committee and as a mentor for the past 20 years – my work owes much to her influence. I would also like to acknowledge Dr Leonie Pihama for her feedback on this chapter and Michelle Boyd of Inkwell Writing Retreats and the October 2017 and March 2018 "Still I Write" cohort for providing a supportive writing space during the early drafting and revision of this chapter.

2 This chapter is based, in part, on work conducted in my doctoral dissertation *Towards a Method of Belonging: Contextualizing Gender Violence in Māori Worlds* (Cavino, 2017).

3 This on top of the pre-existing limits of the record due to it being transcribed from oral testimony by Settlers and written in English.

4 This reading was made possible due to the diligence of my *whanaunga*

Arianna Waller who worked to locate the testimony of the *wāhine* in the Native Land Court files.

5 In the wake of the Land Wars the Crown needed land to reimburse Settler soldiers for their service.

6 It appears the various claimants involved in the original partition case abandoned Settler court adjudication of this process and elected to try to settle amongst themselves. In *kōrero* taking place outside the court, the block is split into five parts and this is later ratified by the court. The terms of the agreement – while technically approved by the various *iwi* claimants in a mediated process that took place outside of court – happened within the deeply coercive confines of the Court's legislative colonial mandate (in this regard the court operates as a site of manufactured consent).

7 Māori Land Court Minute Book. Record No. 65971. Judge Johnson MB No. 6, pp. 47–57; 59–64. Ngapeke Appeal, partition case. September 27, 1897. Hirama Mokopapaki testimony, pp. 48–50.

8 Settler court-sanctioned modalities of "sharing" work here to replace existing cultural systems of management. The latter remain effectively neutralized by what can only be described as a policy of wardship.

9 This relative's residency at *Ngapeke* was precipitated by his losing a Land Court case related to a separate block.

10 Māori Land Court Minute Book. Record No. 65971. Judge Johnson MB No. 6, pp. 47–57; 59–64. Ngapeke Appeal, partition case. September 27 1897.

11 Rahera's testimony also illuminates the ways in which she too takes up a politics of authenticity. Of the men she says: "Ruka is of *Ngāti Pūkenga* but is not a true *Ngāti Pūkenga*. He is mixed up with very many other *hapū*. He had a right to live at *Ngapeke* – but he was connected with many outside *iwi*." Rahera's engagement in the same politics

of disenfranchisement that was previously leveraged against her by the men is a telling example of how the colonial context of land alienation through Settler law spared no-one and seemingly left no relationship or story unscathed.

12 *Wāhine* are also sometimes framed as disastrous to men, as evident in translations of the proverb "*He wāhine, he whenua, ka ngaro te tāngata*" to mean "By women and land, people are lost/war is waged." See Evelyn Stokes for an alternate translation: "But there is another meaning of this saying, Women and land are worth fighting for." See also Joanne Barker's (2011) work on the Martinez vs Santa Clara case. In her analysis she highlights the ways Santa Clara Pueblos women's "out marriages" become hyper-visible (and are used to reverse matrilineal and matrilocal customs – to include land management, customary rights, and the right to belong) while men engaging in the same behaviours (marrying non-tribal members – and in greater numbers) are not subject to the same scrutiny.

13 The apparent inconsistency in testimony between Māori men and women in this case must be read as more than a contestation regarding the relative merits of individual title vs communal land rights. The currency of the court has already been established before Rahera and our other *tipuna* get there – individual title being the only mode of exchange the court is willing to engage (Mikaere, 2011; Parsonson, 2001). Rahera's testimony therefore is not a validation of her political orientation to individual title so much as it is an attempt to secure her own interests and those of her children in a climate where collectivity is already partial and fracturing on the ground. While it is clear that the men testify as to the collective will of the *hapū* (namely, that the land be shared equitably through keeping the title intact rather than partitioned), they are *also* testifying

(to varying extents) that Rahera and her *whānau* fall outside this collective "us." In this way the "share" claimed by the women, their purported property right, is indeed endangered.

14 *Mele* are compositions in chant, poem, and/or song form authored by *Kanaka Maoli. Loea*

mele are compositions that exemplify a particular level of expertise. Importantly this "mastery" encapsulates both the creative and aesthetic properties of the *mele*, along with the knowledge woven into the composition (K. de Silva, personal communication, May 18, 2018).

References

Adichie, C. (2009). Chimamanda Ngozi Adichie: The danger of a single story. TED. [Video file].

Allen, P. G. (1988). Who is your mother? Red roots of white feminism. In Rick Simonson & Scott Walker (Eds.), *The Graywolf annual five: multicultural literacy* (pp. 13–27). St. Paul, MN: Graywolf Press.

Anderson, K. (2016). *A recognition of being: reconstructing Native womanhood.* Toronto, ON: Canadian Scholars' Press.

Archibald, J. A. (2008). *Indigenous storywork: educating the heart, mind, body, and spirit.* Vancouver, BC: UBC Press.

Barker, J. (2011). *Native acts: law, recognition, and cultural authenticity.* Durham, NC: Duke University Press.

Cavino, H. M. (2017). *Towards a method of belonging: contextualizing gender violence in Māori worlds.* Unpublished doctoral dissertation. Syracuse, NY: Syracuse University.

Clothier, H. (1993). *Three Māori women speak: a site for constituting identity.* Wellington, New Zealand: Victoria University.

Deer, S. (2015). *The Beginning and End of Rape.* Minneapolis, MN: University of Minnesota Press.

De Silva, K. (2017). *Loea mele: a brief study of 20th century Kanaka Maoli discussions of mele.* Paper presented at the Native American and Indigenous Studies Association, Vancouver BC, Canada.

Dominy, M. (1990). Maori sovereignty: a feminist invention of tradition. In J. Linnekin & L. Poyer (Eds.), *Cultural identity and ethnicity in the Pacific* (pp. 237–257). Honolulu, HI: University of Hawai'i Press.

Goeman, M. R. & Denetdale, J. N. (2009). Native feminisms: legacies, interventions, and Indigenous sovereignties. *Wicazo Sa Review 24*(2), 9–13.

Graham, J. (2005). He āpiti hono, he tātai hono: that which is joined remains an unbroken line: using whakapapa (genealogy) as the basis for an Indigenous research framework. *The Australian Journal of Indigenous Education 34*, 86–95.

Gray-Sharp, K. A. P. (2007). Taniko: a mana wahine approach to research. *Women's Studies Journal 21*(2), 40–58.

Hall, L. K. (2009). Navigating our own "sea of island": remapping a theoretical space for Hawaiian women and Indigenous feminism. *Wicazo Sa Review 24*(2), 15–38.

Holmes, L. (2012). *Ancestry of experience.* Honolulu, HI: University of Hawai'i Press.

Irwin, K. (1992). Towards theories of Māori feminisms. In R. Du Plessis (Ed.), *Feminist voices: women's studies texts for Aotearoa/New Zealand* (pp. 1–21). Auckland, New Zealand: Oxford University Press.

Kahukiwa, R. & Grace, P. (1984). *Wahine toa: women of Maori myth.* Auckland, New Zealand: Collins.

Kincaid, J. (1988). *A small place*. London: Macmillan.

Lee, J. B. J. (2008). *Ako: pūrākau of Māori teachers' work in secondary schools*. Unpublished doctoral thesis. Auckland, New Zealand: University of Auckland.

Lee-Morgan, J. B. J. (2017). Tikanga Rangahau Webinar Series – Pūrākau as methodology. [Video file].

McFadden, P. (2014). *Patrician McFadden: Culture of romance*. Special Opening Plenary Session of the 4th Annual African Unity for Renaissance Conference [Video file].

Māori Land Court. (1897, September 27). Ngapeke Appeal. Judge Johnson MB No. 6, pp. 45–57, 59–64.

Metge, J. (1998). Time and the art of Māori storytelling. *New Zealand Studies 8*(1), 3–9.

Mikaere, A. (2011). *Colonising myths – Māori realities: he rukuruku whakaaro*. Wellington, New Zealand: Huia Publishers.

Million, D. (2009). Felt theory: an Indigenous feminist approach to affect and history. *Wicazo Sa Review 24*(2), 53–76.

Murphy, N. (2013). *Te awa atua: menstruation in the pre-colonial Māori world*. Christchurch, New Zealand: He Puna Manawa.

Osorio, J. K. K. O. (2004). Gazing back: communing with our ancestors. *Educational Perspectives 37*(1), 14–17.

Parsonson, A. (2001). Stories for land: oral narratives in the Māori Land Court. In B. Attwood & F. Mcgowan (Eds.), *Telling stories: Indigenous history and memory in Australia and New Zealand* (pp. 21–40). Wellington, New Zealand: Bridget Williams Books.

Pihama, L. (2017). Tikanga Rangahau Webinar Series – Kaupapa Māori theory. [Video file].

Pihama, L. & Cameron, N. (2012). Kua tupu te pā harakeke: developing healthy whānau relationships. In Waziyatawin & Yellow Bird (Eds.), *For Indigenous minds only: a decolonization handbook* (pp. 225–244). Santa Fe, NM: School for Advanced Research Press.

Seghal, P. (2018, January 30). "Heart Berries" shatters a pattern of silence. *The New York Times*. Retrieved from www.nytimes.com.

Smith, L. T. (1999). *Decolonizing methodologies: research and Indigenous Peoples*. London: Zed Books.

Smith, L. T. (2017). Tikanga Rangahau Webinar Series – Kaupapa Māori methodology. [Video file].

Te Awekotuku, N. (2003). *Ruahine: mythic women*. Wellington, New Zealand: Huia Publishers.

Te Kawehau Hoskins, C. (1997). In the interests of Māori women? Discourses of reclamation. *Women's Studies Journal 13*(2), 25–44.

Thomas, R. (2005). Honouring the oral traditions of my ancestors through storytelling. In L. Brown & S. Strega (Eds.), *Research as resistance: critical, Indigenous, and anti-oppressive approaches* (237–254). Toronto, ON: Canadian Scholars' Press.

Tuck, E. & Yang, K. W. (2012). Decolonization is not a metaphor. *Decolonization: Indigeneity, Education & Society 1*(1).

Waitangi Tribunal. (2010). *Tauranga Moana 1886–2006: Report on the Post Raupatu Claims. Volume 1. WAI 215 Report*. Wellington, New Zealand: Author.

Whiteduck, M. (2013). "But it's our story. Read it": stories my grandfather told me and writing for continuance. *Decolonization: Indigeneity, Education & Society 2*(1).

Wihongi, H. (2002, January). *The process of whakawhanaungatanga in Kaupapa Māori research*. Hamilton, New Zealand: University of Waikato.

Wilson, S. (2008). *Research is ceremony: Indigenous research methods*. Black Point, NS: Fernwood Publishing.

6 | NAMING OUR NAMES AND TELLING OUR STORIES

Joeliee Seed-Pihama

Introduction

As Māori, when we meet someone for the first time, where they come from will likely be of more importance, than their name. The significance of our collectives and places is exemplified and expressed in a multitude of practices. Our connection to place, to *whenua* (land/placenta), *hau* (wind, vital essence), *wai* (water), *waka* (canoe), and *tāngata* (people) all come before us as individuals and therefore before our names. Evidence of this can be found in *pepeha* (tribal sayings), *mihimihi* (greetings), and *whaikōrero* (formal speech making). These things are often traversed and woven together before the speaker even mentions themselves or their name. However, this does not mean that our names do not matter; in fact, quite the opposite is true. Our genealogical connection with all phenomena in the universe intricately interlinks us, much like a spider web. Therefore, Māori never act or see things on just an individual level. This notion of *whakapapa* (genealogy) is simultaneously understood and embodied by Māori. When we do ask someone's name, how we ask is significant. The Māori word for "who" is "*wai*," which is also our word for "water," and so, when we ask, "*Ko wai tō ingoa?*" ("Who or what is your name?") we are really asking "From whose water do you come?" Huirangi Waikerepuru (2014), a revered Taranaki Elder and scholar, explains this phrase in the following quote:

> Under discussion is *wai* or water, and for Māori it's fundamental. For instance, who's your name? Whose water do you come from? Not, what's your name! So, everything to do with all of life is around water; no water – no life. No *wai*, no *tangata*, no people. And so, for Māori, is to ask the question – *Ko wai tōu ingoa?* Who's your name? Who do you come from? Who's your ancestor? *Ko wai tō tupuna*, your ancestor? *Ko wai tō matua?* Who's your father? *Ko wai tō whaene?* Who's your mother? It's all about water and the connection to every member of the family. (00:01:45)

As Māori, we are never alone or disconnected; we belong, and our names inscribe this upon us. Our names reference the gamut of our connections, beliefs, and values and therefore refer to important aspects such as ancestors, stories, notions of belonging, and our relatives in the natural environment. In that sense, our names provide a collective narrative while also acknowledging the individual (O'Regan, 2001).

This chapter will outline some of my doctoral research, in which I examined the importance of Māori personal names as expressions of Māori language, identity, and as holders of our stories. In this research, I argued that the gift of a Māori name and the assertion of that name over one's lifetime is simultaneously a political act of resistance and an act of normalization – an act of just being Māori. In particular, the stories of how we gift, receive, and carry Māori personal names highlight the power and transformative potential of our names and their stories. I will discuss how the use of *pūrākau* (Māori narrative)[1] as a research method enabled me to build, share, and analyse the naming stories of six generations within my own *whānau* (extended family), to express and position my own voice as a storyteller through creative writing and to also claim space for our cosmogonies as legitimate sources of knowledge for research.

One kind of story I have become deeply intimate with and believe to be integral to the project of storying, and therefore to the agenda of decolonization (Smith, 1999), is our *kōrero ingoa* (naming stories). These are the stories behind our names; of how we choose, give, receive, change, and uphold our names throughout our lives.

Kōrero ingoa: telling our naming stories

Kōrero ingoa are an important source of intergenerational knowledge. These stories make an integral contribution to the ongoing maintenance work that is being done to hold on to our history, values, and practices. Tākirirangi Smith (2012) uses *kōrero whakapapa* to refer to genealogical narratives, and it is from his use of that term that I came upon the term "*kōrero ingoa*" as an appropriate name for the "naming stories" I was gifted by *whānau* participants in my doctoral research.

It was through the telling and sharing of *kōrero ingoa* across my *whānau* that examples of our ability to endure, resist, decolonize, and achieve resurgence were revealed. By "celebrating survival" in this way, as Linda Tuhiwai Smith (1999) terms it, our love for our *ingoa tangata* (personal names) was emphasized, along with the success and well-being that has been achieved and maintained as a result. A clear finding of the research was that the regeneration of our personal names has the potential to conscientize *whānau* and individuals to not only the importance of our names and language but to the power and magic of our ancestral knowledge and stories.

One example of this transformative potential is illustrated in the following *kōrero ingoa* I was gifted by a *whānau* member. In what follows, my aunty retells the story of her daughter's birth and subsequent naming:

> On the day she was born, the day was beautiful but really windy. Mum told me she was going to name my child and I said: "No you're not." Obviously, in my youth thinking, I thought I would get away with not having to be Māori. I thought that next, she would want to keep my baby too. I wasn't willing to give her up. However mum in her wisdom has done both really. She is my mum's baby; she has been almost raised like the youngest child in mums' children. At the birth, mum did a *karanga* as she was born and gave her name in the same breath. I was almost laughing when she did it because she had pipped me at the post. I am glad she did because she gave her moko a fighting spirit. *Kei te whakapiri rāua i a rāua.* She is probably more like Mum than any of us. Sandy is her *Pākehā*[2] name. On her birth certificate, she is Sandy first. This name is the only name that Da and I could agree on. Sandy is my father's name and Da's uncle's name. Funny that the name should come from two men, not women. I chose a *Pākehā* name because I thought in a *Pākehā* world she needed a *Pākehā* name to use if she wanted to. Once again that was my lack of wisdom. She got to about six or seven and told me she hated her *Pākehā* name and to call her Whiti, so Whiti she was. Hurita is her next name – my Nan died while I was *hapū*, so I named her after Nan, which is also mum's name. My Nan was Martha Julia – Mum's name is Maata Hurita, so in honour of my Nan but hating the name Julia I called her Hurita, so she would have both their names. (Seed-Pihama, 2017)

There are many layers to this *kōrero ingoa*, including colonizing and decolonizing experiences that make it an important story to be passed from generation to generation within our *whānau*. Our strong genealogical and spiritual connection with the natural environment and to our *atua* (gods) is beautifully represented in our names. As this *kōrero ingoa* explains, the weather can point to a particular human characteristic or trait that *whānau* may want instilled in their child. The weather on your day of birth can also be seen as a sign from the ancestors of what this child may need or hold within them, and this can be recorded in the name given to that child as a perpetual reminder.

Gabel (2013) asserts that the desire of Indigenous Peoples to reclaim our names brings with it the need to adequately care for our names as *taonga* (treasures). She further argues that the responsibility lies with us to teach our children to be assertive in maintaining the authority and prestige of their name(s). In the above *kōrero ingoa*, the storyteller found that her daughter exemplified this assertiveness and even went so far as to reclaim and reassert her Māori name to first name status after it had been relegated to the position of "other" or "middle." At a young age, around six or seven years old, her family acknowledged and supported her right to use and assert her Māori name. In doing so, she embodied and upheld all the layers of meaning her name implies and references; she *became* her name.

One *pūrākau* proffered in my thesis, which explores the power held in a name, is about our beloved ancestor Māui and how he got his full name, Māui-tikitiki-o-Taranga.[3] The following excerpt from this creation story is about a child seeking out his *whakapapa* (genealogy). In this case, a boy, presumed dead, matures into an adult and decides to seek out his parents, beginning with his mother, Taranga. Giving birth to him on the shore and thinking he has died, Taranga wraps Māui in her topknot and casts him out to sea; hence the name Māui-tikitiki-o-Taranga (Māui of the topknot of Taranga).

Te Rangikāheke, a *Te Arawa* scholar and Elder, recounts the first meeting between Māui and his mother and how Māui was able to prove his identity as follows:[4]

Ā, rongo ana ahau i te rongo haka o tēnei whare, haere mai nei. Otirā i roto anō au i tōu puku, ka rongo au i ngā ingoa o aua mātāmua e tauria ana e koe ki ō rātou ingoa, ā tae noa ki tēnei pō, ka rongo tonu nei au ki a koe e whakahua ana i ō rātou ingoa. Koia ahau ka mea atu nei ki ō koutou ingoa, ko Māui-taha, ko Māui-roto, ko Māui-pae, ko Māui-waho, anā, ko ahau, ko Māui-pōtiki ahau e noho atu nei. Kātahi tōna w[h]aea ka karanga atu ki a Māui-pōtiki. "Ko koe tāku whakamutunga, me te ruahinetanga o taku tinana. Ā, ka mea atu nei ahau ki a koe, ko Māui-tikitiki koe o Taranga." Ā, waiho tonu iho hei ingoa mōna, ā, ko Māui-tikitiki-o-Taranga, ā, ko

Māui-tikitiki-o-Taranga taua māia. (Te Rangikāheke & Thornton, 1992, pp. 28–29)

But when I was in your belly, I heard the names of the older children when you were reciting their names, yes, down to this night I still heard you pronouncing their names. That is why I am going to pronounce your names; there is Māui-taha, Māui-roto, Māui-pae, Māui-waho, and here I am. Māui-pōtiki, sitting here. Then his mother called out to Māui-pōtiki. You are my last-born child from my old woman's body, and I say to you, "you are Māui-tikitiki-o-Taranga." This became his name in the future: that young hero was Māui-tikitiki-o-Taranga. (Te Rangikāheke & Thornton, 1992, pp. 53–55)

This is an important example of a child being named in alignment with his birthing story. In the story, Māui has clearly been taught the story of his birth and how he came to be rescued and raised by his ancestor, Atamumu-ki-te-rangi. The story of how he got his name was clearly deemed a significant one in terms of enabling him to identify and reclaim his *whakapapa* one day.

The connection between the waters of our mother's wombs, as the waters from which we all descend, and our names as important markers of our identity, is brought to life in this narrative. This *pūrākau* reminds us that the learning of *whakapapa*, the building of identity and thus, figuring out where we fit in the world, begins in utero. Our ancestors firmly believed in the ability of babies to learn in utero; as evidenced by the use of *oriori* (song) to teach *tamariki* (children) about their histories, people, sites of significance, and, of course, about their names (Yates-Smith, 1992). Another example of teaching and learning in utero is the *pūmotomoto* flute, which was played directly toward the *kōpū* (uterus) of a pregnant woman to implant songs and their historical and genealogical references into the baby's subconscious (Gabel, 2013; Pere, 1994). Importantly, in this *pūrākau*, Māui clearly remembers the sound of his mother's voice from his time within her, and subsequently, the names of his elder brothers were easily identifiable to him as words he had heard regularly. Consequently, despite never having met his brothers face-to-face, he was able to recognize and claim them as his brothers when he finally met them – through their names.

Maimoatia ō tātou pūrākau

I based the title of this section on the name of a hugely successful song, sung completely in *te reo Māori*, called "*Maimoatia te reo*." Released in 2016, the song encourages us all to "cherish the Māori language"; a message that, I argue, also extends to our stories (Haunui-Thompson, 2016).[5] In my doctoral research, I purposefully spent time deliberating how I could cherish Māori stories in the academic space (and beyond). Although there is every reason to be careful with our stories in the academic sphere, storying has much too important a role to play in our liberation and resurgence to be left in the margins. The magic held therein holds the keys to capturing the hearts of our future generations.

In our stories, we find many answers to the questions of life, especially in our *pūrākau*, which serve to remind us of the first instances of our ceremonies and practices, their importance, and their function. *Pūrākau* also capture the ways in which ceremony and practice have been openly challenged and therefore provide invaluable insight into the intellect of our ancestors (Nock, 2012). Our *pūrākau*, alongside our many other kinds of narratives such as proverbs, traditional chants, and other oral traditions, provide directives for our behaviour and help to guide us in our present context and beyond.

Pūrākau represent an important tool of decolonization, which enables the use of our creation stories as important sources of Māori knowledge. Integral to the unravelling of colonization is our own ancestral wisdom, which can only be found in our stories (in their many forms). A decolonial research agenda demands not only a revealing of the impact of colonization but a focus on unravelling it. *Pūrākau* are like glasses through which we can view, learn, and be taught more clearly by our ancestors, who live on in every recitation. They make the actions of our *atua* and *tūpuna* (ancestors) into "teachable moments" that have applications in a variety of contexts, situations, stages, and ages. In particular, *pūrākau* are a deep pool of knowledge that has been used for centuries by the scholars of our society to philosophize and theorize our world. Several Indigenous and Māori scholars have championed this approach for some time now and it was a deliberate and political decision to follow in their footsteps and assert our cosmogonies as important sources of literature in my research (Archibald, 1997; Kahukiwa & Grace, 2000; Mikaere, 2003; Lee, 2008; Simpson, 2014). (Re)claiming and (re)asserting those stories is to dare to embrace a vision of hope for our *mokopuna* (Jackson, 1998).

I have named the collaborative process I undertook with *whānau* participants in the doctoral research as "story building." Research that seeks to regenerate and reclaim our knowledges often highlights the importance of *mahi tahi* (collaboration); something that was further reinforced during the building of *kōrero ingoa* with *whānau* participants (Smith, 2015). As well as enabling a level of collaboration, a *whānau* approach offered a special opportunity to engage with *ingoa tangata* on a smaller and, therefore, more personal and intimate level. For this reason, every *whānau* participant was also a storyteller in my PhD thesis. As their kin, I was firmly embedded alongside every one of them and this made the research uniquely personal and intimate, not only for us but for the intended readership of my thesis. This level of "personal" may seem overly subjective; however, for Indigenous research, it is, I argue, the norm. Patricia Monture-Angus (1998) argues the "personal" as a "*double understanding*" (p. 10) – that we must both think and feel to truly gain knowledge, which comes from being deeply personal in how and why we conduct research.

The strong relationship and trust already present between myself and *whānau* participants meant that along with a willingness to discuss our names openly and with an open heart, the honesty and *aroha* of their voices came through clearly as a result. Along with being the recipient of such trust and respect came a massive amount of responsibility as a researcher. I struggled with this for the entire journey. I made sure all participants were well informed on a regular basis, that all versions were checked and rechecked with them and that even after the *kōrero ingoa* had been "built," they were informed of any presentations I did using their material. I always asked their permission to use their stories in new contexts.

Becoming a storyteller

Our whole lives are made up of stories. Some stories define us in ways we can never move on from. Of all the powers in the world, storytelling is one of the greatest. Stories are highly political. Those with the power can control whose story is told and how it is told. Scholars discuss the "grand or master narrative" as a form of story told by the colonial machine in the service of the imperial project (Walker, 1999). My people, of the *Taranaki* tribe, have been rehomed, ripped from our lands, and forced to live away from our tribal lands. Our land has been invaded and even occupied by imperial troops. Our stories, our ways of seeing and being, and of expressing ourselves have also been disrupted and re-written by those who forced us from our homes.

Pūrākau as a method can be used as a tool against the grand narrative and also enables us to speak forward, to our *mokopuna*, fortifying them with the wonder of who they are (Mita, 2000). It took me a long time to realize it but those early years with my grandparents, on our land and with our people, carved out a pathway to storytelling for me. Reflecting on it now, I can see that the places they took me, the meetings I attended with them, and the people they surrounded me with, gave me experiences that were deeply grounded in that very ancestral knowledge. My grandparents made sure they had a hand in raising me according to our cultural beliefs and, I think, this was more than an act of cultural survival. My grandparents actively refused to stop being Māori despite all that had been forcibly taken from them, the trauma they had experienced, and the hegemonic and assimilative attitudes and policies that bombarded them throughout their lives. They intentionally and purposefully resisted. An intentional part of their educational plan for me was revealed in the food we collected and ate together, the fires they lit that warmed my face, and the ancestral waters they bathed me in. Their plan was to ensure that being Māori would become as much a part of me as their love is and because of this, being Māori became something I could and would never give up.

My own children have had a very different upbringing, with so much more access to our language and ancestral knowledge in their formalized education than I ever had, and yet my overall aspiration for them is the same as what my grandparents wished for me: for my children to never ever give up loving and living their heritage. My children are fluent speakers of their language; they are educated in their language according to Māori philosophy and political aspirations on a daily basis, and yet, it's not enough. In our colonized and globalized reality where my children see Western culture as "normal," "valued," and "fun," their love of being Māori is still very much at risk. Part of what I see as a key issue behind this is the continued disconnection of our language from its knowledge base. While our language is integral to unlocking the world of our ancestors, the key to unlocking our children's passion for who they are and for the legacy of their ancestors lies in the magic of our stories.

Becoming a mother; birthing, breastfeeding, and raising children throughout my doctoral and research career has also driven my passion for *pūrākau* as method. Leanne Simpson (2011) reminds us about the power of stories and their teachings for mothers. She says: "You are the creator now, you will create life and renew it. This is why these teachings are so important to our young women – when we bring forth new life we are re-enacting this story" (pp. 38–39). Producing creative pieces of writing assisted in my growth and understanding as a "creator" both in and through research and this has had significant impact on my mothering and the researcher I have become. *Pūrākau* as a method supports the use of a range of narratives, both traditional and contemporary, by enabling a multiplicity of voices and allowing stories to be told in different ways. While my approach to the wider work of my PhD was to create a larger narrative of research, I realized that there were many smaller stories, which could make up that narrative. The *kōrero ingoa* of my *whānau* were the most important and powerful source of story, along with the *kōrero ingoa* I found in unpublished and published oral and written sources and in our creation stories. However, perhaps the biggest unexpected discovery for me was that my own creative writing could be an important contribution to the research project, and as I later realized during public presentations, these pieces became particularly useful and compelling.

The writing of those creative pieces also helped in several other important ways, such as enabling me to practice the craft of writing in a style that brought me joy and allowed me to find the pathway between academic writing and our ancestral knowledge. These pieces improved my writing style, enriched my vocabulary (in both *te reo Māori* and English), and enhanced my ability to clarify my thoughts and arguments and to write the research into the reality of what it is to be a *Kaupapa Māori* researcher. Consequently, those creative pieces helped the research to resonate and feel logical – not only on the page but in real life too.

I am a mother, a woman, a grandchild, and I am a storyteller

A little girl sits beside her grandmother in a crowded meeting house, filled to the brim with her relatives. I look over at the glass case by the door and wonder; who built the matchstick ship inside of it? I wonder if I could reach inside and touch it without my grandmother catching me? Suddenly, I'm pulled to my feet, and a pair of *poi* are pushed into my hands.

Hip! Hei! And the drum begins to pound.

Another song, another story. *Poi* flailing this way and that. "I've got to remember to hit my head," I think, in a panic to keep with the rhythm. My grandmother looks over and tells me to turn around and face the people, but I'm way too shy. I just want to crawl between her legs and cling with all my might. Quickly the song is over, and we all sit down. My grandfather is next to speak. Taking his time, he often glances outside as though seeking advice from the trees. He speaks softly at times, bellowing at other times. Only ever stopping to put his walking stick out to block some kid from running around. Funnily enough, all the kids are scared of him, but not me. He is my grandfather, and I am his *mokopuna*. I can do no wrong.

Up we get to sing another song, and I mouth along to the words not really understanding what I'm singing about, although I sure have heard it enough to know many of the words by heart. I love the rhythm of the song, the pounding of the drum and the patter of the *poi*. All around and above me are tufts of white feathers in the hair of every grandmother. Symbols of our identity, our cause, our resistance and of our stories. I look up at the paintings and photos on the walls of our meeting house, and I know I belong to them and to this place. If I listen hard enough, I can still hear my grandfather's voice telling the stories of those paintings and photos, of our ancestors – filling the room with our history and my legacy.

It's my turn now to tell stories made up of stories just like those of my childhood. This time, I am no longer a little girl but a woman and a mother, I am however and always will be their *mokopuna*, and as I write, I can hear the beat of the drum and the pitter-patter of *poi* in the distance.

Conclusion

The renaming of our people was intentional and purposeful on the part of our colonizers. The power to name, or rename, is a specific kind of symbolic violence and power that superimposes and defines what is seen and accepted as normal and legitimate within society. The project of storying our ancestors back into our lived realities and our political aspirations is, therefore, necessary to (re)claiming that power and (re)normalizing our ways of seeing and being in our children. My research reveals that calling our names back from beneath the colonial maps and class rolls of the past is an important site of struggle and a powerful way we can decolonize – *now*.

Our names were, and still are, too powerful, too steeped in our history and identity and therefore were and are intolerable to the white gaze of our colonizers. That is why they attempted to rename us; to erase and remake us in their image and in their name. The use of our *ingoa* (names) to reconnect, anchor, and mark our children with all the glory of our culture and of our ancestors has been undeniably shifted by colonization, and yet we have found successful ways to endure, resist, and thrive. In using decolonization as an overarching aim for this research, I was able to not only begin to find out what happened to our names, who renamed us, how and why, but to also unveil and (re)assert the power of our names and our stories and their importance to our resurgence.

Living a decolonized reality means wearing our names with pride and once again naming our world for ourselves. In calling back our names, several other spaces and knowledges are reclaimed as well. Calling our names back is directly linked to our reconnection with nature, our spiritual beliefs, our ceremonies, our history, and our places of importance. Reconnecting with the function behind our names and naming stories reminds us about where we come from and to whom we belong. These stories return us to the waters from which we descend, where we can once again bathe in their healing caress.

Notes

1 *Pūrākau* is a term commonly used to delineate Māori narratives that are cosmogonic in nature, however, it has also become the name of a storywork-based methodological approach to research method that was founded by Jenny Lee (2008) in her groundbreaking doctoral work.

2 *Pākehā* can be defined as non-Māori New Zealanders, or a New Zealander of European descent.

3 Māui tikitiki a Taranga is the other well-known version of this name.

4 This excerpt from one of the many *pūrākau* about Māui is sourced from the writings of a *Te Arawa* scholar, Te Rangikaheke, also known as Wiremu Maihi or William Marsh. In 1849, he wrote prolifically about our ancestors and their stories for Governor George Grey, a colonial governor and ethnographer, who later published those same narratives in his own books. I chose to reference and source the story from a later publication by Te Rangikāheke & Thornton (1992), although I had located and read the original manuscripts, as Thornton had already transcribed and translated the stories for a wider readership.

5 Please see www.facebook.com/MaimoaMusic/ for further information about this group of singers and their amazing vision.

6 *Poi* – A light ball on a string of varying length which is swung or twirled rhythmically to sung accompaniment. The *poi* has long held a prominent place amongst *Taranaki iwi* (tribe), *hapū* (sub-tribe), and *whānau* (extended family); having been used for many generations to record and pass on important *kōrero* from generation to generation. Likewise, the *poi* was used to share messages and *kōrero* with other tribes, particularly those of a political and/or spiritual significance.

References

Archibald, J. (1997). *Coyote learns to make a storybasket: the place of First Nations stories in education.* Doctoral dissertation, Simon Fraser University. Retrieved from www.collectionscanada.gc.ca.

Gabel, K. A. (2013). *Poipoia te tamaiti ki te ūkaipō.* Doctoral thesis, University of Waikato, Hamilton, New Zealand. Retrieved from http://researchcommons.waikato.ac.nz/handle/10289/7986.

Haunui-Thompson, S. (2016, July 11). "It's a way of thinking" – Maimoatia. *Radio New Zealand.* www.radionz.co.nz/.

Jackson, M. (1998). Research and the colonization of Māori knowledge. In *Te Pūmanawa Hauora, 1999 Proceedings of Te Oru Rangahau: Māori Research and Development Conference* (pp. 70–77). Palmerston North, New Zealand: School of Māori Studies, Massey University.

Kahukiwa, R. & Grace, P. (2000). *Wāhine toa: women of Māori myth.* Auckland, New Zealand: Penguin Books.

Lee, J. B. J. (2008). *Ako: pūrākau of Māori teachers' work in secondary schools.* Doctoral thesis, The University of Auckland, New Zealand. Retrieved from www.rangahau.co.nz/assets/lee_J/leej2008_phd.pdf.

Mikaere, A. (2003). *The balance destroyed: the consequences for Māori women of the colonization of Tikanga Māori.* Auckland, New Zealand: The International Research Institute for Māori and Indigenous Education.

Mita, M. (2000). Storytelling: a process of decolonization. In L. Pihama (Ed.), *The Journal of Puawaitanga. Special issue: Indigenous women and representation* (pp. 7–9). Auckland, New Zealand: Te Whare Wananga o Tāmaki Makaurau.

Monture-Angus, P. (1998). *Journeying forward: dreaming First Nations independence.* Halifax, NS: Fernwood Publishing.

Nock, S. (2012). Ngā Āhuatanga o Ngā Momo Tohu ki te Māori. *Te Kōtihitihi: Ngā Tuhinga Reo Māori. Te Hue Kōrero Tuarua.* 58.

O'Regan, H. (2001). *Ko Tahu, Ko Au: Kāi Tahu tribal identity.* Christchurch, New Zealand: Horomaka Publishing.

Pere, R. (1994). *Ako: concepts and learning in the Māori tradition.* Wellington, New Zealand: Te Kōhanga Reo National Trust.

Seed-Pihama, J. E. (2017). *Ko wai tō ingoa? The transformative potential of Māori names.* Thesis, Doctor of Philosophy, PhD. University of Waikato, Hamilton, New Zealand. Retrieved from https://hdl.handle.net/10289/11310.

Simpson, L. (2011). *Dancing on our turtle's back: stories of Nishnaabeg recreation, resurgence and a new emergence.* Winnipeg, MB: Arbiter Ring Publishing.

Simpson, L. B. (2014). Land as pedagogy: Nishnaabeg intelligence and rebellious transformation. *Decolonization: Indigeneity, Education & Society 3*(3), 1–25. Retrieved from: www.decolonization.org/index.php/des/article/view/22170/17985.

Smith, L. T. (1999). *Decolonizing methodologies: research and Indigenous Peoples.* London: Zed Books.

Smith, L. T. (2015, September 11). Heritage and knowledge: decolonizing the research process. *[Video file].* Retrieved from: www.youtube.com/watch?v=-dfE_p_mxQ.

Smith, T. (2012). Aitanga: Māori precolonial conceptual frameworks and fertility: a literature review. In P. Reynolds & C. Smith (Eds.), *The gift of children: Māori and infertility* (pp. 3–37). Wellington, New Zealand: Huia.

Te Rangikāheke & Thornton, A. (1992). *The story of Māui: by Te Rangikāheke; edited with translation and commentary by Agathe Thornton.* Christchurch, New Zealand: Department of Māori, University of Canterbury.

Waikerepuru, H. (2014, May 20). *Cultural bridge: Māori values around wai (flow or water)*. [Audio podcast]. Retrieved from http://m.waterwheel.net/03/16/88/-4998816031.mp4.

Walker, R. (1999). The development of Maori studies in tertiary education in Aotearoa/New Zealand. In M. Peters (Ed.), *After the disciplines: the emergence of cultural studies* (pp. 187–198). Westport, CT: Bergin and Garvey.

Yates-Smith, A. (1992). *Hine! E Hine! Rediscovering the feminine in Māori spirituality*. Unpublished doctoral thesis. Te Whare Wānanga o Waikato, Hamilton, Aotearoa.

7 | INDIGENOUS LAW/STORIES: AN APPROACH TO WORKING WITH MĀORI LAW

Carwyn Jones

Introduction

Working with Māori law[1] requires the legal practitioner to work with Māori stories. Māori law is not written in statutes or reported in volumes of judicial decisions. It is part of a cultural system that is based on oral tradition, recorded in different forms such as *waiata* (songs), *whakairo* (carvings), *karakia* (prayers/chants), and *kōrero pūrākau* (histories and stories). In this chapter, I explore one possible approach to working with Māori law through an analysis of Māori stories. Using Māori stories to understand, discuss, and apply Māori law enables Māori law to be explored on its own terms. That is, by adopting this approach, Māori law is not framed by Western perceptions of law or filtered through a common law lens.[2] Indigenous storywork (Archibald, 2008; Lee-Morgan, 2009) helps to articulate an internal perspective of Māori law, which necessarily builds on the cultural and experiential groundings of Māori communities (Christie, 2009, p. 195). In this chapter, I suggest a tentative framework to help to draw out law from Māori stories and illustrate its application to the story of two of my ancestors, Kahungunu and Rongomaiwahine. The intention is to show that understanding Māori law through Indigenous storywork can contribute to the decolonization of legal theory and practice and to Māori law being recognized as comprising dynamic and sophisticated legal systems that are relevant and applicable to the full range of legal issues we face as Indigenous Peoples.

Stories of law

Stories, as I use the term in this chapter, include what might be described as myths and legends, as well as histories of identifiable ancestors and communities that are closer in time to our own generation. I refer to all of these as stories because, for the purposes of understanding and working with Māori law, the important characteristics of a story are its meaning and purpose, not whether it is one hundred per cent verifiable fact. To provide some parameters for the consideration of law in the story of Kahungunu and Rongomaiwahine, it is helpful to first set out something of the context of the common law and Māori legal systems.

The basic framework of English common law was established in the century and a half after the Norman conquest of 1066 (Glenn, 2010, pp. 237–287). A key feature of common law systems is the role of judge-made law that is built up by precedent over time. This has led to lawyers developing a particular way of reading judicial decisions and judges developing a particular way of writing those decisions (Davies, 1987; Bruner, 2003). It developed according to the worldview, values, and social, economic, and environmental imperatives of the communities within which it operated. Māori law has its roots in the Pacific and developed from a system of law and social organization that the first people to arrive in Aotearoa brought with them from Hawaiki[3] (Waitangi Tribunal, 2011, pp. 1–7). It reflected the values and objectives of those who came from Hawaiki. This law necessarily adapted to meet the new circumstances found in Aotearoa, perhaps at roughly the same time that the common law system was bedding-in on the other side of the world.[4]

The Māori legal system, therefore, developed law that not only differed from common law in substance; its processes for creating, amending, repealing, applying, and enforcing law were also different. This may seem an obvious point to make but it is an important one that is not always clearly recognized. It is important in the present context because it follows that, to properly examine Māori law, it is necessary to do so through a Māori lens, using a Māori analytical framework.

Anishinabe legal scholar, John Borrows, has identified basic sources of Indigenous law that he suggests may be applicable to Indigenous legal systems in what is now known as the North American continent (Borrows, 2010, pp. 23–55). I suggest a similar categorization could be applied to Māori law to assist our understanding of the operation of Māori legal traditions.[5]

Law of the spiritual world

As with Borrows' categorization (Borrows, 2010, pp. 24–28), the first source I have identified here is the law of the spiritual world. Understanding the spiritual dimension of Māori law is fundamentally important. Not only does it explain aspects of the enforcement and effectiveness of Māori law (the nature of the obligations to which participants within the legal system feel themselves to be subject) (Benton, Frame & Meredith, 2013, p. 404), but it also explains necessary components of concepts such as *mana* (power/authority) and *kaitiakitanga* (guardianship) (Marsden, 1992). Managing the spiritual dimension and the relationships with *atua* (the Māori gods) is an integral and everyday aspect of Māori law.

Law of the natural world

The second source of Māori law that I have identified is law that comes from the natural world. As with John Borrows' category of Indigenous natural law, there are two strands to this source of law (Borrows, 2010, pp. 28–35). First, there are laws that have developed from practical experience and close observation of the natural world. These are often rules around the management of natural resources. For example, in order to maintain the sustainability of certain bird species, there may be a prohibition placed on hunting at certain times of the year or in certain circumstances (Benton, Frame & Meredith, 2013, p. 310). There are also laws which, while also derived from close observation of the natural world, may be applied more by analogy or metaphor. For example, laws which regulate relationships between people or between people and the natural environment may be based on analogies drawn from observed relationships between bird and plant life. Key statements of legal principle will often be expressed as a metaphor from within the natural world, whether or not the legal principle itself directly derives from the natural world (McRae, 2017, p. 93).

Law of the rūnanga

Māori law also deploys deliberative law-making processes. The authority of Māori communities rests in the collective, rather than with individuals. Legal decision-making, whether in relation to the creation or application of law, therefore aims to draw on that collective authority. Although *rūnanga* came to be the term adopted by the colonial government to describe authoritative Māori decision-making bodies, the concept itself is one that is traditionally Māori (Benton, Frame & Meredith, 2013, pp. 343–362). The relatively diffuse and de-centralized nature of executive authority in the Māori world means that not only are there opportunities for deliberative legal discussion but, in fact, this becomes a necessity for effective law-making.

Law of the rangatira

Although executive authority is relatively de-centralized in the Māori world, Māori law can sometimes derive from a declaration made by an authoritative source. For example, leaders, or *rangatira*, might be recognized as having the authority to impose or remove prohibitions on hunting or access to territory. This means there are examples of positivistic sources of law to be found within the Māori legal world. However, it would be rare if such law was not also supported by other sources or perhaps even had its origin, subsequently forgotten, in another source of law, such as law that is derived from patterns of the natural world.

Law of the ancestors

Precedent does not operate in Māori law in the same way it does under common law (Durie, 1994). However, past action is still an important source of Māori law. The key principles (as outlined below) that underpin the Māori legal system – and, in fact, the Māori world – can, in some senses at least, be understood as packages of information that transmit to following generations' wisdom that has been built up by the ancestors (Mead, 2016, pp. 13–28). Ancestors are a key source of Māori law. Perhaps the key distinction from the common law system of precedent is that instead of the application of specific legal rules, Māori law focuses on the expression of values. This provides greater flexibility and often allows for significant variations of practice to develop between different places, communities, or circumstances (Durie, 1996, p. 451).

These sources of law set the scope and provide the reference points for undertaking a legal reading of Māori stories.

Key principles of Māori law

There are a small number of principles that are central to the Māori world and are also essential to examining Māori stories as legal texts and through a Māori legal lens. These key principles, outlined below, frame the ways in which we approach Māori stories as legal texts. Before turning to a discussion of the use of *pūrākau* as a key tool of Māori legal analysis it is necessary to provide a brief explanation of these five principles.

Whanaungatanga

One of the key features of the Māori worldview is the centrality of relationships to all aspects of society. The principle of *whanaungatanga* captures this fundamental centrality and also provides the conceptual framework for effectively viewing all relationships as kin relationships. Relationships define rights and obligations not only between individuals and communities but also between past, present, and future generations, and they reflect rights and obligations between people and *atua*, and people and the natural world. The practices and processes of Māori law must therefore be understood through a relational lens (Waitangi Tribunal, 2011). Individual rights to land and natural resources did not exist independently of the wider collective right of the community.

Mana

The principle of *mana* sits at the heart of Māori understandings of leadership, authority, and accountability. The Māori term derives from an ancient Oceanic concept that was used to describe supernatural power (Benton, Frame & Meredith, 2013, p. 154). The spiritual aspect of *mana* has remained an important part of the concept. However, this really only represents one strand of *mana*. Often, *mana* is described as deriving from three core sources:

- *mana atua* – *mana* that comes from the sacred power of the gods;
- *mana tupuna* – *mana* that comes from one's lineage, the inherited mana of one's ancestors; and
- *mana tangata* – the power and authority that one achieves through one's own skill, knowledge, and actions.

Mana is a central motivating factor behind social interactions of all kinds in *te ao Māori* (the Māori world) (Kawharu, 1989, p. xix; Mead, 2016, p. 33).

Manaakitanga

Manaakitanga is closely connected to the concept of *mana*. The etymology of the word illustrates this connection. The root word, "*manaaki*," is a conjunction of the words "*mana*" and "*aki*." "*Mana*" has been described above. "*Aki*" is a Proto-Polynesian word that expresses the concept of reciprocal action. The implication is that the generosity encompassed in the concept of *manaakitanga* enhances the *mana* on both sides of the relationship, i.e. those who fulfil their obligations to show kindness or provide hospitality as well as those who accept that kindness or hospitality (Benton, Frame & Meredith, 2013, pp. 205–209). *Manaakitanga* does not simply reflect a sense that there is a social expectation that people will be kind and generous. It encompasses legal obligations, which might be thought of as obligations that are created through the recognized legal processes of the community and will be subject to enforcement through that community's legal institutions. *Manaakitanga* also incorporates the rights necessary to fulfil those obligations, which have a direct bearing on the maintenance of relationships and the exercise of authority in *te ao Māori*.

Tapu/Noa

Tapu and *noa* are key institutions in the maintenance and application of Māori Law. They may be understood as complementary opposites, though ultimately both concepts are about the recognition of the spiritual aspect of all things. *Tapu* and *noa* therefore have social and religious foundations as well as operating as key legal institutions. Bishop Manuhuia Bennett described *tapu* as follows (see Benton, Frame & Meredith, 2013, p. 409): "Tapu is a spiritual institution set up for political purposes, it is a form of control, and controlled behaviour patterns, behaviour standards."

"*Tapu*" is often translated as "sacred," though perhaps something that is *tapu* would more accurately be described as being subject to restriction because of its spiritual dimension. *Noa* is the key institution for managing *tapu*. If *tapu* reflects something that is of special status that must be set apart or subject to restrictions, then *noa* reflects a normal state of affairs where there is balance and where interactions can occur free of restriction. In this sense, *noa* and *tapu* always go together (Mead, 2016, pp. 34–38).

Utu

Utu embodies the principle of reciprocity. It reflects the constant motivation of Māori Law to achieve, maintain, and restore balance. *Utu* is often reductively characterized as "revenge." It is true that part of the principle of *utu* requires that offences or wrongs are punished but the principle of *utu* also requires that the provision of goods or services is reciprocated (Metge, 2002). *Utu* is central to Māori gift exchange practices. These practices not only serve as a means of trade and commerce; they are also important in the establishment and maintenance of relationships. The principle of *utu* is therefore closely connected with the principle of *whanaungatanga*. The various aspects or applications of *utu* illustrate the importance of this principle to the system of Māori Law. As described above, *utu* plays a central role in commerce, maintaining relationships, providing compensation or redress, and punishing wrong-doing (Firth, 1929).

The key principles briefly described above provide the basis for the analytical framework for working with Māori stories, which I now turn to consider.

Kōrero (story/talk) Analysis Framework

Lawyers in common law systems are trained to use a case analysis framework in order to derive legal rules from judicial decisions and determine the applicability of precedent. The case analysis framework helps common law lawyers sift through the text of a judgment and identify matters such as the *ratio decidendi* (the reason for the decision, being "the point in the case that determines the judgement" (*Black's Law Dictionary*, 1979, p. 1135) or "the principle that the case establishes" (*Barron's Law Dictionary*, 1984, p. 385)); *obiter dicta* (parts of the judgment that are not central to the reason for the decision and therefore do not act as a binding precedent); and the material facts (the key factual circumstances of the case to which the law is applied and which provide the key parameters for the application of precedent).

As outlined above, Māori law is different from common law in both form and substance. The processes by which Māori law is created, applied, and recorded are different from those of common law. It is, therefore, not possible to take a process designed to help the legal reader to analyse common law judgments and apply it to records of Māori law, such as those contained in Māori stories. The common law case analysis framework provides a useful tool for synthesizing legal rules and principles from across a range of decisions about how law is to be applied within the common law legal system (Weaver, 1991, pp. 545–561). It helps participants in common law processes to see clearly the law contained in the judgment and to use and apply the law, as well as indicating how to challenge the law and shape it. In order to help focus on the legal dimensions of Māori stories, I have identified some key questions that a reader of Māori law can use as a basic analytical framework.[6] This "*Kōrero* Analysis Framework" is intended to help articulate Māori legal process and principles as part of the discipline of law, to understand the relevant aspects of *tikanga Māori* as law.[7]

While drawing on the common law case analysis framework as a concept, the *Kōrero* Analysis Framework is not merely a modified version of the common law approach. The *Kōrero* Analysis Framework is grounded in the Māori stories to which it is intended to apply and has been developed from a *tikanga* base, which places key principles (*whanaungatanga, manaakitanga, mana, tapu/noa,* and *utu*) at the heart of the Māori legal system. This framework asks the legal reader of a Māori story the following questions:

1. Who is involved in this story? What are the relationships that are involved?
2. In this story, do you see expressions of key principles such as *whanaungatanga* (centrality of relationships), *manaakitanga* (value of nurturing/caring for others), *mana* (power and authority), *tapu* and *noa* (respect for the spiritual and everyday dimensions of all things), and *utu* (reciprocity)? Are there examples of key principles being breached? If so, what are the consequences?
3. Why do people in the story do what they do? Are their actions determined by:
   a. Key values/principles?
   b. Past action (precedent)?
   c. Their relationships to one another?
   d. Actions or statements of people in leadership roles?
   e. Something else?
4. What is the central message of this story?
5. If you were to re-tell this story, what would you see as the essential points?

This framework is intended to suggest some aspects of the story that help us to understand the way in which Māori legal traditions operate and the kind of legal principles and reasoning that underpin their development.

The overall aim of using this framework is to explore Māori knowledge relating to law and legal institutions, with the specific aim of making Māori law more accessible and more readily able to be applied to legal issues that Māori communities face. The internal perspective of this framework places the emphasis on working with Māori legal concepts and Māori models of legal analysis. Furthermore, one of the important dimensions of this approach is that it situates Māori law as part of a living and dynamic legal system within the field of legal research.

Kahungunu and Rongomaiwahine

As an example of the kind of stories to which this framework can be applied, I have reproduced the story of Kahungunu and Rongomaiwahine – two important ancestors of my own people:[8]

The story of Kahungunu and Rongomaiwahine's romance has been told many times. Kahungunu had heard reports of Rongomaiwahine's beauty and high birth, but when he arrived at *Nukutaurua*, on the *Māhia* Peninsula, he found that she was already married to Tamatakutai. In an attempt to impress her people, he gathered enormous quantities of fern root, tied them into bundles with vines, and rolled them down a hill. Such were the quantities that it became like a landslide, blocking the doors of the house.

Kahungunu then went up onto a hill and watched the *karoro* (shags) diving. He practised holding his breath, counting "*pepe tahi, pepe rua, pepe toru ...*" (count one, count two, count three ...) until the birds reappeared. Then Kahungunu went diving, holding his breath for as long as the shags had done. He filled several baskets with enough *pāua* (a type of shellfish) for all the occupants of the village. When he surfaced from his final dive, he had covered his chest with *pāua*, and everyone was very impressed. The hill has since been named *Puke Karoro*.

Having gained the approval of Rongomaiwahine's people, Kahungunu set out to create discord between Rongomaiwahine and her husband Tamatakutai. One night he surreptitiously broke wind near the sleeping couple, causing an argument between them. In the morning Kahungunu joined Tamatakutai in the sport of surfing in a canoe. After several trips Kahungunu took over the steering, and capsized it on a particularly large wave. Tamatakutai fell out and, unable to swim, was drowned.

One day Kahungunu asked Rongomaiwahine to dress his hair for him. As she was fastening his topknot, the tie broke. Kahungunu took from his plaited belt some flax that had been grown at *Kawhainui*, near *Tauranga*. After softening the flax in water, Rongomaiwahine used it to tie his topknot. Kahungunu then stood up, and facing north said:

E te pūtiki wharanui o Tamatea i mahue atu rā i runga o Tauranga.
Here is the binding broad-leaved flax of Tamatea that was left at Tauranga.

It was from this remark that Rongomaiwahine and her people finally knew the true identity of Kahungunu, and he became her permanent husband. They settled at *Maungakāhia*, their *pā* at *Māhia*, where Kahungunu eventually died.

Many of Rongomaiwahine's descendants on the *Māhia* Peninsula identify themselves as *Ngāti Rongomaiwahine* rather than as *Ngāti Kahungunu*: they believe her to be of superior lineage.

Even at a very simple level, the story of Rongomaiwahine and Kahungunu provides some basic information about law and legal process. The *Kōrero* Analysis Framework helps the legal reader to focus on the legal dimension and draw out the legal principles at play. A basic application of the *Kōrero* Analysis Framework to this story might look something like the following:

1. Who is involved in this story? What are the relationships that are involved?

This story identifies three named ancestors: Rongomaiwahine, Kahungunu, and Tamatakutai. At one level, the relationships between these three individuals can be described in relatively straightforward terms. Rongomaiwahine and Tamatakutai are living as husband and wife before Kahungunu arrives and disrupts their relationship. Kahungunu and Tamatakutai might be described as rivals for the affections of Rongomaiwahine. Eventually, through both fair means and foul, Kahungunu displaces Tamatakutai. It is not specifically mentioned in the account above, but Kahungunu and Rongomaiwahine subsequently went on to have five children and became the eponymous ancestors of the *iwi Ngāti Kahungunu* and *Rongomaiwahine*.

However, if the legal reader adopts a Māori legal lens, then the relationships involved might be considered in more depth. It is clear from the account above that Rongomaiwahine's people play a key role in events. When examining Māori stories as legal texts, the reader should be careful to look beyond the individual protagonists to take account of the network of relationships within which those individuals sit. In the story of Rongomaiwahine and Kahungunu this requires the legal reader to examine the *whakapapa* (genealogy) of Rongomaiwahine, Kahungunu, and Tamatakutai – the communities that each of these individuals bring to their interactions in the episode described above, and to consider the other marriages of Kahungunu to women of high rank throughout the East Coast area and the relationships those formed both before and after his marriage to Rongomaiwahine. Kahungunu's

whakapapa is not recounted in depth in this story, but there are important details included, which clearly identify for the reader that where
he comes from is important. The named ancestors in this account
all sit within a complex network of kin relationships that extend to
their own ancestors as well as to their descendants. There are relationships between Rongomaiwahine's people and Kahungunu's people
that pre-date those individuals meeting and the events recounted in
the story. In a Māori legal text, those pre-existing relationships are
not merely background context but are crucial to fully understanding
people's actions.

2. In this story, do you see expressions of key values? Are there examples of key principles being breached? If so, what are the consequences?

Expressions of key values can be identified in the story of Rongomaiwahine and Kahungunu. The story's primary theme could be said
to be *whanaungatanga*, the centrality of kin relationships in the Māori
world. As noted above, the relationships involved extend beyond the
individuals named in the account. *Whanaungatanga* and *mana* are
both given expression through what the story tells us about the site
of decision-making authority. In this instance, the marriage between
the two ancestors, both from chiefly lines, was not a decision only for
the two individuals involved. The wider community had both a stake
and a say in whether the marriage would take place. This illustrates
the relational nature of individual rights in the context of the rights of
the collective.

A persuasive factor in gaining the approval of Rongomaiwahine's
people is Kahungunu's ability to provide food for the community.
These are skills for which he is famous, as illustrated by the following
whakatauki:

> Ko Kahu-hunuhunu he tangata ahuwhenua mōhio ki te haere i ngā
> mahi o uta me te tai.
> Kahu-hunuhunu is an industrious man and one who knows how to
> manage works both on land and at sea.

This provides a clear expression of the value placed on *manaakitanga*
and, when considered alongside other stories, this helps the legal
reader to identify key principles and mechanisms of gift exchange and
Māori forms of contract. Kahungunu's study of the diving shags may

also point to the importance in Māori law of a close observation of the natural world in determining appropriate ways of acting, perhaps in the context of resource management.

The principles of *tapu* and *noa* are also apparent. Re-tellings of this story usually include the detail about Rongomaiwahine dressing Kahungunu's hair, as does the version above. A person's head is understood to be the most *tapu* part of their body. This detail then reflects a level of intimacy between the two, and most likely an equality of status, such that they can engage in this way without breaching *tapu*.

The other question of *tapu* and *utu* arises from Kahungunu's treatment of Tamatakutai. For many people, the death of Tamatakutai is seen as a breach of *tapu* and one that has never properly been redressed in accordance with the values of reciprocity and balance that are part of the principle of *utu*. Where there is division and ill-feeling between the *iwi* of *Rongomaiwahine* and *Ngāti Kahungunu* today in relation to current political and commercial matters, this, some would argue, can be explained by the fact that appropriate action has never been taken to redress the breach of *tapu* occasioned by Tamatakutai's death.

3. Why do people in the story do what they do?

As described above, the key principles of *tikanga Māori* are given expression in the story of Kahungunu and Rongomaiwahine and provide a frame of reference for the protagonists' actions. Perhaps the two main principles that determine people's actions in this story are *whanaungatanga* and *mana*. Ultimately, although sometimes characterized as a love story, the account of Kahungunu and Rongomaiwahine is highly political. This is about creating a strategic match and connecting two powerful, chiefly lines. It is the principle of *whanaungatanga* that provides the mechanism to do this and it is the principle of *mana* that provides the motivation. The history of Kahungunu, the *tipuna*, is sometimes portrayed as the story of a young man who travels far and wide, seemingly without purpose, having liaisons with women all around the island, and finally meeting the beautiful Rongomaiwahine. The truth is probably altogether more strategic, albeit less romantic. When one examines Kahungunu's journey and the connections he made through marriage, it seems clear that he carefully identified women of rank in each district in order to cement relationships with different communities and ultimately establish *whakapapa* rights for his descendants. An important piece of the Rongomaiwahine story is that it was, of course, she who had the *mana* and authority and rights to lands and resources in and around *Māhia* and *Nukutaurua*, not Kahungunu. The political nature of their marriage is also evidenced by the involvement of Rongomaiwahine's community in accepting the match, and the recognition by both Rongomaiwahine and Kahungunu that it was appropriate that the community have a say in this matter.

The key principles of *tikanga Māori* clearly play an important role in determining people's actions within this account. Other matters can also be identified, although they are not always explicit or obvious. For example, there is reference to past action and events though precedent is not directly applied as an authoritative rule in the way that it would be under the common law doctrine of *stare decisis*. In the above account, Kahungunu reveals his identity by stating:

> E te pūtiki wharanui o Tamatea i mahue atu rā i runga o Tauranga.
> Here is the binding broad-leaved flax of Tamatea that was left at Tauranga

This is a statement about his own origins, which reaches into the past to reference his father, Tamatea, and connections to place and the natural world. For those who are aware of the history of the ancestors involved, this short reference also points to the journeys of Tamatea and the *whakapapa* of Kahungunu. For those knowledgeable about *whakapapa*, this explains the genealogical connection between Kahungunu's people and Rongomaiwahine's people, which sets the framework for the relationship of rights and obligations within which the protagonists operate (McRae, 2017, pp. 42–78).

4. What is the central message of this story?

This story places a strong emphasis on the importance of the match between Kahungunu and Rongomaiwahine. It is commonly told as a reminder of the foundation of the now many communities of Hawkes Bay and *Wairarapa* that descend from the union of these two ancestors, each a leader in their own right. The key message of the story might be understood to be a reinforcement of the centrality of relationships within the Māori world and the necessity of understanding the way in which relationships shape networks of rights and obligations. Kahungunu had no rights to the lands of the district independent of Rongomaiwahine, but the rights and obligations of the descendants of these famous ancestors was established by *whakapapa* and developed over generations of active relationships with the land of the region.

Alongside the central message, it is helpful to note other key messages, which may be given greater priority, depending on the purpose of the storyteller and the requirements of the circumstances in which the story is deployed. For example, recognition of the ability of Kahungunu as a provider of food and resources speaks to the value placed on leadership in that field. There is also the sinister removal of Tamatakutai, which, as noted above, is still raised in contemporary discussions between the *iwi* of *Rongomaiwahine* and *Ngāti Kahungunu*.[9]

5. If you were to re-tell this story, what would you see as the essential points?

As previously mentioned, the purpose for which this story is told in any given circumstance may lead to some points being given greater emphasis and others being de-prioritized. The general framework of the story remains the same: Kahungunu arrives from outside of the district, sets his sights on marrying Rongomaiwahine, gains the approval of her community through feats of resource gathering, disrupts the existing relationship between Rongomaiwahine and Tamatakutai (including through cunning and somewhat underhand means), and eventually marries Rongomaiwahine, a union that is subsequently recognized as one of the most strategically important on the East Coast (Mitchell, 1972, p. 79). In a common law judgment, these might be referred to as the material facts.

There are also some other specific details, which usually appear in accounts of this story but which do not appear to have any bearing on the central narrative. One example is the episode in which Rongomaiwahine dresses Kahungunu's hair, leading to his statement of his own identity (Mitchell, 1972, p. 79). This is such a particular detail that it must be assumed to signify an important point to the reader. As noted above, this episode gives an insight to knowledgeable readers, through a very concise statement, of Kahungunu's origins and the journeys of his father. It also serves as a reminder of the *tapu* nature of the relationship that was formed between Kahungunu and Rongomaiwahine. These matters would probably not be identified as material facts in common law case analysis and yet they are matters of importance in explaining the Māori law that is recorded in this story.

Conclusion

Both common law and Māori law use stories and narratives to give expression to the application of legal rules, principles, and processes. Common law developed stories – sometimes about common law itself – that served the objectives of the English communities within which it was founded, and later communities from other parts of the common law world. Māori law comes from different sources and was developed in response to the circumstances and aspirations of Māori communities. Its stories are different from the stories of common law, and working with Māori law requires the application of a set of conceptual tools that are grounded in the Māori world. The *Kōrero* Analysis Framework that I have tentatively sketched out in this chapter is grounded in key Māori sources of law and legal principles and is designed to provide a Māori legal lens for working with Māori law stories. The example of the story of Kahungunu and Rongomaiwahine illustrates the way in which this framework could be applied to draw out law from Māori stories and help to articulate an internal perspective of the Māori legal system. Developing this internal perspective allows for Māori legal traditions to be understood on their own terms and made accessible as law. It reveals Māori legal traditions as important legal tools within their own right and enables Māori law to be more regularly and effectively applied to the full range of legal issues faced by Māori communities.

Notes

1 I use the term "Māori law" to capture the idea of fundamental infrastructure that underpins the Māori legal order. That is not to deny the existence of multiple Māori legal systems that operate within different communities. However, there are elements of the way in which Māori law operates that remain relatively consistent across Māori communities, even where the particular substantive legal rules or practices may vary.

2 Common law legal systems are those that derive from English legal traditions, such as the New Zealand state legal system. Law is often a central component of the imperial apparatus and common law has been an effective instrument of colonization in many parts

of the world, including Aotearoa. One of the important aspects of articulating Indigenous law *as law* is to challenge the hegemony of imposed legal structures.

3 In Māori oral traditions, Hawaiki is the ancestral homeland from which the first arrivals came to Aotearoa.

4 It is estimated that the first human arrival in Aotearoa New Zealand occurred around 1200 (Anderson, 1991, pp. 767–795).

5 The categories that I use mirror the categories that are proposed by Borrows. However, they draw on Māori institutions and a Māori frame of reference to provide a distinctive Māori gloss.

6 This framework is based on the key principles of Māori law as described in

this chapter, developed with reference to Indigenous storywork methodology, and has been refined through a number of workshops aimed at testing the applicability of this analytical framework.

7 I have drawn inspiration for developing the *Kōrero* Analysis Framework from the work being undertaken by Indigenous legal scholars in Canada, such as Val Napoleon, Hadley Friedland, and John Borrows, who have been working with First Nations communities to explore

the law contained within their own stories (Borrows, 2016; Napoleon & Friedland, 2016).

8 As recounted on the *Te Ara – The Encyclopedia of New Zealand* website www.teara.govt.nz/en/ngati-kahungunu/ page-4.

9 For example, the *iwi* of *Rongomaiwahine* has been in a long-running dispute with *Ngāti Kahungunu Iwi* Incorporated over the allocation of fishing quota under the Māori Fisheries Act 2004.

References

Anderson, A. (1991). The chronology of colonization in New Zealand. *Antiquity 65*, pp. 767–795.

Archibald, J. (2008). *Indigenous storywork: educating the heart, mind, body, and spirit.* Vancouver, BC: UBC Press.

Barron's Law Dictionary. (2nd ed.). 1984, at 385.

Benton, R., Frame, A. & Meredith, P. (2013). *Te Mātāpunenga: A compendium of references to the concepts and institutions of Māori customary law.* Wellington, New Zealand: Victoria University Press.

Black's Law Dictionary. (5th ed.). 1979, at 1135.

Borrows, J. (2010). *Canada's Indigenous Constitution.* Toronto, ON: University of Toronto Press.

Borrows, J. (ed.). (2016). *Windsor yearbook of access to justice. Special issue: Indigenous Law, Lands, and Literature*, 13.

Bruner, J. (2003). *Making stories: law, literature, life.* Cambridge, MA: Harvard University Press.

Christie, G. (2009). Indigenous legal theory: some initial considerations. In B. J. Richardson, S. Imai & K. McNeil (eds.), *Indigenous Peoples and the law: comparative and critical perspectives* (pp. 195–232). Oxford: Hart Publishing.

Davies, M. (1987). Reading cases. *Modern Law Review 50*, pp. 409–431.

Durie, E. T. (1994). Custom law (unpublished).

Durie, E. T. (1996). Will the Settlers settle? Cultural conciliation and law. *Otago Law Review 8*, pp. 449–465.

Firth, R. (1929). *Primitive economics of the New Zealand Maori.* London: Routledge.

Glenn, P. H. (2010). *Legal traditions of the world.* (4th ed.). Oxford: Oxford University Press.

Kawharu, I. H. (1989). Introduction. In I. H. Kawharu (ed.), *Waitangi: Māori and Pākehā perspectives of the Treaty of Waitangi.* Auckland, New Zealand: Oxford University Press.

Lee-Morgan, J. (2009). Decolonising Māori narratives: pūrākau as a method, *MAI Review 2*, article 3.

McRae, J. (2017). *Māori oral tradition: He Kōrero nō te Ao Tawhito.* Auckland, New Zealand: Auckland University Press.

Marsden, M. (1992). *Kaitiakitanga: a definitive introduction to the holistic world view of the Māori.* Wellington, New Zealand: Ministry for the Environment.

Mead, H. M. (2016). *Tikanga Māori: living by Māori values.* (2nd ed.).

Wellington, New Zealand: Huia Publishers.

Metge, J. (2002). Returning the gift: *Utu* in intergroup relations. *Journal of the Polynesian Society 111*, pp. 311–338.

Mitchell, J. H. (1972). *Takitimu*. Wellington, New Zealand: Reed Publishing.

Napoleon, V. & Friedland, H. (2016). An inside job: engaging with Indigenous legal traditions through stories. *McGill Law Journal 61*, pp. 725–754.

Waitangi Tribunal. (2011). *Ko Aotearoa Tēnei: a report into claims concerning New Zealand law and policy affecting Māori culture and identity* (Wai 262). Wellington, New Zealand: Legislation Direct.

Weaver, R. L. (1991). Langdell's legacy: living with the case method. *Villanova Law Review 517*, pp. 545–561.

8 | *WHĀNAU* STORYTELLING AS INDIGENOUS PEDAGOGY: *TIAKINA TE PĀ HARAKEKE*

Leonie Pihama, Donna Campbell, and Hineitimoana Greensill

Introduction

Hūtia te rito o te harakeke
Kei hea te kōmako e kō
Kī mai koe ki a ahau
He aha te mea nui o te ao?
Māku e kī atu
He tangata, he tangata, he tangata

Pluck the centre shoot from the flax bush
Where will the Bellbird sing?
You ask me
What is the most important thing in the world
I will say
It is people, It is people, It is people

This chapter is grounded on an ongoing programme of research and transformative praxis, *"Tiakina Te Pā Harakeke."* The aim of the research is to provide insights into ways in which *whānau* (extended family relationships) talk about and share their experiences of *pūrākau* as pedagogy. *"Tiakina Te Pā Harakeke"* is a *Kaupapa Māori* research. *Kaupapa Māori* provides an approach that is distinctively Māori and which affirms *te reo Māori* (Māori language), *tikanga* (Māori cultural practices), and *mātauranga* (Māori knowledge). It is an Indigenous research approach that interrogates issues through both a Māori and a decolonizing lens (Smith, 1999b). Within this project this included *whakawhiti kōrero* (open conversations) with Māori knowledge experts and *hui* (cultural gatherings) where those involved had the opportunity to share knowledge and traditional stories related to raising *tamariki* (children) and *mokopuna* (grandchildren) in ways that aligned to our cultural beliefs and practices.

"Tiakina Te Pā Harakeke" literally means to nurture the *harakeke* (an indigenous species of flax) plantation. *Harakeke* is a plant used extensively by weavers for *kete* (baskets), *whāriki* (mats), *kākahu* (clothing),

and many other daily and ceremonial uses. *Harakeke* is also *rongoā*, a traditional medicine and healing source. Just as it has multiple uses for weavers, *harakeke* also has multiple applications for healers. To *tiaki* (nurture) the *harakeke* plant is to ensure the conservation of plants for the wellbeing of future generations. *Te Pā Harakeke* also provides shelter, the plant itself may be woven to provide shelter and protection from the elements.

In the context of *whānau* wellbeing within Aotearoa, this *whakataukī* (proverbial saying) has served for many generations of Māori as an expression of the importance of healthy human relations. *Hūtia te rito*, the *whakataukī* that opens this chapter, highlights the importance of *harakeke* to our wellbeing as Indigenous people and in particular the centrality of the wellbeing of future generations. It highlights that crucial to the sustenance of *Te Pā Harakeke* is the centre shoot or *"te rito"* which represents the central importance of the child. The removal of the centre shoot is tantamount to the potential destruction of the plant itself. A key learning being that children are the centre of our *whānau*, they are critical to our survival as a people and anything that harms a child is destructive to the *whānau* as a whole.

Te Pā Harakeke is an understanding that reaches into the core of *whānau* wellbeing. It is a broad and encompassing term, which includes a direct link to creator, ancestors, and universe. *Te Pā Harakeke* embraces the collective values that nourish all *whānau* members, enhances the wellbeing of *tamariki* (children) as *taonga* (treasures) within our *whānau*, *hapū* (subtribal groupings), and *iwi* (tribal nations). This notion, when applied within our lived understandings, maintains that the whole of the *whānau* need to be nurtured, to ensure wellbeing for our *tamariki* and *mokopuna* (grandchildren).

Underpinning the *"Tiakina Te Pā Harakeke"* project is the belief that *tikanga* (Māori values and protocols) and *mātauranga* (Māori knowledge and understandings) can assist *whānau* and others to identify, learn, and practise positive, culturally enriched approaches to childrearing as defined and practised by our *tūpuna* (ancestors). It is within those cultural notions that we may find guidance to support us in raising our *tamariki* within a contemporary context where many *whānau* have been forcibly dispossessed of our land, language, and cultural knowledge. Māori knowledge holders refer to the position of *tamariki* as being of particular importance within Māori society. Rangimarie Rose Pere (1988) writes,

Tamariki: Tama is derived from Tama-te-ra the central sun, the divine spark; ariki refers to senior most status, and riki on its own can mean smaller version. Tamariki is the Māori word used for children. Children are the greatest legacy the world community has. (p. 4)

"*Tiakina Te Pā Harakeke*" has been focused on exploring ways in which *tikanga* and *mātauranga* are harnessed in contemporary Māori contexts to provide safe, vibrant, and enriched childrearing practices and *whānau* ways of being. The wellbeing of *whānau* requires processes of decolonization and the regeneration of Indigenous knowledge to operate simultaneously (Smith, 1999a).

Pūrākau

Pūrākau, as a form of Māori narrative and storytelling, have always been critical to Māori society. In *Te Ao Māori*, when Māori cultural, social, political, and economic systems were dominant and functioned to ensure *whānau*, *hapū*, and *iwi* were strong and cohesive, our people maintained traditional systems of intergenerational knowledge transmission of which *pūrākau* was one (Lee, 2015). Indigenous storytelling processes are fundamental to understanding our world (Archibald, 2008). As Leanne Simpson (2011) states "our elders tell us that everything we need to know is encoded in the structure, content and context of these stories and the relationships, ethics and responsibilities to be our own Creation Story" (p. 33). Being "our own Creation Story" requires us to live our lives in ways that align to the fundamental values and cultural epistemologies that our ancestors have gifted us. These ways of being are embedded within our *pūrākau*.

For Māori, *pūrākau* are fundamental to understanding our natural world and social experiences and as such are crucial to sharing *mātauranga* (Māori knowledge) that ensures our survival and cultural sustainability (Lee, 2015), providing both historical and contemporary information that shapes our cultural identities and understandings. Smith et al. (2017) refer to stories as one form of Indigenous knowledge transmission:

Indigenous people talk about knowledge in a wide variety of ways. Indigenous knowledge can be spoken about as stories and songs, as visions, prophesies, teachings and original instructions, as genealogies and memories … The stories may serve to reinforce major knowledge narratives through motifs, morals, principles and values that are accessible and understood by each generation of the community. (pp. 137–138)

Pūrākau are most well understood as traditional stories, such as the stories of creation involving Ranginui and Papatūānuku; the power of Hineahuone who held the first female essence; in the feats of Māui; the adventures of Tāwhaki; and the strength of *tūpuna wahine* (female ancestors) such as Ruaputahanga who took control of their lives when faced with abuse (Biggs, Hohepa & Mead, 1967; Jones & Biggs, 1995; Kahukiwa & Grace, 1984). There are also those that tell of *ngārara* (reptiles), *taniwha*, whales, and *tuatara* as supernatural beings (Biggs, Hohepa & Mead, 1967). *Pūrākau* also tell of the histories and traditions of *whānau*, *hapū*, and *iwi*, including the formation of personal or tribal relationships, alliances, struggles, and battles. The people who held these *pūrākau* within each *iwi*, *hapū* and/or *whānau* were held in high esteem as the position and distinctiveness of their group rested on this learned knowledge (Lee, 2008).

Pūrākau were always treated as treasured and precious teachings, they not only contained valuable knowledge about the environment but were fundamental to our identity – *pūrākau* provided and informed the uniqueness of us as groups of people. As Smith points out (2002) "[Māori] Words have *whakapapa*, they are from a particular state of existence, they have origins, and the stories told about the words give us meanings" (p. 38).

As Lee (2015) argues, *pūrākau* are not considered to be fixed traditional narratives that only exist in the past. *Pūrākau* can, and should, be narratives that we continue to craft to provide the information and inspiration core to our identity. Today, *pūrākau* are critical in teaching and learning, particularly for *whānau* because they are concerned with the transmission of knowledge, culture, and worldviews. In relation to the *"Tiakina Te Pā Harakeke"* research programme, *pūrākau* are a critical means by which to impart key messages to children about how to be and live as Māori. Often these *pūrākau* are based on Elders' experiences, they are narratives that caution, encourage, direct, and impart knowledge and wisdom.

One example of a traditional *pūrākau* that provokes thought, reflection, and for *tamariki* to consider how to make good choices and manage their own behaviours is the story of Rona. The *pūrākau* of Rona and *Marama* (the moon) is a well known one amongst our people. In collaboration with the moon itself, Rona is a guardian of the tides, of planting, and of menstrual cycles (Murphy, 2013). In this *pūrākau*[1] Rona goes, with a *tahā* (gourd/calabash), in the night to collect water for her children and as she journeys to the spring clouds cover the moon and she trips over tree roots in the dark. Rona curses the moon. The moon angered at her reached down and grabbed her, in an attempt to stay on the ground Rona grasped a *Ngaio* tree but the moon was too strong and pulled Rona and the tree into the night sky, Rona still holding the *tahā* in her other hand. As time passed her children were concerned and went in search of their mother, calling out "Rona, where are you?" to which Rona replied "I am here, I am with the moon and the stars." Now at night, and especially on the full moon you can see Rona in the moon, holding the *Ngaio* tree in one hand and the *tahā* in the other.

This *pūrākau* provides us with a range of teachings and learnings. Within *Te Ao Māori* there is a fundamental belief in the *mana* (prestige, authority, power, influence) and *tapu* (sacredness) of words, where words have their own inherent power and their own inherent sacredness, as do the people being spoken to. The power of words is highlighted in sayings such as "*he tao rākau ka taea te karo, he tao kupu e kore e taea te karo* – the thrust of a spear can be avoided, but not the thrust of words" (Pihama et al. 2015, p. 35). To curse or demean is a serious offence and is considered a transgression of the *mana* of another person, or in this case the moon. Such transgressions have been traditionally responded to through specific cultural practices. Where some may consider the moon's reaction as severe, within an oral culture where words carry *mana* and *tapu*, their misuse is considered an act of abuse that can have serious consequences, as was the case in this situation. The power of this story is encapsulated in *whakataukī* such as, "*Kia mahara ki a Rona*" which was referred to in this project by a number of knowledge holders. This *whakataukī* is a *kōrero whakatūpato*, a cautionary statement, that states "Remember Rona," which is described by Pihama et al. (2015) as "a reminder to us to be careful of what we say or do" (p. 20).

Pūrākau as pedagogy

The role of *pūrākau* in the teaching and learning of our children was emphasized within "*Tiakina Te Pā Harakeke*," including both the role of ancestral stories and storytelling from within a contemporary context. Pedagogy is, in Māori terms, referred to as "*ako.*" *Ako* is one way through which we may view *pūrākau* as a means of sharing, learning, and teaching for the wellbeing of future generations. The transfer of knowledge, language, protocols, practices, ceremonies is essential to the wellbeing of Māori people. *Ako* as a Māori pedagogical process is highlighted in *Te Ao Māori* as being an interrelationship, not only between learners and teachers, but within the range of relationships of *whānau, hapū* (sub-tribal groupings), and *iwi* (tribal groupings). It is within these reciprocal relationships and giving regard to the *mana* of Māori knowledge that knowledge is both produced and transmitted.

> Māori knowledge was highly valued; it was seen as vital for the social, economic, political as well as spiritual sustenance of whānau (family), hapū (sub-tribe) and iwi (tribe) groupings. The mana (power and prestige) of each group was dependent on the way in which the knowledge of each group was protected, developed and practiced. The way in which knowledge was transmitted was through the process of ako. Ako was based on the knowledge that pertained to the interests of the wider group, knowledge that ensured the physical and spiritual wellbeing, the uniqueness of each iwi. (Pihama et al. 2004, p. 16)

Rangimarie Rose Pere (1994) asserts that all forms of *ako* come about through carefully negotiated relationships. Those relationships are within *whānau* and between people but they should not be reduced purely to "*tangata* (human) -centric" relationships as our connections to land, seas, rivers, mountains, animals, and the spiritual domain are equally influential in defining, and informing, our processes of *ako*. *Ako* also provides a framework for culturally defined appropriate teaching and learning strategies that connect with the cultural and life circumstances of Māori (Smith, 1997). *Ako* has been referred to within Māori educational contexts, and as a key principle of *Kaupapa Māori* theory and methodology, and as Māori culturally defined pedagogical practices (Lee, 2008, 2015; Pihama, 2001; Smith, 1997).

Within contemporary educational contexts we have a growing body of work highlighting the role of traditional knowledge and pedagogical forms as key to both formal and informal learning for Māori (Hohepa, 1999; Pihama et al., 2004; Royal-Tangaere, 1997). These pedagogies have been embedded within Māori educational initiatives such as *Te Kōhanga Reo* (Māori language nests) and *Kura Kaupapa Māori* and *Wharekura* (Māori immersion schooling) and inform the ways in which learning and teaching take place drawing upon *ako* as the framework within these contexts (Hohepa, 1999, 2015; Royal-Tangaere, 1997).

Pūrākau is utilized within contemporary Māori educational initiatives, and is considered a central part of *ako*, an activity in which every person in the *whānau* is engaged throughout their lifetime (Lee, 2003, 2015; Nepe, 1991; Pere, 1994). Apart from some formal teaching and learning that took place between *tohunga* (experts) and *tauira* (students) in the *whare wānanga* (traditional houses of learning) context, *ako* is not bound by age, gender, or social status. Learning and teaching is inclusive, extensive, cooperative, reciprocal, and obligatory. Metge (1984) refers to the all-encompassing nature of *ako* as "education through exposure" (p. 3). She describes teaching and learning as "informal, semi-continuous, embedded in the ongoing life of the community, open and inclusive" (Metge, 1984, p. 3). Everyone was in a constant state of teaching and learning because the collective, not only the individual, gained to benefit through *ako* and the transmission of knowledge (Nepe, 1991). The sharing of *pūrākau* was considered one of the cultural pedagogies that operationalized *ako* within both formal and informal contexts. The extensive archive of *pūrākau* that our ancestors have left for us provide us with a depth of understanding that we can access to support our language regeneration and cultural revitalization movement here in Aotearoa.

Whānau storytelling as Indigenous pedagogy

Recognizing *pūrākau* as inherently pedagogical is significant in the discussions shared by *whānau* involved in this research programme. Passing down historical knowledge is a practice that aligns to our desire and need to understand our past in order to locate ourselves in the present and shape our dreams for our future. *Whānau* talked about *pūrākau* as having a clear intent to provide guidance or give direction,

> Nō reira ko ngā pūrākau, kei te whakarerekē aua pūrākau me te pakiwaitara. Ko te pūrākau ko aua tūmomo kōrero, he tohutohu o roto hei whakaaro mā te kaiwhakarongo, nō reira ko aua pūrākau o taku kuia. Hei whakaako i a au ki te tika o te mahi. (*Whakawhiti kōrero*)[2]

Our *tūpuna* actively shared historical knowledge in all contexts where children heard the stories and histories as a part of both daily and ceremonial activities.

> Our *kaumātua* and adults taught freely and openly in front of children. They didn't exclude them from *kōrero*. They spoke freely and openly

and *tamariki* were around and they either absorbed it in which case they were ready to hear that *kōrero*, to learn from those *kōrero* or they didn't because it went off the top of their head because they weren't ready for those kinds of *kōrero*. (*Whakawhiti kōrero*)

Through colonization the denial of *te reo Māori* has had a detrimental effect on the ability to share *mātauranga Māori*. The establishment of schooling as a system of social control, focused on ideologies of assimilation and Christianizing, actively seeking to marginalize Māori knowledge, language, and culture as a part of a broader denial of Māori sovereignty (Simon, 1998; Simon & Smith, 2001). This process has continued with *pūrākau* being positioned as myths and legends (Lee, 2008), the impact of which has continued within the contemporary experiences of our people within the education system.

> The way that I internalized the information was really through storytelling. And I think that's an element that's sort of beginning to miss out for our children because a lot of our stories are being treated by the education system by schools as fairytales. Yet to us they are a profound part of our religion, our beliefs, our values and all the things that are important. (*Whakawhiti kōrero*)

Another example that highlighted a contemporary experience of racism in schooling is a story that has been handed through one of the *whānau*. In this context a mother and a daughter were reflecting on how being Māori within a *Pākehā* schooling context was experienced differently by different *whānau* members.

> _____ always tells the "fried bread" story. He tells the story like it's the saddest story in the world, and we always look at him like it's not a sad story, that was you. But he always said that Nan used to make fried bread and put butter and golden syrup on it and wrap it in newspaper and send it along to school. So he would fire it in the rubbish or behind the bushes or something, instead of unwrapping his newspaper and all the stuff running out. For him, that was horrible to feel. That was a motivating thing for him, he felt that. The rest of us would just take the bread and eat it. (*Whakawhiti kōrero*)

Given the pedagogical nature of *pūrākau* it is unsurprising that many *pūrākau* have emerged in the course of this research. *Pūrākau* have no set format, they can be short and direct, long and descriptive, informal and pointed. However, *pūrākau* always engage the learner and serve to teach Māori ways, practices, and principles. Most often, the *pūrākau* were a retelling of stories or experiences to draw attention to a particular way of seeing or being in the world. In particular, the *pūrākau* pointed to the relationships between children and adults within *whānau*, the roles that adults as *whanaunga* played in caring for and teaching children, and the place of children within the collective. These *pūrākau* not only became part of the knowledge that emerged from the *whānau* that were interviewed, but also a tool for teaching, learning, and sharing within the community gatherings that were held.

Particular *pūrākau* were told by the *whānau* involved and discussions emerged to highlight how within their experiences their Elders or *whānau* members would seek to provoke new ways of thinking and understanding, as well as to encourage *tamariki* to make choices and decisions that were an outcome from their understanding the knowledge being imparted. One story shared gave insights into the sanctity of *tamariki* and an understanding that smacking was not acceptable within her *whānau*.

> One of the stories I tell about Pani is that if I was "naughty" Pani would hit herself. You know, she would stand there and smack her hand and say to me "you're a naughty girl" but she would smack her hand. When she was dying, a couple of years ago, I went up to the hospital and she died in my arms. She was 77. She was 25 years older than me ... We called her Aunty Pani but she was my cousin and I asked her about that when she was dying in hospital and she said to me with a look of absolute horror on her face "to hit you would have been akin to a sin and oh no I couldn't hit you. If you did wrong it was because I wasn't vigilant enough with you," so that's how she thought. (*Whakawhiti kōrero*)

Alongside *whānau* sharing contemporary stories and experiences, the sharing of ancestral stories to inform and reveal meaning and learning is highlighted throughout the discussions. The role of *pūrākau* in the teaching and learning of our children was emphasized within the project, including both ancestral stories and storytelling from within a contemporary context.

> Storytelling for me was a real thing. We'd sit under a *pūriri* tree in the hot hot sun. I'd go to sleep and wake up and she'd be chanting *pōpō e tangi ana tama ki te kai* ... you know that be going for 15 minutes

and no sooner she started I'd be asleep and I'd wake up and she'd be doing something else still going on with the storytelling. But you know I think the integration of that information, the story of Māui which I grew up to think they were fairytales, she would tell the story of Māui and Hinenuitepō, the way that you relate to nature you must not be hostile to nature and the consequences of trying to change nature is what happened to Māui. He dies in the end by trying to return through the womb. (*Whakawhiti kōrero*)

I'll talk about maybe one of the Māui stories or talk about Tāne and I say this is what happened back then and they say "far we didn't know that" yeah well that's why it still happens now. There might be a little bit of a change but these are the things that we do now and I talk about what happened in those stories. (*Whakawhiti kōrero*)

Whānau talked of the ways in which these histories were transmitted through repetitive storytelling between generations, enabling each generation to share the stories orally through hearing the details repeated consistently through their lives.

I think the richness of the land became a part of me … my grandmother, her background was *Tūhoe* in the *Urewera*, but she and her family left their lands because of the policies of the Crown, so it's very political and I listened to stories over and over and over again and repetition is an important part of the Māori way of passing on the stories and the hurt and the pain of the people. (*Whakawhiti kōrero*)

She had lots of beautiful stories to tell. And she'd also reflect, she'd often say how much I reminded her of our *kuia* who was a *matakite*. So she was the time of *Te Kooti* … So she'd talk a lot about those things. Those stories are inside me so although I never knew many of these old *kuia* and *koroua* I feel that they guide me today. I'm receptive to them guiding me. (*Whakawhiti kōrero*)

We were really fortunate in that we had loving parents and *Māmā* was a creative storyteller. Very artistic, very feminine and *Pāpā* was her rock. *He tika hoki te kōrero o ahau* about *Māmā* being like a sea flowing of water very much her personality … a lot of stories about *patupaiarehe* and the *whakatūpato* about *patupaiarehe* but *Māmā* was also fascinated with those other realms and the closeness of those other realms and so some of her stories were also of her own weaving and of her own creation. Those stories came when we were locked in a car with her, when we were travelling from one part of the country to the other with her and it was just me and *Māmā*, or me and *Māmā* and another *tuakana*, or me and *Māmā* and another *teina*, and sometimes they related to where we were and *whanaunga* who live in those places and stories about that particular *whanaunga*, full of stories you know and *Pāpā* was a storyteller and very eloquent as well. His was always about *kai*, about nurturing family, *whānau*. (*Whakawhiti kōrero*)

It has been highlighted within the *whānau* discussions that sharing stories and histories to babies in the womb was a key practice. *Pūrākau* gave insights into *whakapapa*, providing a sense of belonging and insights in to the centrality of relationships and shared with children from birth.

That makes me think about Kōkā, one of the things that she talked to me about, was that when her mother was pregnant with her, her grandfather would talk to her in the womb and talk to her like she was an ancient being. That she was an ancient wise being and he would share his stories in his recollections in his memories with her to get close to her whilst she was in the *whare tangata* and so when she came into *te ao mārama*, that bond had already been forged during that time. (*Whakawhiti kōrero*)

I think it starts with knowing who you are fully. As full as of sense as possible, so *ā-whakapapa, ā-papa kāinga, ā-rohe, ā-whānau, ā-hapū, ā-iwi*. You have to have a full sense of who you are in order to pass that on to your child ... Giving a child a sense that they've come from a line of people who carried a particular responsibility, a particular *kaupapa* or made a particular contribution to their *hapū*, their *whānau* or whatever. (*Whakawhiti kōrero*)

Closing comments

The urgency of needing to return to storytelling and sharing as a process of strengthening both current and future generations has been articulated regularly by *whānau* involved in this research.

There are too many young people in this world at a complete loss as to what they've come from. They have this sense that they are inherently bad because they've not known anything else but in fact, scratch the surface and start to help this kid reclaim their stories you know and they actually find all kinds of interesting ways to reframe the way they think about themselves because that *tipuna kōrero* matters. It helps people to navigate themselves about the way they think about themselves. (*Whakawhiti kōrero*)

So I had all those connotations of stories, all those [heroes], our heroes. And you know it was equivalent to Shakespeare, all the love and the hate and the war and chivalry and all those things in our stories. So our children today I think are missing out. But, I think we're starting to restore it in *kōhanga reo*. (*Whakawhiti kōrero*)

The use of *pūrākau* as sources of traditional knowledge to draw upon as guidelines, templates, warnings, or examples of Māori values, beliefs, principles, practices, and behaviours enables a pathway for raising children that is grounded upon ancestral knowledge that can be applied in the contemporary context that our *tamariki* find themselves in. They are a foundation that our ancestors have left for us to help inform current and future generations. *Tūhoe* Elder Kaa Williams spoke of the power of *pūrākau* in raising our children.

> Kei roto katoa ngā kōrero mō tēnei mea o te tohi, mō ruapūkenga mō ngā whakaaro ka whakatō ki roto i ngā tamariki mehemea ka akohia ērā me te mārama ki ngā kōrero, ātaahua.[3] (Williams in Pihama & Daniels, 2007, documentary interview)

We need to be active in both our remembering and our sharing of those *pūrākau* as a part of our daily lives. As Linda Tuhiwai Smith (1999b) reminds us, it is in the telling of and listening to our *pūrākau* that we can come to understand more fully our own ways, our place, and ourselves.

> For many indigenous writers stories are ways of passing down the beliefs and values of a culture in the hope that the new generations will treasure them and pass the story down further. The story and the storyteller both serve to connect the past with the future, one generation with the other, the land with the people and the people with the story. (p. 145)

Within *Te Ao Māori* we have an archive of *mātauranga Māori* sources such as *pūrākau* and *whakataukī* that provide us with insights and knowledge about ways of being, values, behaviours, actions, relationships, protocols, and ceremonial rituals. We also have a growing revitalization movement that is revealing ways of more deeply understanding the sacred place of our children within our *whānau, hapū, iwi*, and communities. The resurgence of *pūrākau* as Indigenous pedagogy is an essential component to that process. The remembering and regeneration of our *pūrākau* is a decolonizing project. For *whānau*, reclaiming the knowledge gifted by our *tūpuna* through the retelling and sharing of our *pūrākau* is an act of *rangatiratanga*, it is an assertion of our self-determination as Indigenous Peoples to tell our stories, our way.

Notes

1 Where there are varying *iwi pūrākau* related to this story I have chosen to base this discussion on my reading of the *te reo Māori* version provided by Biggs, Hohepa & Mead (1967) as within *te reo Māori* the story is not layered with the colonial gendered translations that we seen in most English versions recorded by early ethnographers and anthropologists.

2 Translation: There are *pūrākau*. *Pūrākau* differ from *pakiwaitara*. *Pūrākau* are stories that contain advice for the listener like the stories of my *kuia*. As guidance for me to know what is right.

3 *Whakawhiti kōrero* refers to the *whānau* discussions that were shared within the research project. Translation: Within our stories, the practice of dedicating a child is there, of raising a child. If one learns and understands the stories, it's stunning.

References

Archibald, J. (2008). *Indigenous storywork: educating the heart, mind, body, and spirit.* Vancouver, BC: UBC Press.

Biggs, B., Hohepa, P. & Mead, S. M. (1967). *Selected readings in Māori.* Wellington, New Zealand: A. H. & A. W. Reed.

Hohepa, M. (1999). *Hei Tautoko i te reo: Māori language regeneration and whānau bookreading practices.* Unpublished PhD thesis. Auckland, New Zealand: The University of Auckland.

Hohepa, M. (2015). Kia Mau Ki Te Aka Matua: research Māori development and learning. In L. Pihama & S. Tiakiwai (Eds.), *Kaupapa Rangahau: a reader* (pp. 109–117). Hamilton, New Zealand: Te Kotahi Research Institute.

Jones, P. & Biggs, B. (1995). *Ngā Iwi o Tainui: The traditional history of the Tainui people.* Auckland, New Zealand: Auckland University Press.

Kahukiwa, R. & Grace, P. (1984). *Wahine Toa: women of Māori myth.* Auckland, New Zealand: Collins.

Lee, J. (2003). Ngā Tohutohu: A pūrākau approach to Māori teacher narratives. In *Teacher Education Forum of Aotearoa New Zealand (TEFANZ) Conference Proceedings.* Massey University, Palmerston North, New Zealand.

Lee, J. (2008). *Pūrākau: Māori teachers' work in secondary schools.* Unpublished EdD thesis. Auckland, New Zealand: The University of Auckland.

Lee, J. (2015). Decolonising Māori narratives: Pūrākau as a method. In L. Pihama, S. J. Tiakiwai & K. Southey (Eds.), *Kaupapa Rangahau: a reader. A collection of readings from the Kaupapa Māori Workshop Series* (p. 95–104). Hamilton, New Zealand: Te Kotahi Research Institute.

Metge, J. (1984). *Learning and teaching: He tīkanga Māori.* Wellington, New Zealand: Department of Education.

Murphy, N. (2013). *Te Awa Atua: menstruation in the pre-colonial Māori world. An examination of stories, ceremonies and practices regarding menstruation in the* pre-colonial Māori world – based on a Masters Thesis. Hamilton, New Zealand: He Puna Manawa.

Nepe, T. (1991). *Te toi huarewa tipuna: Kaupapa Māori, an educational intervention system*. Unpublished MA thesis. Auckland, New Zealand: The University of Auckland.

Pere, R. (1988). Te Wheke: Whaia te Maramatanga me te Aroha. In S. Middleton (Ed.), *Women and education in Aotearoa* (pp. 6–19). Wellington, New Zealand: Allen & Unwin, Port Nicholson Press.

Pere, R. (1994). *Ako: concepts and learning in the Māori tradition*. Wellington, New Zealand: Te Kōhanga Reo National Trust Board.

Pihama, L. (2001). *Tīhei mauri ora: honouring our voices: mana wahine as Kaupapa Māori theoretical framework*. Unpublished PhD thesis. Auckland, New Zealand: The University of Auckland.

Pihama, L. & Daniels, N. (2007). *Te Taonga o Taku Ngākau*. Māori Television Documentary. Auckland, New Zealand: Māori and Indigenous Analysis.

Pihama, L., Greensill, H., Campbell, D., Te Nana, R. & Lee, J. (2015). *Taku Kuru Pounamu*. Hamilton, New Zealand: Te Kotahi Research Institute.

Pihama, L., Smith, K., Taki, M. & Lee, J. (2004) *A literature review on Kaupapa Māori and Māori education pedagogy*. A Report to ITP New Zealand, Auckland, New Zealand: The International Research Institute for Māori and Indigenous Education.

Royal-Tangaere, Arapera (1997). Māori human development learning theory. In P. Te Whaiti, M. McCarthy & A. Durie (Eds.), *Mai i Rangiātea* (pp. 46–60). Auckland, New

Zealand: Auckland University Press and Bridget Williams Books.

Simon, J. (Ed.). (1998). *Ngā Kura Māori: the native schools system 1867–1969*. Auckland, New Zealand: Auckland University Press.

Simon, J. & Smith, L. T. (2001). *A civilising mission? Perceptions and representations of the New Zealand native schools system*. Auckland, New Zealand: Auckland University Press.

Simpson, L. (2011). *Dancing on our turtle's back: stories of Nishnaabeg Re creation resurgence and a new emergence*. Winnipeg, MB: ARP Books.

Smith, C. W. (2002). *He pou herenga ki te nui: Māori knowledge and the university*. Unpublished PhD thesis. Auckland, New Zealand: The University of Auckland.

Smith, G. H. (1997). *The development of Kaupapa Māori: theory and praxis*. Unpublished PhD thesis. Auckland, New Zealand: The University of Auckland.

Smith, L. (1999a). Kaupapa Māori methodology: our power to define ourselves. A seminar presentation to the School of Education. Vancouver, BC: University of British Columbia.

Smith, L. T. (1999b). *Decolonizing methodologies: research and Indigenous Peoples*. London: Zed Books.

Smith, L., Maxwell, T. K., Puke, H. & Temara, P. (2017). Indigenous knowledge, methodology and mayhem: what is the role of methodology in producing Indigenous insights? A discussion from Mātauranga Māori. *Knowledge Cultures* 4(3), 2016, pp. 131–156.

9 | *PŪRĀKAU* FROM THE INSIDE-OUT: REGENERATING STORIES FOR CULTURAL SUSTAINABILITY

Jenny Bol Jun Lee-Morgan

Introduction

This chapter emerged out of a paper I presented about *pūrākau* at an international symposium on *pūrākau* and Indigenous storywork in Aotearoa New Zealand, 2017.[1] *Pūrākau* literally refers to the *pū* (base or foundation) of a *rākau* (tree). As I have previously argued (Lee, 2008) and presented again, conceptualizing of stories as fundamental to our sustenance and growth, as soil and water are to trees, offers precious cultural clues to understanding the importance of *pūrākau* in our lives, including our research. This presentation, however, was inextricably bound in the context and location of the Indigenous storywork symposium that preempted my thinking about *pūrākau* from the inside-out.

Held at the *Waikato-Tainui* Research and Development College, the symposium was located in the heart of my own tribal territory of *Waikato-Tainui*. The theme was *"Kimihia te mea ngaro"* (Seek that which is lost) – a well-known *tongikura* (proverbial saying) of the leader and prophet, King Tāwhiao in the latter half of the nineteenth century.[2] This was a period characterized by the violence of colonization, culminating in invasion by colonial troops and the unjust confiscation of 1.2 million acres of our most valuable land by the Settler government. Our tribal territories were decimated, and our communities were reduced from being prosperous people with a thriving economic export base, to a tribal group that was mostly landless, homeless, and poverty stricken (O'Malley, 2016). At a time when many of our people were "forced to live as refugees from war" (O'Malley, 2016, p. 419), *"Kimihia te mea ngaro"* was uttered by Kingi Tāwhiao as a sign of hope and promise (Kirkwood, 2000). "From the inside-out" speaks not only to the methodology of *pūrākau* as recovery and revitalization, but in the context of the devastation colonization has caused to the "inside" that includes our lands, hearts, minds, bodies, and spirits.

In this chapter, *pūrākau* as methodology (Lee, 2009; Lee-Morgan, 2017) is framed by the referents of Indigenous storywork (Archibald, 2008) and decolonizing research methodology (Smith, 2012). This chapter introduces some key methodological considerations through the conceptual framework of *te pū o te rākau* (the core of the tree). As the title of this article suggests, *pūrākau* as methodology is examined from the inside-out, challenging Western research conventions with its preoccupation on "data" gathering, "data" observation, and "data" analysis – which could be viewed as working from the outside-in. With decolonial intent, *pūrākau* encourages us to begin in a different place – the heart. However, the inside is not always an easy place from which to start. I open with a historical reminder about our stories as the "researched" to signal caution and the need to always remember the decolonizing dimension of our methodologies.

Risky research stories

As Indigenous Peoples, we know that revealing what is on the "inside" is risky business, especially in research. Wielded as an instrument of colonization, the damage resulting from research on Indigenous Peoples worldwide, which included stolen, contrived, or rejected cultural and intellectual knowledge, is well documented (Grande, 2004; Said, 1978; Smith, 2012; Thiong'o, 1986). In Aotearoa, our *pūrākau* were among the first to be infiltrated, documented, and published, usually by male Eurocentric anthropologists and ethnographers who primarily targeted Māori men (Lee, 2008; Mikaere, 2017). Misappropriation, misrepresentation, and misinterpretation characterized the early collection of *pūrākau*. In turn, these distorted stories contributed to an epistemological confusion and destabilization of our spiritual beliefs, reinforcing the social and structural disarray created by the imposition of colonization on our lands (Jackson, forthcoming; Lee, 2009; Mikaere, 2017).

Much like the symbol of the Trojan horse, many of our *pūrākau* became a form of disruption and destruction from the inside-out. Ani Mikaere's (2017) analysis of the way Christianity covertly influenced many of our creation *pūrākau* is a good example of colonizing our core cosmological and spiritual beliefs through the promotion of versions of *pūrākau* that were conveniently close to Christian stories. As a consequence, Ani Mikaere (2017) argues that the balance between male and female elements in traditional *Māori* society was destroyed; the active and powerful female elements were omitted from our stories of creation. Instead, female figures were cast in passive roles where their power and sexuality was neutralized. Today, many of the colonial and Christian-influenced *pūrākau* reinscribe gendered and heteronormative views in our contemporary understanding of our theories, everyday practices, routines, and rituals (Cavino, 2017; Mikaere, 2017; Pihama, forthcoming).

Like Indigenous stories all over the world, our *pūrākau* were selected, framed, elevated, and legitimated through "research" and popularized as myths and legends. Worse still, these contrived stories were taught back to us as fables through our school curriculum for generations (Bishop & Glynn, 1999; Lee, 2008; Mikaere, 2011). In many cases, not only did we become implicated in the perpetuation of these same stories, but the reinterpreted colonized messages they contained were then internalized by us. Just as the Christian ethos continues to heavily influence our practices today, so too does the lasting impact of fragmented knowledge, packaged and represented in narrow ways such as myth and legends. The logic of colonial sensibilities, through their treatment of our *pūrākau*, has had a profound effect. Not only have our traditional understandings of our world been severely diminished, but our hearts too have been affected – our faith and confidence in our stories and ultimately ourselves. Linda Smith describes this process of disruption as part of the impact of imperialism and colonialism that is "an epic story telling of huge devastation, painful struggle and persistent survival" (2012, p. 20). Decolonizing methodologies insist that a critical part of our work as researchers is to identify, expose, and rectify the normalizing of the objective, invisible, or neutral "imperial gaze." Research that produced these dominant discourses continues to frame our stories, stereotype our identities, limit our thinking, and impede our lives as Indigenous Peoples.

In the same way it is sometimes difficult to recognize the colonizing frame in the reproduction of *pūrākau*, the demarcation as insiders or outsiders in research is often blurred. As Linda Smith (2012) recognizes, Indigenous researchers are positioned simultaneously as insiders and outsiders in our own communities. Indigenous researchers located in universities are referred to as the "outside-within" or "insider-within," a term that not only signifies the ambivalent positionality of Indigenous researchers within the colonizing practices of universities, but that this dilemma remains problematic (Battiste, 2008; Bishop, 2011; Collins,

1991; Smith, 2012). For instance, Brayboy and Deyhle (2000) discuss the challenge of reconciling the expectation of ethnographic researcher "distance" to Indigenous cultural understandings of cooperative relationships. Brayboy and Deyhle (2000) describe the complexities of negotiating the identities of the "good researcher" and "good Indian," but reconclude that researchers must always be cognisant of the positionality. They state, "Researchers in these [Indigenous] communities must guard against the imposition of methods of collecting, analysing, and reporting 'fact' in ways that are not culturally sensitive and that fail to safeguard the lives of the people they study" (Brayboy & Deyhle, 2000 p. 168). A *pūrākau* methodology raises the same ethical considerations (as does *Kaupapa Māori* research) about our inescapable position as insiders in our communities as well as our universities and institutions, and the nuances in the insider-outside binary.

As Jo-ann Archibald (2008) points out, in Indigenous storywork the insider-outsider positionality is intimate and layered. In addition to the complexity of the position of the researcher within or outside Indigenous and professional research communities, there is the interrelationship between the storyteller, story listener, and story itself. In addition, Archibald distinguishes storytellers and Elders who live "good" cultural traditions, and provide "good teachings" (2008, p. 13). Archibald places an emphasis on what I would describe as a "good heart," love, and compassion in the sharing of Indigenous stories. In her reference to Walter Lighting, of the *Samson Cree* Nation, she states "the compassionate mind combines physical, spiritual, emotional and intellectual learning with humility, truth and love" (p. 2). On the many edges of the Indigenous research endeavour, the distinction between the outside and the inside (especially with matters to do with a good heart) are not clearly demarcated, and getting it wrong can be risky. Linda Smith's (2012) cautionary guidance to get the story/stories "right," the inside-out quandary also points to the varied cultural expectations and ethical considerations (beyond those required by academia) that we must try to adhere to if our research is to be respectful and truly transformative for our communities. Therefore, it is with some caution I proceed to present what *pūrākau* might offer as an Indigenous storywork methodology.

Rākau: teachings from our trees

As Māori, our origins are in the natural world, including the trees. One of the most famous children of Papatūānuku (Earth Mother) and

Ranginui (Sky Father) is Tāne Mahuta (God of the Forest). There are numerous *pūrākau* about Tāne's memorable feats, including the story of separating his parents from their tight embrace so there would be space and light for their descendants to develop – the trees, the shrubs, the ferns, and eventually all living things. In this particular *pūrākau* he takes the form of an enormous tree that grows with power and strength to push his parents apart. It was also Tāne Mahuta who created the first woman, Hineahuone, with whom he begat the first child. There are multiple *pūrākau* about Tāne; epistemological designs that provide a deep insight into the ontological constructs of our world, our wisdom, and our potential. At its simplest level, the *pūrākau* of Tāne Mahuta tell us that we are the trees, and the trees are us.

To get a sense of our trees, it is important to imagine the landscape of the islands that make up Aotearoa to understand the cultural concepts afforded to us by our native trees. Pre-colonization, our natural environment was dominated by bush with a rich and unique ecosystem of flora and fauna. Our native trees formed a dense and dark bush, abundant with birds, insects, lizards, and small creatures. In the context of the *ngahere* (bush), trees grow. An indicator of the relationship between our trees can immediately be detected in our language. Literally, the two words that make up *ngahere* can be broken down to *nga* – "the" – and *here* – "binds or ties." The bush is the place where all the trees and living things are connected, or the place where everything is bound together, an ecosystem. One example of the significance of connection is the way in which our trees grow. Unlike many trees in forests around the world, our native trees do not have taproots. Taproots are roots that young trees usually produce to anchor themselves to the earth while they are developing their main root system. In Aotearoa, our young trees do not have taproots because the older and more established trees provide support to the young ones. Without taproots, the young trees literally depend on each other to grow.

A living demonstration of *whanaungatanga* (extended familial relationships), our *rākau* illustrate the importance of connectedness, support, and cooperation. Our *rākau* have great social skills, and rarely prospered in isolation. One well-known *whakatauki* (proverb) about *rākau*, reads:

E kore te totara e tū noa i te parae, engari me tū i roto i te waonui a Tāne.
The great *totara* does not stand alone in the field but stands within the great forest of *Tāne*. (Mead & Grove, 2003 p. 36)

We know already from our *pūrākau* of creation that we are all connected; everything in the natural world is bound together by *whakapapa* (genealogies) that tell us of the relationships to all living things, including people and the metaphysical realm. Jo-ann Archibald (2008) illustrates the inter-relatedness of all things through the concentric circles that represent the holism evident in Indigenous philosophies. In Indigenous storywork, Archibald (2008) depicts the "synergistic influence" of the intellectual, spiritual, emotional, and physical dimensions of Indigenous oral tradition that go beyond individuals (and singular stories) and are intimately intertwined with our families, communities, tribal groups, and nations. Similarly, *pūrākau* signals the deeply relational nature of our stories.

Pūrākau are relational

So what might this relational nature of our *rākau* tell us about our *pūrākau* in the context of research? In my mind, it makes sense that in order for *pūrākau* to grow, they actually require other *pūrākau* – that there is an interdependence among *pūrākau*. At one level, this requires the storyteller to engage with the *pūrākau* of the listener. In order to ensure the *pūrākau* is most effective, to cultivate growth and understanding, the astute storyteller will be aware of the stories of the listener. *Pūrākau* only begin to make most sense alongside other *pūrākau* of knowledge, of experience, of understanding, of empathy – because *pūrākau* are always pedagogical, and *pūrākau* are connected. A simple example can be seen in our stories of Māui. Māui is a well-known figure throughout Polynesia, famous for his many adventures. However, one only begins to fully appreciate the depth of Māui by understanding the story of his birth (he was thought to be a stillbirth), his place as the youngest brother, his many feats, and the circumstances of his death.

In the research domain, we are often challenged by the idea that we are going to arrive at the real story, the true story, the evidenced story, when in fact the diversity of stories from various perspectives provide a richer, fuller, more colourful, and probably more life-like portrait. This doesn't mean that one *pūrākau* may be more helpful as a critical analysis than another, or that one *pūrākau* might better address the complexities of a particular situation than another. Perhaps, because at the heart of *pūrākau*, like Indigenous storywork, is not the "truth" of the story. However, *pūrākau* conceptually caution us to think carefully about engaging in research that aims to produce the definitive *pūrākau*, or immutable truth. In my view, our *pūrākau* will only find meaning and richness alongside other *pūrākau*, because perhaps, at its heart is not the "truth," but how people feel about their story, and how the story makes them feel at that point in time. Similarly, Brayboy and Deyhle (2000) argue that because our identities, contexts, and lived experiences (within an Indigenous community) can be so different, "multiple and different interpretations can be valuable simultaneously" (p. 168). To this end, *pūrākau* methodology is not formulaic; rather it is research that needs to be carefully considered and creatively crafted for context. At a fundamental level, to conduct research and indeed undertake a *pūrākau* methodology without strong relationships (to the *kaupapa* and the communities to which the *pūrākau* belong) and good heart may render the research fruitless and simply ignored. Worse still, it may continue to perpetuate the colonizing approaches that put our stories and ourselves at risk.

The interdependent relationships of our trees have prompted me to reflect more deeply about the methodological processes of *pūrākau* research. Currently, I am involved in a two-year research project, called "*Te Manaaki o te Marae*:[3] The Role of the *Marae* in the Auckland Housing Crisis." This project uses a *pūrākau* approach, and is centred on the people at *Te Puea Memorial Marae* (TPMM). While I belong to this *marae* through my *whānau*, I was not strongly connected to this *marae* growing up on the west side of the Auckland region. However, stories of my great grandmother and grandmother still abound, and many of my aunties are still there. Although it is a *mana whenua marae*,[4] it located within the precincts of urban Auckland and also serves the wider Māori community. In 2016, TPMM made headlines by voluntarily (and unassisted by any government funding or agency) welcoming homeless families and individuals (of all ethnicities and cultures) requiring emergency housing. It was a public affair, because this cultural act of *manaaki* (that encompasses both kindness and responsibility) made visible the reality of homelessness at a time when the government refused to acknowledge homelessness as a serious issue (Lee-Morgan & Hoskins, 2017). Moreover, TPMM disrupted dominant discourses about the housing "situation" in Auckland, and called it to the attention of government officials and the general public by naming the housing "crisis."

When we (Rau Hoskins and I as co-Principal Investigators), initially approached the *marae* to be involved in this research, we asked how might this research be useful to them. Their first response was, "We want the story of our *marae* to be told." In that short and seemingly simple phrase are great and complex expectations. Whose story? The Board of Trustees, the *kaumātua* (Elders), the *marae* beneficiaries, the *whānau* (if so, whose *whānau*?), the government agencies (who are now supporting the *marae*), the chairperson and key strategist, and/or the *whānau* needing homes? When I naively asked "Which story?" many of them said, "yep, all that, we are so glad you are going to do it, and you better get it right." In many ways, our ability to *whakawhanaunga* (enact familial relationships) and our cultural skills are the key ena-blers to crafting the *pūrākau* they want to be told, not my position as the insider-outsider researcher. For example, when I asked Hurimoana Dennis, the Chairperson and Programme Leader, if I could make a regular research meeting time with him (in my mind to ensure we pro-vided regular updates and kept abreast of the activities at the *marae*), I was refused and told to just "hang out." It was a good reminder to me that working from the inside-out is an expectation. After the first three months of going to the *marae* a couple of days each week I had not undertaken any scoping research, any interviews, any observations, or collected any documentation. Instead, I planted myself among the *pūrākau* that already existed and hoped to be sheltered, protected, and helped to grow within the context of the *marae*.

Pūrākau, like Indigenous storywork, also raises a number of ques-tions about our conventional research practices that are usually constrained by funding, time, and deliverables. Such practices expect an interview to be a discrete block of time, and that words and tran-scripts or visual observations will be the only encryptions of meaning. Usual Western research practices often treat (and sometimes rightly so) interviewees as anonymous profiles, who provide interesting and insightful vignettes. Within this qualitative paradigm, a thematic analysis might be undertaken and common and key themes might be identified. If this is working from the outside-in, what does it mean to work, in this case, from the inside-out? In my view, strong *pūrākau* research requires one to be able to understand the complexity and dynamics of *whanaungatanga* (family relationships) and the relation-ality of the researcher as the listener, and then as re-storyteller to the interviewee/s, their communities, and the story itself.

In turn, an inside-out approach poses a new set of questions. How do contemporary *pūrākau* connect to our *tūpuna*, to our *marae*, to our *whenua?* How do they connect to each other? Who are you choosing to listen to? Who is choosing to speak to you? And what are they choosing to say? Can you hear the stories that are being told to you that are not spoken, and when the recorder isn't on? And how do you engage in story that connects and binds you? *Whanaungatanga*, an inherent quality among our *rākau*, guide us to think more deeply about the relationships between our *pūrākau*, the relationships of us as Indigenous storywork researchers to our research, to our participants, each particular context including the land, the tribal groups, and communities. In my view, the strength of one's relationships is critical to the integrity of our *pūrākau* as research, and to the ability to contribute meaningfully as a researcher to our communities.

Regenerating *pūrākau*

Another characteristic of our native *rākau* is their sheer strength and vitality. The magnificence of the *kauri* tree is perhaps most well known. With their ability to grow more than 50 metres high and 16 metres in diameter, *kauri* can also live for hundreds of years. This resembles the potential strength and longevity of *pūrākau*. Our oral traditions ensured that our tribal versions of Tāne Mahuta and others were firmly established, sustained, and regenerated for hundreds of years.

One of the ways our *pūrākau* have been sustained is in their production, whether it be stories told around the fire at home, at a gathering at the *marae*, or more recently through various multimedia. I have argued previously (Lee, 2008) that our people were adept in crafting *pūrākau* for a particular purpose, to pack a purposeful pedagogical punch or adhere to the protocols of new contexts. The portrayal of *pūrākau* was important, to enlist an audience that would continue to think about the story long after it was finished. In some cases, this may mean providing lots of detail and emotion, and in others it might be short, swift, and matter-of-fact, depending on the circumstances and pedagogical intent of the storyteller.

One of the groups that understood the importance of the portrayal of *pūrākau* as part of *Māori* tradition was *Māori* artists. In 1973 the establishment of the "*Māori* Artists and Writers Society" marked the intention of *Māori* practitioners to pioneer new ways of using traditional forms in contemporary settings. In *Māori Artists of the South Pacific* (Mataira, 1984), Ford remarks:

Old images were broken down and reformed, new materials replaced
the traditional ones and the content looked both backward into
the past and forward into the future. The exact copying of previous
designs was not seen as the only means of conserving the old. Instead,
the ancient custom of treasurable uniqueness became the justification
and motivation for the new symbols and shapes to express each new
venture. (p. 9)

Each person profiled in Ford's book, including *Māori* writer Patricia
Grace and poet Hone Tuwhare, did not aspire to be a copycat of
templates of the past but to use the tools and new media to re-create
the uniqueness of our treasures. Following a *Māori* creative tradition of modifying, extending, and expressing with artistic sensitivity and inventiveness, they worked to ensure our culture and our stories survived and were sustained. Today, *Māori* have continued to
explore *pūrākau* through print, film, theatre, new media, and digital
technologies.

In my view, if *pūrākau* as research are to be critical to our understanding and the regeneration of our cultural selves as *Māori*, then
we must also explore the portrayal, the format, the conventions of
pūrākau. Like Indigenous storywork, *pūrākau* (traditional and contemporary stories) aim to provoke pedagogical responses of the heart,
mind, body, and spirit. The strength and vitality of *pūrākau* rests in our
ability to look forward to the past, to the inside, to the core and connect to our storied lives today. Ani Mikaere writes,

> The perception of time means that our creation stories cannot be
> locked into the distant past or relegated to the status of myth or
> folklore. The present is merged with the past and the future in a
> timeless cycle of repetition and reinforcement as each successive
> generation comes to appreciate the genius of stories in light of their
> own experience. (Mikaere, 2011, p. 321)

For the continuity of our *pūrākau* narratives to remain, it is accepted
that stories will be reshaped by each generation, determined by the
shifts in their circumstances, issues, and priorities.

The function of *pūrākau*, including *pūrākau* research, is not only to
craft *pūrākau*, but to remember, and to connect critical events from
the past to present concerns and to future scenarios. Our ability as
researchers to recognize the *pūrākau* in our land, our water, our place

names, our ancestors' names, our events, and their relevance to our research is critical. In this book, Hayley Cavino describes *pūrākau* as a discursive geography, where stories not only define a place and space, but can also simultaneously produce and inscribe place and space with new meanings. *Pūrākau*, as a process and product of our research, have the potential to live a long, strong life.

Concentric rings of growth

In an interview about *pūrākau* with celebrated *Māori* songwriter and artist, Ruia Aperahama, he pointed me directly to the rings of the tree – in particular, its core. The concentric rings around the core of a tree indicate phases of growth, another generation. In his view, like *rākau*, *pūrākau* develop from the inside out. *Pūrākau* are always connected to those that have gone on before, and those that are still to be spoken. In this way, *pūrākau* are a shared narrative of the collective self, a type of communal consciousness and memory that produces an evolving narrative. While each generation determines the way they will tell the story, they are always linked to the *pū*.

So, what is the *pū*? What is at the core of the story you are researching, the story you are wanting to tell or are listening to? The words of Kīngi Tāwhiao "*Kimihia te mea ngaro*" echo, providing covert cultural messaging that demands we re-search, think, and feel more deeply to discover what is at the heart of the story. Another *whakataukī* about the trees that again points to our ancestors' understanding of the importance of the core, is:

> Ruia taitea, kia tū ko taikākā anake
>   Cast aside the sapwood, and let the heartwood alone stand. (Mead & Grove, 2003, p. 351)

In reference to the *totara* tree (*Podocarpus totara*), a majestic native tree that can reach up to 30 metres and grow for more than 1,000 years, the *taikākā* or heartwood is most valued. Whereas the pale brown living sapwood soon decays, it is the heartwood that provides the main structure and support of the tree, and is most durable. In this sense, the *pū o te rākau* indicates stories whose function is to support the life of the tree; *pūrākau* ensure our endurance as a culture and as a people.

Māori filmmaker, the late Merita Mita, reminds us of the *pū* and the importance of our stories:

We must not overlook the fact that each of us is born with a story, and each of us has responsibility to pass those stories on. To fortify our children and grandchildren, and help them cope with an increasingly material and technological world, we have to tell them the stories which re-enforce their identity, build their self-worth and self-esteem, and empower them with knowledge. (Mita, 2000, p. 8).

Undoubtedly the purpose of *pūrākau* is to preserve our connection to our *tūpuna*, through our consciousness of the present and the inevitability of the future. *Pūrākau* is an exploration and exposition of culture and identity that can seamlessly move in time and space. Story is our core; it provides the structure of the tree, it determines how the tree will look and ultimately grow. Similarly, in a person, your core is your *puku* (stomach), the place your power is generated from to carry out any movement, and to Māori considered the seat of your emotions. *Pūrākau* teach us what is core to understanding our world, to guiding our engagement with our environment, and our interactions with each other.

Jo-ann Archibald also identifies the notion of working from the "core" (of a tree) in Indigenous pedagogy in her discussions with Elder Dr Ellen White, of the *Snuneymuxw* Coast *Salish* Nation. Ellen (cited in Archibald 2008) says:

They said you learn the base, the very basic, the inside, the stem, and the core. It sort of sounds like it when you translate it, the core of what you are learning and then expand out. The teacher will already know that – it is like a big tree, never mind the apples or if it's the flowers, we're going to learning inside first and then out, they said. Never from outside first. (p. 53)

Jo-ann Archibald was faced with a similar challenge, rather than meaning making by proceeding from the "outside surface to the depths" (p. 54), she set out to think more deeply about the "core" for Indigenous storywork. One of the learnings that Ellen also shared with Jo-ann Archibald, that is significant here, is "it is important to take time to sit, think about, and *feel* what we have learned" (p. 53; my emphasis).

The simplicity found in nature, in our ecosystem, and our native trees, directs us as *Kaupapa Māori* researchers to consider that if we strip away all the layers of complexity, what is at the core? How will this *pūrākau* facilitate the relationships, growth, development, strength, and vitality that will enable the next generation to prosper as *Māori*? What are the conditions required for our *pūrākau* to propagate? In the contemporary research domain, the conditions required to craft safe, ethical, pedagogical *pūrākau* may take time to create. There are multiple threats to the integrity of our stories as Indigenous Peoples, ranging from academic and funding structures and conventions to the specific (and sometimes unrealistic) requirements of communities themselves. However, the question remains: how do we make that space and create those conditions in our work, in our department, in our field, in our homes, and in our lives for *pūrākau* to flourish?

The healing qualities of *rākau*, particularly the many rescue remedies they provide, can only be understood when you understand a *rākau* intimately. In the same way, *pūrākau* can be used and created to heal the heart. In my study of *pūrākau* I have been fortunate to experience their healing power with many of the Elders I interviewed, including Ngapare Hopa (*Tainui, Tūwharetoa*), Tom Roa (*Ngāti Maniapoto, Waikato*), and Aroha Yates-Smith (*Te Arawa*). Underpinned by our existing (and often long) relationship, their extensive cultural knowledge and understanding of tribal lands and histories, combined with their strong listening skills and intuitive sensibilities, created powerful moments of revelation and/or emotional and spiritual strengthening. Being privy to the rendition of ancient as well as personal *pūrākau* by these Elders was a stark reminder of the power of *pūrākau* through our lived "inside" experiences. Similarly, at a recent symposium about Māori approaches to trauma-informed care[5] Hinewirangi Kohu-Morgan, a *kuia*, musician, poet, and artist, told an inspiring personal *pūrākau* of healing that was powerful enough to uplift an audience of 150. With the aid of a PowerPoint presentation consisting of images and text, her *pūrākau* spanned generations and was laced with song and poetry and animated with emotion and humour that pierced the heart, mind, body, and spirit.

It is not, however, my intention to romanticize *pūrākau*. Rather there is a continued need to be circumspect about the reproduction of many of our traditional stories, and contemporary creations. Decolonizing methodologies demand a critical lens that shows many of our *pūrākau* need to be rescued. For example, as much as we may delight in the production of the Disney movie *Moana* entirely in the *Māori* language, this is a new formation of colonization. Characters and storylines based on traditional *pūrākau* and stories from our respective islands of Polynesia are hybridized, commodified and commercialized, and consumed for their entertainment value. With millions of dollars behind the movie creation that is shown on a big screen with bright lights, and wonderful song and music, the story is captivating and dominating in the minds of the young target audience. Our *Māori* children delight in seeing cartoon images that look like themselves, and speak our own language for the first time. While the gendered roles of male and female have shifted in the movie, my own young daughters proclaim they want to be just like "Mooanna" (as pronounced in the American English version), and my young sons think Māui "is kind of dumb." We are not just reclaiming *pūrākau* as a methodology; in many cases, we are also rescuing our *pūrākau* from new and enticing colonizing configurations to protect the *pū* of the *rākau*.

Conclusion

It is not a coincidence that *pūrākau* just happens to be one of the words for stories in *Māori* language. As Kenyan theorist and activist Ngugi wa Thiong'o reminds us in his advocacy for linguistic decolonization, "each language, no matter how small carries its memory of the world" (cited in Mikaere, 2011, p. 292). As he suggests, the memory of the world is not only in each language, but in each word. It is the connection of our language that is the key to opening the door to the worlds and knowledge of our ancestors – that enables us to theorize about the meaning, the intent, and the practice of *pūrākau* today. When we look to our natural world, to our trees, to the inside for clues about how to understand *pūrākau* as methodology, there is a wealth of information to ensure regeneration for our cultural sustainability. From the inside, *pūrākau* are stories that matter; stories not just of, but for survival, for courage, for strength, for resilience, and for vitality. Stories for healing – they too have rescue remedies. Stories of the heart, they teach us about compassion, generosity, reciprocation, and responsibility. Stories of struggle and stories for *tino rangatiratanga*.

"From the inside-out" is a call to decolonize our *pūrākau* practices, and better understand our cultural constructs within our Indigenous frames of reference such as storywork. *Pūrākau* methodology from the inside-out encourages radical research processes and the courage to return to our own frameworks that provide some clear guidelines for ways of being, thinking, knowing, and researching. While *pūrākau* makes up part of a knowledge system, and is a pedagogical tool and a creative practice, *pūrākau* as methodology is also research approach and skill. The art of *pūrākau* in research yearns for stories that are powerful, provocative, and pedagogical. Finally, from the inside-out also hints at something we don't often talk about in research: the heart, how we feel, and how we make people feel on the inside. At our best, *pūrākau* tellers, listeners, practitioners, and researchers are always conscious of the inside and outside, because like our trees, *pūrākau* are always and only relational.

Notes

1 *"Kimihia te mea ngaro: Pūrākau and Indigenous Storywork"* Research Symposium, hosted by Te Kotahi Research Institute, The University of Waikato, held at Waikato-Tainui College for Research and Development, 19 September 2017. Symposium presenters were: Jenny Lee-Morgan, Wiremu Doherty, Jason De Santolo, Jo-ann Archibald, Tracy Bear, and Ruia Aperahama.

2 King Tāwhiao was the second Māori king, his reign was from 1860 to 1894.

3 A *marae* refers to a traditional Māori meeting space, often understood as the whole complex of buildings around the marae courtyard.

4 A *mana whenua marae* refers to a *marae* that belongs to the tribal people of that land or territory, as opposed to an urban and/or pan tribal *marae*.

5 *"He Oranga Ngākau: Māori Approaches to Trauma Informed Care"* Symposium and Thought Space Wānanga, hosted by Te Kotahi Research Institute, Holiday Inn Auckland Airport, 8 May 2018.

References

Archibald, J. (2008). *Indigenous storywork: educating the heart, mind, body and spirit.* Vancouver, BC: UBC Press.

Battiste, M. (2008). Research ethics for protecting indigenous knowledge and heritage: institutional and researcher responsibilities. In N. K. Denzin, Y. S. Lincoln & L. T. Smith (Eds.), *Handbook of critical and Indigenous methodologies* (pp. 497–510). Thousand Oaks, CA: Sage Publications.

Bishop, R. (2011). *Freeing ourselves.* Rotterdam: Sense Publishers.

Bishop, R. & Glynn, T. (1999). *Culture counts: changing power relations in education.* Palmerston North, New Zealand: Dunmore Press.

Brayboy, B. & Deyhle, D. (2000). Insider-outsider: researchers in American Indian communities. *Theory into Practice 39*(3), 163–169.

Cavino, H. (2017). *Towards a method of belonging: contextualizing sexual violence in Māori worlds.* Unpublished PhD dissertation. Syracuse, NY: Syracuse University.

Collins, P. (1991). Learning from the outsider within: The sociological significance of Black feminist thought. In M. Fonow. & J. Cook (Eds.). *Beyond methodology: feminist research as lived research* (pp. 35–59). Bloomington, IN: Indiana University Press.

Grande, S. (2004). *Red pedagogy: Native American social and political thought.* New York, NY: Rowman & Littlefield.

Jackson, M. (forthcoming). In the end: the hope of decolonisation. In E. McKinley & L. Tuhiwai Smith (Eds.), *Handbook of Indigenous education.*

Kirkwood, C. (2000). *Tāwhiao – King or Prophet.* Hopuhopu, New Zealand: Waikato Raupatu Lands Trust.

Lee, J. (2008). *Ako: pūrākau of Māori teachers' work in secondary schools.* Unpublished PhD thesis. The University of Auckland, New Zealand.

Lee, J. (2009). Decolonising Māori narratives: pūrākau as a method. *MAI Review 2*(3), 79–91.

Lee-Morgan, J. (2017). Pūrākau: Hei kaupapa rangahau mana motuhake Māori! In A. McFarland & N. Mathews (Eds.), *He kete Whakawaitara he whakatara ā-rangahau* (pp. 48–60). Wellington: NZCER.

Lee-Morgan, J. B. J. & Hoskins, R. (2017). Kāinga tahi, kāinga rua: A Kaupapa Māori response of Te Puea Memorial Marae. *Parity 30*(8), 13–14.

Mataira, K. (1984). *Māori artists of the South Pacific.* Raglan, New Zealand: Ngā Puna Waihanga.

Mead, H. & Grove, N. (2003). *Ngā Pēpeha o ngā Tīpuna: The sayings of the ancestors.* Wellington, New Zealand: Victoria University Press.

Mikaere, A. (2011). *Colonising myths Māori realities: He Rukuruku Whakaaro.* Wellington, New Zealand: Huia Publishers.

Mikaere, A. (2017). *The balance destroyed.* Ōtaki, New Zealand: Te Wānanga o Raukawa.

Mita, M. (2000). Storytelling: a process of decolonisation. In L. Pihama (Ed.), *The Journal of Puawaitanga. Special Issue: Indigenous Women and Representation* (pp. 7–9). Auckland, New Zealand: The University of Auckland.

O'Malley, V. (2016). *The great war for New Zealand: Waikato 1800–2000.* Wellington, New Zealand: Bridget Williams Books.

Pihama, L. (forthcoming). Colonisation and the importation of ideologies of race, gender and class. In E. McKinley & L. Tuhiwai Smith (Eds.), *Handbook of Indigenous education.*

Said, E. (1978). *Orientalism.* New York, NY: Vintage Books.

Smith, L. T. (2012). *Decolonizing methodologies: research and Indigenous Peoples.* (2nd ed.). New York, NY: Zed Books.

Thiong'o, Ngũgĩ wa. (1986). *Decolonising the mind: the politics of language in African literature.* London: Heinemann.

MĀORI GLOSSARY

Aotearoa	New Zealand
aroha	love
atua	gods/the Māori gods
hapū	sub tribal groupings/pregnant
harakeke	an indigenous species of flax
hau	wind, vital essence
Hineahuone	the female element who comes from the soil
hui	cultural gatherings
ingoa	names
ingoa tangata	personal names
iwi	tribal nations
kāinga	home
kaitiakitanga	guardianship
kākahu	clothing
karakia	prayers/chants
kaumātua	Elders
kaupapa	initiative
Kaupapa Māori	Māori initiative/a decolonizing methodology local to Aotearoa
kauri	native tree
kete	baskets
kōpū	uterus
kōrero	story/talk
kōrero ingoa	naming stories
kōrero pūrākau	histories and stories
Kura Kaupapa Māori/Wharekura	Māori immersion schooling (primary/secondary)
mahi tahi	collaboration
mana	power/authority/prestige/influence
mana atua	*mana* that comes from the sacred power of the gods

mana tangata	the power and authority that one achieves through one's own skill, knowledge, and actions
mana tupuna	*mana* that comes from one's lineage, the inherited mana of one's ancestors
mana wāhine	Indigenous feminist
manaaki	kindness and responsibility
manaakitanga	nurturing/caring for others
Māori	Indigenous people of Aotearoa
marae	Māori meeting space, often understood as the whole complex of buildings around the *marae* courtyard
Marama	the moon
mātauranga	Māori knowledge and understandings
Māui	Māori ancestor
mihimihi	greetings
mokopuna	grandchildren
ngahere	bush, forest
ngārara	reptiles
noa	a normal state of affairs where there is balance and where interactions can occur free of restriction (in contrast to *tapu*)
oriori	song
Papatūānuku	Earth Mother
pepeha	tribal sayings
pū	base or foundation or core
puku	stomach
pūmotomoto	flute
pūrākau	traditional oral narratives/storytelling
rākau	tree/the wood, branches, and leaves
rangatira	chief/leader
Ranginui	Sky Father
raupatu	confiscation

rūnanga	council/assembly
taikākā	heartwood
tamariki	children
Tāne Mahuta	God of the forest
tangata	human
tāngata	people
taonga	treasures
tapu	sacredness/something that is of special status that must be set apart or subject to restrictions
tauira	student
te ao Māori	the Māori world
Te Kōhanga Reo	Māori language nest
te pū	the origin or foundation, the roots
te pū o te rākau	the core of the tree
te reo Māori	Māori language
tiaki	nurture
tikanga Māori	Māori custom/Māori cultural practices/Māori values and protocols
tino rangatiratanga	self-determination
tipuna/tūpuna	ancestors
tipuna wahine	female ancestors
tohunga	experts
tongikura	proverbial saying
totara	native tree
utu	the principle of reciprocity
wāhine	women
wai	water
waiata	songs
waka	canoe
whaikōrero	formal speech making
whakairo	carvings
whakapapa	genealogy
whakatauki	proverb/proverbial saying
whakawhanaunga	to enact familial relationships
whakawhiti kōrero	open conversations
whānau	extended family
whanaunga	blood relation

whanaungatanga	centrality of relationships/familial relationships
whare wānanga	traditional houses of learning
whāriki	mats
whenua	land/placenta

PART III

INDIGENOUS STORYWORK IN AUSTRALIA

Jason De Santolo

In this continent Indigenous Peoples were colonized in the late eighteenth century. Despite diverse experiences there is a strong shared story of resistance. Oral traditions celebrate resistance in hundreds of our languages while carefully worded historical journals (in English) witness the reprisals. It is here we become conscious of the unearthly violence of the "Settler" story, a foundational pillar of the colonial project of Australia. Like in other parts of the world, colonization involved deliberate acts of genocide and a murderous intent to exterminate and exploit not only Indigenous Peoples but their pristine life-sustaining lands and waters. This story of invasion is therefore one of social, cultural, and environmental destruction, the impacts of which have resonated across the generations.[1] Every year, on Australia Day, the story of invasion is overcome by stories of survival. Storytelling is about emotional resonance to Country, it evokes creation and survival in each breath.

Indigenous storytelling is a profound form of resistance for the heart, mind, body, and spirit. From sacred songlines as law to the revitalization of traditional fire practices, Elders are now choosing to share and revitalize these ancient practices at a crucial moment for Mother Earth. Just as we are embarking on a quest for climate justice we are witnessing new forms of theoretical warfare, from challenging the foundations of literary theory, to breaking down ethical protocols of higher education. Story is a way forward in the decolonizing movement as deep meaning-making encounter, as expansive creative collaboration. Collaboration breaks down imperialistic boundaries and reimagines collective will according to Indigenous-inspired strategies of transformation. Indigenous movements and campaigns grow organically and resist ongoing systemic issues: the revival of languages and cultural practices, the forced removal of Aboriginal children, deaths in custody, and the targeting of Indigenous homelands by extractive industries. The resurgence of Indigenous storytelling is at the heart of these self-determination movements. Storywork is able to forge new political alliances that bind community movements to place. It activates and holds the most dynamic of our ancient practices in their rightful place – Country. In similar ways, Indigenous storytelling is an expansive relational way of being in Country and as such it resonates strongly across transdisciplinary and decolonizing research realms. These storywork chapters offer us a glimpse into the resurgence of story as an ongoing moment of transformational resistance.

Indigenous storytelling: decolonizing institutions and assertive self-determination – implications for legal practice – Larissa Behrendt

Larissa Behrendt positions and grounds Indigenous storytelling deeply within her *Eualeyai* and *Gamillaroi* heritage. This chapter highlights how relational responsibilities inform the way of story, as being, as connection to ancestral knowledge and power, as assertive self-determination. Unpacking this assertion, Behrendt realizes the transformational energy of standpoint in challenging colonization and patriarchy in everyday institutional contexts. Stories carried law as "Law Stories" – they recognized and were imbued with interconnectedness and they have survived the anti-storytelling agenda of colonization. The project of reclamation is posed as giving voice to humanity in processes of social justice as reflected in the deeply inspired storywork supporting the Bowraville families' 20-year-plus struggle for justice for their murdered children. This heartfelt call for justice stories a further call for unity in our self-determination movements across the oceans for "Our sovereignty is strongest when we are strongest in ourselves. We are strongest in ourselves when we are with each other" (Behrendt, Chapter 10, this volume).

The limits of literary theory and the possibilities of storywork for Aboriginal literature in Australia – Evelyn Araluen Corr

In this chapter Evelyn Araluen Corr expertly tackles the dangers and limits of conventional literary theory. Relationships between literature and theory emerge where Western traditions of the colonial (intellectual) project seek to dominate, revealing a stark absence of Aboriginal and Torres Strait Islander voices in the post-colonial Australian discourse. For Araluen Corr storywork has potential as combative recovery and interpretation projects for overcoming literary theory projects of silencing and erasure. This chapter takes us into a powerful space, where storywork illuminates and holds potential as a relational, place-based, and storied language for the generative discourses and practices emerging through Indigenous literary theory.

Lilyology as a transformative framework for decolonizing ethical spaces within the academy – Nerida Blair

This chapter focuses on the transforming of ethical spaces within the academic institution through Nerida Blair's unique Lilyology framework. Lilyology is both metaphor and philosophy – it images waterlilies, sweet potatoes, spiders, and brick walls as a transformative storytelling practice and decolonizing methodology for engaging Indigenous knowledge. In this context, Blair articulates the enactment of Lilyology as strategic intervention within a University Human Rights Ethics Committee. Blair challenges conventional understandings of the Indigenous "Acknowledgement of Country" ceremony – providing key insights into what is often a hidden process of research – a closed door, or as Lilyology frames it: "*the brick wall.*" For Blair, storywork permeates Lilyology, as reverence for privileging of Indigenous Knowings, as holistic, synergized, and interrelational elements of story that interact and impact on each other.

Putting the people back into the country – Victor Steffensen

In this chapter Victor Steffensen shares insights into a unique Aboriginal cultural revitalization methodology. Steffensen shares his experience of training in the bush with the late Awu-Laya Elders George Musgrave and Tommy George. The storying of this methodology is part of Steffensen's way of honouring and acknowledging the mentorship of these revered Elders. What emerges through these Elders' teachings and living knowledge systems is Praction, aptly named by the Elders as a deep interrelational way of being in Country by combining action with practice. Steffensen's chapter offers for the first time a framing of a methodology to get people back on Country through the revitalization of ancient fire practices, using shared knowledge principles, and the recording of traditional knowledge projects. When Indigenous knowledge is applied the right way it activates and heals the land and the people. Storywork here is about knowledge journeys through the bush, activated at grassroots level and using living knowledge principles that educate and harness technologies alongside some of the oldest Indigenous knowledge systems in the world.

The emergence of *Yarnbar Jarngkurr* from Indigenous homelands: a creative Indigenous methodology – Jason De Santolo

This chapter reflects upon a creative doctoral journey into the transformative power of ancient song renewal. For De Santolo these ancient song traditions are bound within the eternal guardianship role held by *Garrwa* over their homelands through original laws and practices. Sourced in the *Yigan* (the dreaming creation), passed down through ancestors, Elders, family, clan, these vibrant cultural powers are intergenerational (Hoosan, 2018). Song traditions guide the enactment of original laws and practices and now ground *Garrwa* as they mobilize against extractive industries. De Santolo asserts that these songs transcend the dominion of the colonial project, yet are still threatened by the ideologies and extractive systems that underpin it. In this chapter De Santolo reflects upon *Yarnbar Jarngkurr* (talking and storying) as a journey of emergence orientating *Garrwa* video practice (music videos) into greater resonance with the Indigenous storywork principle of interrelatedness where there is a "synergistic interaction between storyteller, listener, and story" (Archibald, 2008, p.32). This paper offers a creative Indigenous methodology for community researchers, creatives, activists, and water protectors operating in complex Indigenous knowledge spaces.

Note

1 The Indigenous population in Australia is around 800,000 and 3.3 per cent of the total population and is made up of Aboriginal and Torres Strait Islander peoples. Australian Bureau of Statistics (2018), www.abs.gov.au/ausstats/abs@.nsf/mf/3238.0.55.00.

Reference

Archibald, J. (2008). *Indigenous storywork: educating the heart, mind, body and spirit.* Vancouver, BC: UBC Press.

10 | INDIGENOUS STORYTELLING

Decolonizing institutions and assertive self-determination: implications for legal practice

Larissa Behrendt

Introduction

Our sovereignty is strongest when we are strongest in ourselves.
We are strongest in ourselves when we are with each other.

I am descended from emu women and we are ancient storytellers. We have an oral history that provides a unique cultural worldview. Storytelling is a transformative practice and nowhere is that more true than within the institutions of our society, including universities and the legal system. Indigenous perspectives can challenge the assumptions within these institutions that have been crafted with the values of the dominant, colonial culture by offering alternative perspectives and standpoints. A key strategy in this is the use of our storytelling as a methodology. Storytelling not only challenges or decolonizes institutions, it is a way of reasserting Indigenous voice, perspective, and experience. Storytelling is an act of sovereignty that reinforces Indigenous identity, values, and worldview.

I am a *Eualeyai* and *Gamillaroi* woman and my personal totem is the *dinewan* (emu), my clan totem is the long-necked turtle (*girrabirrii*) and my spiritual totem is the lyre bird. In this introduction, I am telling you a story of more than just what my name is and where I am from, that I am descended from emu women. I am also telling you something of my worldview and value system.

Our personal totem reminds us that we are descended from our animal totem and it is this animal that is our ancestor. We have responsibilities for looking after that animal – we can't eat its meat, for example – and the personal totem reminds us of our interconnection to our environment and the natural world. Our clan totem reminds us that we are connected to other people, that we have responsibility to and for them and our spiritual totem is our connection to our ancestors.[1]

Aboriginal people in Australia when they meet you will ask you where you are from as a way of fitting you into our kinship network – which we do by family name, place, and nation group. There is power in asserting our place in the natural world and in our kinship network as we introduce each other. It is an assertion of sovereignty. To me, and it is a personal definition, sovereignty is our identity, our nationhood, our culture, and our worldview. An assertion of these things is our assertion of our sovereignty.

Worldview and standpoint

This positioning with its coded worldviews is also a foundation of the process of decolonizing the academy through Indigenous scholarship. The Western tradition assumes neutrality or objectivity by a scholar and a researcher (Robinson, 2015).[2] It is suspicious of subjectivity. Indigenous approaches to knowledge are completely the opposite. They understand that where you are placed – your positioning or your standpoint – will fundamentally influence the way you see the world.

Indigenous standpoint notes up front that we, as individuals, are shaped by our cultures, cultural values, and experiences with society's institutions. And this is true no matter what background someone has and it challenges those who do not reflect on the values, biases, and assumptions they bring into their work. In this way, Indigenous standpoint theory plays an important role in challenging the assumptions around neutrality that are actually a way of reinforcing power structures of colonization and patriarchy.

Storytelling as methodology

Acknowledging the richness and honesty that background and perspective bring to work within the academy also highlights the importance of storytelling. Storytelling is ancient and potent. It is our most instinctive and human form of communication, of teaching, of persuasion, of validation, of healing, of transformation. It has a particular resonance in oral cultural traditions like those of Aboriginal and Torres Strait Islander Nations.

Indigenous methodology that places research in context provides an opportunity to relate the nature of that context and that is most effectively done through the act of narrative or story. Relation of life story and experience becomes an important context for Indigenous scholars but also plays an important role in the academy.[3] It illuminates experiences that those who do not come from that background might not otherwise be exposed to. It allows for the comparison of experience and a depth at which issues that are conceived at an abstract level – child removal, contact with the criminal justice system, racism – remain within a human context.

Storytelling also plays a key role in our resilience as the world's oldest living culture *and* in our assertion of sovereignty *and* in the countering of the colonial narratives, the colonial stories, which have spread across our lands. Reasserting our stories on our land is a way of reasserting our ownership. This is an important role within the academy, in spaces that have been unwelcoming and alienating for Indigenous people and in disciplines that have privileged colonial perspectives over Indigenous ones. It is also important in the context of academic institutions that have sought to research Indigenous people and their culture and have used that research in ways that are unethical and in ways that undermine the interests and well-beings of Indigenous subjects or deprive them of intellectual property rights to their knowledges.

Introduction of Indigenous storytelling into the academy as a methodology and as a source of knowledge is an important way of countering structural privileges. An example is the use of Indigenous cultural stories – often referred to as Dreamtime stories – as a source of knowledge. Aboriginal people hold our laws and governance structures within these cultural stories – I think of them as law stories though they contain a lot of other insights than just within the legal context.

The emu story from my country has a moral about not letting your vanity distract you from your responsibilities as a parent; the story of the echidna is a cautionary tale about ensuring that you share your resources; the story of the seven sisters constellation is about the bonds of family and the importance of following the laws. These stories contain our codes of conduct and reinforce the worldviews that are structured through our totemic systems.

The values of Aboriginal culture are reflected in our laws and can be seen in our ways of settling disputes. Recognizing the interconnectedness of people in the community, our disputes were negotiated with that understanding that a broad range of people have an interest in the outcome. Everyone would get a chance to speak and to put their position forward.

The result would be reached by consensus and at the heart of this process is the understanding that relationships are critical and need to be protected and preserved as we go forward. Disputes were always held on Country, on the land, to ground us. This process stands in deep contrast to the colonial legal system. The most obvious difference is that ours is an oral tradition of storytelling and colonial legal systems are written – they place the emphasis on the written word, on legal precedent. Disputes are settled in a way that only considers the evidence of the individual parties before the court. Decision is arrived at by judgement. It is authoritarian. It is individually focused, not community minded.

We have so many reasons to be sceptical about these imposed legal systems that are clearly colonial and now seek to be normalized as the national laws of our country. We know the tool that they were in the colonization process but I want to explore this role a little bit more. Our laws were dismissed by colonial states and they used *their* legal systems to try to legitimize this. They didn't want to recognize our legal systems because to do that would be to recognize our sovereignty, our culture, our laws, our connection to our land. So colonial institutions, like the legal system, build in a wilful blindness about these elements of Indigenous culture.

The anti-storytelling agenda of colonization

The colonial legal system works tenaciously to counter our stories and dismisses Indigenous story in several ways. It treats law stories, which are an assertion of ownership and sovereignty, as little more than children's stories. It rejects the oral nature of the narratives as being less credible that those contained in text.

And at the same moment the stories of Indigenous people are dismissed as part of the colonial project, it privileges their own narratives and stories. A clear example of this is the construction of *terra nullius* whereby the deep connection to land that Aboriginal and Torres Strait Islander Nations had – which was evidenced by stories that they ignored and gave no weight to but within their own legal system created a self-confessed "legal fiction," a story of settlement of land over which no one had a claim.

This legal fiction remained in Australian law until 1992 when the High Court decided in the *Mabo* case that there was a form of Aboriginal title or native that was retained by Indigenous Nations in certain circumstances. Until then, the concept of *terra nullius* was used to justify the absolute claiming of Indigenous lands in Australia by the British – and then the Australian state. And while the doctrine of *terra nullius* was overturned in relation to native title, the High Court was clear that there was no recognition of Aboriginal sovereignty that flowed as a result of this recognition.

The court in disconnecting our land from our governance system used the metaphor of a skeleton saying that Aboriginal rights can only be recognized by the colonial legal system to the extent that their recognition would not fracture the skeleton of the law.[4] In other words, only to the extent that it does not disturb the colonial power balance.

The colonial legal system claims that it is objective, that it is not biased. It even proclaims that justice is blind. And it holds that the traditions in the colonial legal system are legitimate because they are steeped in history and rooted in ancient Greek and Latin traditions. The lineal story goes something like this – there was the Stone Age, then there was the Bronze Age and then there were the Greeks and then the Romans, the dark ages, then the Renaissance, and then the Enlightenment, and all of this leads to the implied superiority of European cultures especially over those that never progressed out of the Stone Age. The strong civilization dominates and the weaker ones are subsumed or disappear into the mists of history. It is, they claim, just like Darwin's theory of evolution.

The point that is worth underlining is that this lineal storytelling is also in direct conflict with our own tradition of Indigenous storytelling. Our storytelling is not linear; it is circular. We know that there are cycles, that there are high points and low points of our history. Just as the seasons go in cycles, just as our lives go in cycles, so too does our history as peoples.

The dismissal of Indigenous knowledges and other cultures deprives colonial societies of the knowledges that would ensure survival and sustainability. The cities we inhabit now, the infrastructure that goes through our lands, the destructive activities that disrupt our ecosystems will one day be gone and this land will still be our land. And our stories will still connect us to it. The Social Darwinism which so infected Western intellectual traditions through so many of its disciplines and was adopted as a key philosophy that infected the colonization project was deeply arrogant. It fails to consider that there is anything to be learned from cultures even though they have existed for over 60,000 years, especially about sustainable use of resources, stable government, and strong community values.

Reclaiming Indigenous stories

The colonial legal system is dismissive of storytelling because it is deeply challenged by it. Disconnecting law from story disconnects law from personal story. Storytelling humanizes. It gives voice to people. An important part of the decolonization process, especially as we work in the structures of the dominant culture like the legal system, is to advocate for broader law reform but to never lose sight of the colonial law's dominating power. And one way to subvert the dominant colonial legal system is to rely upon our traditional laws and their values and processes to guide our advocacy.

I want to use an example of this in the work I have done with my colleagues from the *Jumbunna* Institute of Indigenous Education and Research at the University of Technology Sydney. Between a period of several months over the summer of 1990 and 1991, three Aboriginal children – Colleen Walker, aged 16, Evelyn Greenup, aged 4, and Clinton Speedy Duroux, aged 16, were murdered on the Aboriginal reserve on the edge of the town of Bowraville in New South Wales. When the children first went missing, their parents knew that something was wrong but when they took their complaints to the police, they were not taken seriously.

When Clinton's body was found a few weeks after his disappearance, police started to investigate but instead of sending in homicide detectives, they sent in investigators who had child welfare experience. There has only ever been one suspect in this case – a white man who engaged in a pattern of behaviour whereby he would bring alcohol on to the reserve, put drugs in the alcohol, and sexually assault young Aboriginal women. He had allegedly attempted this on Colleen, on Evelyn's mother, and on Clinton's girlfriend. He was charged but the failings in the police investigation meant the man was acquitted. The police overlooked critical evidence in the period that they didn't take the disappearances seriously.

The families of Colleen, Evelyn, and Clinton have fought to have the case brought back into court and get a conviction. When I was approached by Colleen's aunt to see what could be done to assist, the families had already been engaged in a 20-year struggle. I'd always been aware of this case. The murders occurred while I was in law school and they symbolized to me as an Aboriginal young person the very deep failings of our criminal justice system that was locking up Aboriginal men and women at disproportionate rates for offences such as being drunk in public and swearing but a white man who allegedly murdered three Aboriginal children could walk free.

So when I was approached, I was keen to be involved. I travelled to meet the families with Craig Longman, the head of our Litigation Unit, and Jason De Santolo, the head of our New Media Unit to meet with the members of all three families. They were frustrated that the case had seemed to stall. The Department of Public Prosecutions (DPP) had advised the New South Wales Attorney General that the cases shouldn't be sent back to court. What ideas, they asked, did we have on how to break this impasse?

In our conversation, one of the answers came from them. They had noticed that the only time there had been movement in their case was the two occasions on which the mainstream media had done stories about them. Could we, they ask, do our own documentary to once again raise the profile of the case? Part of our thinking too was that the legal arguments about why the case couldn't go forward that were being asserted by the DPP had taken the real heart out of these cases by the legal wrangling over the definition of "fresh and compelling evidence." This was not a case that should be best defined by legal arguments. This was a case about getting justice for three sets of parents who had their children murdered and about putting a child serial killer behind bars – and this was a more compelling argument than any other legal one. The documentary was a way in which we could emphasize that important concept by putting the story into the words of the parents. And no lawyer could argue the rightness of this case as powerfully as they could.

It was also apparent that there was a view amongst the officials that, after 20 years, these parents should just get over it and get on with it. I often wondered when I saw that attitude expressed whether those people would have the same view if these had been white parents who were grieving white children. In their own words, it is clear that these parents were never going to forget their children – they lived with their presence every day. Jason De Santolo produced the film and we had advice from Pauline Clague who is from that area and now an adjunct professor at *Jumbunna*.

We also researched other avenues to pursue. One was a parliamentary inquiry and while there had never been one into a case like Bowraville, the families decided to lobby for that. And they did. And they got one.[5] One of the first steps that the NSW Legislative Council

Standing Committee on Law and Justice undertaking the inquiry did was to watch the video to get a sense of the story and the families – and to hear their point of view. And then they went to Bowraville and spent time with the families before asking a single question.

When the Standing Committee on Law and Justice delivered its findings, every member of that committee spoke with passion about the need to get justice in this case and what was striking was how each said something like, "As a parent, I could not imagine how I would feel if this had happened to my child" or "I put myself in their shoes." The important thing these comments revealed was that the parliamentarians saw their commonality as parents; they didn't see this simply as an Aboriginal case. They saw the humanity – the personal story. And once they could do that – once they could put themselves in the shoes of the parents – there was political will to finally do something.

Our team, through Craig Longman's Litigation Unit, also wrote a new application to the Attorney General that was submitted on behalf of the NSW Police Force. Two had been made previously and rejected. So what could we do differently to try to get a different result? We decided not to start with the legal argument but to start with the story – to talk about the impact on the families and the communities, about the need to put a serial killer behind bars. And then we got onto the legal arguments. As a strategy, we also got the police to submit the application. In the past, the families had submitted them. But the strategy was discussed with them and they knew it would be harder for the Attorney General to say no to the police than to them. The application was successful and the man was arrested early in 2018 and the case is preparing to go to court.

Our approach in Bowraville is consistent with our research practice as Aboriginal people:

- We didn't get involved in the case, even though we felt strongly about it, *until we were asked.*
- Along the way, we gave suggestions to the Bowraville families about their options or how to achieve what they wanted but we never made decisions for them.
- We did not speak for them but found ways to have their voice elevated. The documentary did that.

We were able to use the recorded interviews we made for the documentary as the basis of the written applications to the parliamentary inquiry, which allowed us to put the perspectives of the families forward – in their own words – without having to re-traumatize them with telling the parts of the story that still cause them great grief. The documentary is also being used by the NSW Police now as a training resource on what not to do when investigating a murder case in the Aboriginal community (Behrendt, 2014).

Storytelling as self-determination

This is the self-determining role that storytelling can play – it takes our voices from the margins and puts them in the centre. That should be a guiding part of our process. The first question we should ask ourselves as researchers is: how is this research building the capacity of the community? Our second is: how can we mobilize the resources of the university to do the work that the community needs done? And in thinking about storytelling as a methodology, the questions we ask are:

- What is the human impact of the law/policy?
- Who has the power / who is powerless?
- Who needs to be empowered to speak?
- Who has the real authority to speak?
- Whose STORY is it?
- How can we help storytellers enact the intent of the story?

Within *Jumbunna*, we have sought to ensure an integration of research, practice (through litigation), and storytelling (through new media). Our best work occurs when we pull all three together. The Bowraville case is an example of how we have used Indigenous knowledges and methodologies within the colonial legal system to try to achieve justice. This is an important part of the decolonization process.

Storytelling as sovereignty

Indigenous storytelling is the counter-narrative of colonization. Indigenous story deconstructs and shifts power (Raheja, 2010). There are two roles we play as we navigate our way as researchers and as lawyers. We work to decolonize by transforming colonial structures. And we act to assert our sovereignty – our values and our cultures. Our cultures teach about the importance of balance and our challenge is to find the balance – the balance that is personally right for us – between those two tasks. But there is an ongoing challenge to the assertion of our sovereignty in this context – it is the need for us to stay true to our values and knowledges, our teaching and learnings.

As we go into the academy and work to decolonize spaces, we need to ensure that we do not lose our own perspective, our own connection to our community. I found myself challenged by this as a young legal scholar. I did my doctoral studies at Harvard and the research question of my thesis was how to recognize Indigenous sovereignty in Australia. It was important for me to do my studies overseas. When I mentioned my thesis topic to Australian legal scholars, even those who had made their career in Indigenous law, they were dismissive and said it was not a good topic for a thesis because it would never happen.

But in a university where there was no unconscious bias to deal with *on my issues* my supervisor said, "that's a great topic – it looks at the way in which an historically marginalized group can be recognized in a democratic society." So I approached my subject in a systematic way. What did international law say about sovereignty and the claiming of sovereignty over Aboriginal lands. When I took the efforts of my first three months' research to my supervisor, he was incredibly dismissive. "Who would care about that?" he asked. "What do Aboriginal people want?"

And he was right. That was the question. Our sovereignty cannot be defined by international laws – the very laws constructed by the colonial powers to justify their actions. Instead, the content had to come from the aspirations of Indigenous people. And so I reframed my questions and always remembered how I had been seduced by the discipline that I had originally entered because I wanted to work to change it. It is easy to be seduced. It is hard to rock the boat – it takes emotional energy and it makes career progression harder. The "troublesome" Aboriginals do not get ahead the way that "the good ones" do.

After over 20 years in the academy I have seen traps for Indigenous researchers and lawyers. The most dangerous trap is to move away from the strong grounding of their culture. That's when they stop being an agent of transformation and merely are co-opted into the system. This tends to happen to younger people, who are drawn into the apparatus of the system, lose a critical capacity, and become complacent cogs in the wheel. The second pitfall is the seduction of title and accolade. It is clear in our own community where people develop a pathological need to be acknowledged by the colonizer. They seek government appointment and affirmation to bolster their self-esteem and sense of self. This also seems to be symptomatic of a loss of connection to Aboriginal community and culture.

Linda Tuhiwai Smith speaks of the need for nurturing. Indigenous cultures that value wellness and healing. And yet with each other, we are harsh (Smith, 2014). The work of trying to transform is hard, emotionally draining, and often heartbreaking. I struggle with this as the head of a research unit where my team work on cases of child removal, deaths in custody, and with victims of crime (Smith, 1999). We cannot create a place of subversion and transformation within the academy without creating a culturally safe place. A key part of our role in developing and supporting our researchers is to ensure that their wellbeing is being looked after and that their connection to their culture and cultural values kept strong.

A final reflection

As Aboriginal researchers, we do not assume to be objective. We know there is no such thing. If we thought our position in the world could be passive we wouldn't introduce ourselves by our nations, our clans, our kinship networks. We place ourselves in the world as an act of sovereignty and it reinforces our worldview. In our research approaches, we take this on by not pretending that we are neutral. We are proud advocates and activists for our people. We march and protest. We publish and critique. We confront wilful blindness and we will not be silenced. We research to empower our community and build our communities. We research to honour the history and battles of our ancestors and we research to arm the next generation of warriors.

Our most powerful tool in this is the assertion of our sovereignty, our unapologetic stance that our Aboriginal culture, our philosophies, our values are the things that define us as we work in the institutions of the colonizer – whether that is within the courts, within the bureaucracy, or within the academy. For our next generation of young warrior scholars: keep moving forward with the important work you are doing, support each other, hold onto our sense of community and connectedness. Take the time to write one email or note to one of our warriors who you admire and tell them. Let them know they have your support, that we are all in this battle together. Let them know that you are thinking of them. Let them know the community values them. Not only will you make the person who receives your letter of encouragement and support stronger, you will feel yourself becoming stronger.

Our sovereignty is strongest when we are strongest in ourselves. We are strongest in ourselves when we are with each other.

Notes

1 See also Graham Smith's (2015) work on *Kaupapa Māori* praxis which has been deeply influential in Indigenous scholarship. Pihama, Tiakiwai and Southey (2015).

2 See also, Robinson (2000).

3 See the influential work of Jo-Ann Archibald on storytelling (Archibald, 2008).

4 Justice Brennan's judgment contains the metaphor of the skeleton of the common law and the need not to break it. Mabo v Queensland (No.2) (1992) 175 C.L.R. 1 at 28–30.

5 See NSW Legislative Council Standing Committee on Law and Justice. *Family Response to the Murders in Bowraville*. Report no. 55. 6 November 2014. Chair: David Clarke MLC.

References

Archibald, J. (2008). *Indigenous storywork: educating the heart, mind, body and spirit*. Vancouver, BC: UBC Press.

Behrendt (Director) & De Santolo, Longman, Cavadini (Producers). (2014). *Innocence betrayed*. [Documentary]. Australia: Frontyard Films/Jumbunna/NITV. Distributed by Ronin Films.

Mabo v Queensland (No.2) (1992) 175 C.L.R. *1 at* 28–30.

NSW Legislative Council Standing Committee on Law and Justice. (2014) *Family response to the murders in Bowraville*. Sydney. Report no. *55*. 6.

Pihama, L., Tiakiwai, S.-J. & Southey, K. (2015). *Kaupapa rangahau: a reader*. Waikato, New Zealand: The University of Waikato.

Raheja, M. (2010). *Reservation reelism: redfacing, visual sovereignty, and representations of Native Americans in film*. Lincoln, NE: University of Nebraska Press.

Robinson, A. M. (2000). *White privilege: talkin' up to the white woman – Indigenous women and feminism*. St Lucia, QLD: University of Queensland Press.

Robinson. A. (2015). *The white possessive: property, power and Indigenous sovereignty*. Minneapolis, MN: University of Minnesota Press.

Smith, G.H. (2015). *The dialectic relation of theory and practice in the development of Kaupapa Maori praxis*. Hamilton, New Zealand: Te Kotahi Research Institute.

Smith, L. (1999). *Decolonizing methodologies: research and Indigenous Peoples*. London: Zed Books.

Smith, L.T. (2014). *Keynote: He Manawa Whenua Te Kotahi Research Institute, University of Waikato* [Video File]. Retrieved from www.youtube.com/watch?v=BUm3DVsek-I.

11 | THE LIMITS OF LITERARY THEORY AND THE POSSIBILITIES OF STORYWORK FOR ABORIGINAL LITERATURE IN AUSTRALIA

Evelyn Araluen Corr

In telling you all of this in this way, I am resigning myself and you to the idea that parts of my telling are confounding. I care about you understanding, but I care more about concealing parts of myself from you. I don't trust you very much. You are not always aware of how you can be dangerous to me, and this makes me dangerous to you. I am using my arm to determine the length of the gaze. At the same time that I tell, I wonder about the different endings, the unfurled characters, the lies that didn't make it to the page, the anti-heroes who do not get the shine of my attention ... Yes, I am telling you a story, but you may be reading another one. (Tuck & Ree, 2013, p. 639)

The concept of the discipline is even more interesting when we think about it not simply as a way of organizing systems of knowledge but also as a way of organizing people or bodies ... The colonizing of the Other through discipline has a number of different meanings. In terms of the way knowledge was used to discipline the colonized it worked in a variety of ways. The most obvious forms of discipline were through exclusion, marginalization and denial. Indigenous ways of knowing were excluded and marginalized. (Smith, 1999, p. 70)

As articulated by *Ngāti Awa* and *Ngāti Porou* academic Linda Tuhiwai Smith's pioneering work on decolonial Indigenous methods and practices in research and education, the university – here referring both to pedagogical and research structures of Settler-colonial tertiary education institutions – is underpinned by a range of beliefs and assumptions regarding Western authority over Indigenous lands, bodies, knowledges, cultural practices, and histories. Certain disciplines, such as anthropology, have been interrogated by Indigenous scholars for their more direct role in structures of ongoing dispossession and genocide, simultaneously erasing, extracting, and testing beliefs and methods from and on Indigenous communities (Smith, 1999, p. 68). Literary studies, as a sprawling and multifaceted discipline which

striates semiotics, hermeneutics, linguistics, cultural and critical theory, philosophy, historiography, psychoanalysis, anthropology, and
bears the potential and opportunity for engagement with most other
forms of discourse, has at times been protected from suspicion of these
empirical underpinnings by its own disciplinary ambiguity. However,
the epistemological premise that constitutes theory's effectiveness as
a tool of analysis – the assumption that a given social condition is an
essentially arbitrary discursive product of particular mechanisms – is
also a limitation when it comes to Aboriginal literature and realities.
Paul de Man, one of deconstructive theory's leading figures, con-
figures conventional theory as an "unreliable process of knowledge
production" in which the totalizing rhetorical principles of theory
aspire to prevent all discourses from directly approaching lived experience (de Man, 1982, p. 20). This suggests that theory is innately
ill-equipped to recognize or reconcile the priority of Indigenous contexts and knowledges to Aboriginal writing. Moreover, in its practice,
theoretical reading often goes further – assuming not only that textual
expressions of cultural and political identity are transparently amenable to discursive interpretation, but also that this interpretation will
itself be ethical, or somehow abstractly beneficial. This underestima-
tion of literature's power to operate as a force of imperialism has been
a central concern in postcolonial critique for the last half century, and
the critical legacy of Palestinian scholar Edward Said has demonstrated that literary status cannot isolate the cultural object of the text
from the political conditions of the colonial project. As much effort
has gone into understanding the power wielded by textual representations of the Other in the work of Said, Gayatri Spivak, and Chinua
Achebe, as has been invested in exploring writing as a potential for
decolonization and consciencism in the work of Frantz Fanon, Ngũgĩ
wa Thiong'o, Édouard Glissant, and Aimé Césaire.

Australian postcolonial discourse, however – which emerged and
acted with little to no participation from Aboriginal and Torres Strait
Islander scholars in the 1980s, and has in fact been extensively rejected
by Indigenous writers – failed to account for the ongoing cultural and
political implications of the Australian Settler-colonial state. As a result
it has been subject to extensive international criticism from Indigenous
writers and academics for issues such as an insistence on depoliticized
definitions of marginalization, in which both Settler and Indigenous
identities are subject to multiple modernities of the same oppression,

and for attempts to "discipline" Indigenous writers and activists for their rejection of the orthodox techniques of postcolonial theory – particularly those who have emerged from nations, unlike Australia, that have experienced a national decolonial event (Allen, 2002, p. 30). The insistence on a material and political framing of postcoloniality as a potential of a decolonized future, but not a possibility for a thoroughly colonized present from Aboriginal writers and academics, is in no way a rejection or misunderstanding of theory's instructive or liberatory potentials. Rather, it is an assertion of the central importance of material sovereignty to Indigenous conceptions and expressions of self. This is a sovereignty that Australian post-Federation and post-Mabo writing has attempted to register metaphorically through what Bob Hodge and Vijay Misha have called the "Aboriginal archipelago" of visual and political exclusion alongside a ubiquitous symbolic presence (Hodge & Mishra, 1991, p. 30). However, it is rarely taken up as a material or intellectual responsibility for the postcolonial critic, and instead is deferred to supposedly non-institutional space, efforts, and individuals. Elsewhere, I have argued that the relationship between Western traditions of literature and theory is inconsistent with global discourses and practices of decolonization:

> Literature is a term we apply to the textual products of the West, or those texts that reinforce accepted narratives of the other. For those who live in a perpetually compromised position regarding the sovereignty of our ancestral homelands, for whom the West came with guns and disease, literary theory usually signifies a binary of applicability: either it is unconcerned with our material realities and processes of cultural production, or it has seized upon our creations for its tropes and metaphors. At worst, literary and poetic theory is elitist, ahistorical, esoteric and universalizing. (Araluen, 2017)

These critiques are, of course, generalizations of the multiple forms and functions that literary theory as we understand it today has adopted since its establishment in the twentieth century. These origins were influenced significantly by structuralist linguistics and the rise of the formalist New Criticism movement in the 1940s and 1950s. Introductions to literary theory emphasize the diversity and flexibility of approaches and intended outcomes in the practice of reading, framing, and questioning literature, and cite a range of historical and hermeneutical roots to such practices. Many of these theories, as Smith demonstrates in her critiques of Hegel, Freud, and several other major prophets of modern critical and literary theory, are structurally and conceptually embedded in the intellectual products of nineteenth-century imperialism, such as notions of civilization and the Other, reflecting geographic and economic forces of appropriation, expropriation, and incorporation (Smith, 1999, p. 69). Under these conditions, in which a wide range of concepts capable of influencing literary representation and interpretation can be framed, distributed, and standardized as legitimate analytical tools, literary theory is shaped by the same structures of power and exclusion that have, since 1770, provided and sustained an intellectual discourse justifying the dispossession of Aboriginal peoples. It should thus be regarded with suspicion by Aboriginal scholars.

With little interest in or strategies available to engage with Aboriginal critical knowledges – an issue observed and critiqued by Michelle Grossman and a range of Aboriginal and Torres Strait Islander writers in *Blacklines: Contemporary Critical Writing by Indigenous Australians* (2003) – literary theory in Australia has carried on largely without accountability to the political and cultural conditions that shape Aboriginal textual production. As an early career researcher, and one of a small number of Aboriginal academics working in literature in Australia, I have struggled to discover and apply any relevant literary theory to Aboriginal texts that does not erase political or cultural forms of difference. I and my colleagues aim for complex, nuanced, and evolving bodies of literary theory informed by Indigenous knowledges and principles, which may affirm Terry Eagleton's assertion that "properly understood, literary theory is shaped by a democratic impulse rather than an elitist one; and to this extent, when it *does* lapse into the turgidly unreadable, it is being untrue to its own historical roots" (Eagleton, 2008, p. viii).

The opportunity for theory to liberate, as opposed to containing meaning and interpretation, has been investigated through global discourses of Indigenous literary scholarship, particularly in the work of Chadwick Allen (*Chickasaw*), Alice Te Punga Somerville (*Te Ati Awa*), Daniel Heath Justice (*Cherokee*), and Craig Womack (*Creek-Cherokee*). Allen and Te Punga Somerville have both advocated for juxtapositional or trans-Indigenous modes of engagement with a diverse range of Indigenous texts and contexts. These thorough reconceptualizations of comparative literary practice resist the homogenizing effects of collectivizing diverse textual expressions and minority experiences, by embracing entangled and unstable relationships of Indigenous subjects to Indigenous texts. This approach emphasizes the productivity of comparative and relational reading over the closure of formal exegesis (exegesis used here in a literary theory and praxis context). Allen argues that such approaches need not sacrifice the historical and cultural specificity that can be brought to localized readings of Indigenous texts; nor do they neglect projects of recovery and interpretation with which many Indigenous literary scholars are concerned. By prioritizing an Indigenous global, Allen argues, we decentre the terms and boundaries of literature as they are framed by colonial discourses and institutions, and create space for Indigenous communities to benefit from Indigenous-led conversations around representation and narrative (Allen, 2012, pp. xiii, xv, xxi). Te Punga Somerville's work on Indigenous comparatives furthers the anti- and de-colonial goals of Allen's juxtapositional, trans-Indigenous methodology, by emphasizing Indigenous relations before and beyond mutual experiences of colonization. In *Once Were Pacific: Māori Connections to Oceania* (2012), Te Punga Somerville articulates the complexity and duality of Māori identity in relation to ancestral, oceanic, and political contexts of kinship by exploring a literary history of Māori–Pacific relations. In situating her own subjectivity and experience as a Māori scholar, this study defies a Western focus on objectivity and individualist subjectivities in comparative work, and replaces it with politics of sovereignty and relation.

Although not explicitly situating his work in the language of juxtapositional or trans-Indigenous methodologies, Justice's *Why Indigenous Literatures Matter* (2018) engages in the same practice of reading across a variety of texts to examine shared and disparate experiences of contemporary Indigenous identity. Further, his work seeks to destabilize the notion of Indigenous literatures reacting to, and in some way being determined by, colonization, as opposed to responding to colonialism in a broader context of ongoing relation to land, community, and culture (Justice, 2018, p. xix). The book is structured by four central questions to which Justice contends Indigenous literatures and the reading of those literatures can respond. How do we learn to be human? How do we behave as good relatives? How do we become good ancestors? How do we learn to live together? (Justice, 2018, p. 28). By replacing traditional notions of literary theory with questions about the role that literature plays in Indigenous responsibilities to land, community, and culture, Justice is simultaneously able to relate aesthetic and instructive values and to expand what is considered readable in Indigenous contexts.

Like Allen, Te Punga Somerville, and Justice, Womack's *Red on Red: Native American Literary Separatism* (1999) emphasizes the multiple ontologies that constitute Native identity in Womack's own *Muskogee Creek* and *Cherokee* context; a multiplicity he carries through to argue against the notion of there being fixed, "authoritative" acts of Native literary criticism. His argument for "Native literary separatism" is a push for Native sovereignty to be recognized in literary domains, and is concerned with the benefit literary discourse can give to Native communities when it is led by Native knowledge and principles. He writes:

> I wish to suggest that literature has something to add to the arena of Native political struggle. The attempt, then, will be to break down oppositions between the world of literature and the very real struggles of American Indian communities, arguing for both an intrinsic and extrinsic relationship between the two. I will seek a literary criticism that emphasizes Native resistance movements against colonialism, confronts racism, discusses sovereignty and Native nationalism, seeks connections between literature and liberation struggles, and, finally, roots literature in land and culture. This criticism emphasizes unique Native worldviews and political realities, searches for differences as often as similarities, and attempts to find Native literature's place in Indian country, rather than Native literature's place in the canon. (Womack, 1999, p. 11)

In a criticism such as this, Womack argues, Native people can discuss the conditions and implications of aesthetics, mimesis, and evocation as they are relevant in their specific tribal contexts, without answering to Western assumptions of the primitive or the supernatural (Womack, 1999, pp. 16–17). Published almost two decades ago, the Creek-centred methodologies and readings of *Red on Red* have been highly influential in global discourses of Indigenous literary studies, providing a model for the politicization of Indigenous texts without deferring to the colonial comparatives of representation to which Allen, Te Punga Somerville, and Justice each refer. Essential to each of these approaches to the forms, functions, and possibilities of Indigenous literatures is the centring of Indigenous sovereignty in the writing, distribution, and reading of Indigenous texts. By locating Indigenous presence within, around, and in the imagination of the text and its possibilities – a practice not required by postcolonial discourse – Indigenous literary methodologies articulate their own demands from literature and the dialogues that surround it.

This is not to suggest that Allen, Te Punga Somerville, Justice, and Womack exclude all forms of non-Indigenous critical and literary theory. Although, as Womack observes, the recovery and construction of Indigenous history and narrative is a more pressing concern than the deconstruction (and therefore recirculation) of non-Indigenous representations and reading practices, many Indigenous scholars engage directly with theorists such as Jacques Derrida and Erich Auerbach to examine the structures and discourses of power in which these histories and narratives have been presented. Even without explicitly identifying with the paradigms of Indigeneity being employed here, these theorists themselves have often been subject to conflicting politics of identity and nationhood, including racial or cultural exclusion from the state's sovereignty. Therefore they can provide valuable counter-hegemonic strategies, or languages of anti- and de-coloniality. The value of this work emerges from its understanding and experience of imperial power, and the forces of dispossession and displacement shared across communities whose sovereignty has been compromised by the state in structures of what *Unangax* scholar Eve Tuck and K Wayne Yang refer to as external and internal colonialism (Tuck & Yang, 2012, pp. 4–5). Attempts have been made by Indigenous and non-Indigenous academics alike to apply theories from these racialized and postcolonial contexts to Aboriginality in Australia, with varying success.

Before arriving at conclusions regarding the use and value of literary theory in its various forms, we must first ask where, and to what ends, theory is used and is of use in the context of Aboriginal literature in Australia. Stephen Muecke, Paddy Roe, and Krim Bentarrak's collaborative project *Reading the Country: Introduction to Nomadology* (1984), is perhaps the earliest, and remains one of the most explicit, attempts to curate Aboriginal presence and voice through literary and cultural theory. This text, which includes song, poetry, interviews, paintings, and vast sections of theoretical framing and philosophizing, departs from the anthropological structures that had previously laid claim over the distribution of Aboriginal song. Instead the book presents an entirely new paradigm of disciplinary containment through the various intellectual and poetic exercises employed primarily by Muecke to translate his encounters with *Goolarabooloo* Elder Roe into a textual and archival object. Muecke not only reads Roe's songpoems, he reads Roe's otherness, and from this he presents a theory of "nomadology," adapted from French philosophers Gilles Deleuze and Félix Guattari. Even when this notion of nomadology – meaning both a sense of movement and placedness – is rejected by Roe, Muecke is reluctant to give up the term and the structuring possibilities it entails (Bentarrak, Muecke & Roe, 1984, p. 213). Seven years later in 1991, Hodge and Mishra's framework of "Aboriginalism" is similarly occupied by notions of otherness, and is a similarly poor model for the potential relationship between theory and representation in the reading of Aboriginal texts. "Aboriginalism" co-opts the language and colonial positionalities of Orientalism to insert Indigenous experience into Said's analytical model, replacing terms such as "the Orient" and "the Orientalist" with "Aboriginality" and "the Aboriginalist." Although the intent and application of this project is noble enough, its attempt to configure Settler subjectivity as what Said refers to as the "interpreter, exhibitor, personality, mediator, representative (and representing) expert" through the appropriation of a discourse inextricably bound to the struggle for political and human rights for dispossessed Palestinians still fails to advance any decolonial strategies with which to address the particular concerns and realities of Aboriginal experience (Said, 1978, p. 284). More to the point of this discussion, it is not the object of Orientalism, nor its neologized cousin Aboriginalism, to frame the various ways in which Aboriginal people represent themselves textually. Although projects such as *Eualeyai/Kamillaroi* lawyer and academic Larissa Behrendt's *Finding Eliza: Power and Colonial Storytelling* (2016) and Liz Conor's *Skin Deep: Settler Impressions of Aboriginal Women* (2016), which analyse, deconstruct, and demythologize Settler representations of Indigenous Peoples as the colonized Other, make use of the anti- and de-colonial languages of Said's work, these resistances are more importantly narrative *recoveries* of Aboriginal presence and agency. Deconstructive texts such as these attempt to resist further perpetuating epistemological and ontological models that hold colonizing powers at their centre, by pushing imperialism to the periphery of Aboriginal experience and representation. Jonathan Dunk's "Reading the Tracker: The Antinomies of Aboriginal Ventriloquism" (2017) demonstrates the value of literary and critical theory in the deconstruction and destruction of colonial imaginings of Aboriginality. However, it ultimately concludes that Western theory cannot, and indeed should not, claim authority over Aboriginal knowledges. In reading the heavily curated document disseminated by the *Sydney Morning Herald* in 1849 as "The Statement of Jackey Jackey" for the epistemological crisis of colonial subjectivity which forecloses all autonomous presence of *Galmarra*, the *Wonnarua* tracker whose testimony of Edmund Kennedy's 1848 Cape York expedition was widely circulated after it ended in Kennedy's death, Dunk performs what he argues is the only possible benefit of theory in relation to Settler representation of Aboriginal subjectivity and experience – the breaking apart of Settler strategies of sublimating Aboriginal presence into Western terms of reference and control. This approach differs from the more conventional forms of historicism usually framing Aboriginal presence in the colonial archive, which rely on positivist assumptions that a scholar can access some sort of empirical truth outside of subjectivity or standpoint in such texts. Where historicism would claim to "know" something of *Galmarra* through his curated account, deconstruction is more concerned with the various strategies of silencing and concealment that distance *Galmarra* from his textual representation. The goal of such deconstruction, Dunk argues, is the "honest light" of a critical scholarship working to dismantle its own assumptions and structures, opening space for Aboriginal readers and writers to establish new representations and terms of engagement, conceding that "without an equable form of epistemological compromise or treaty – such as that underwriting other forms of comparative literary study – this is all the tools of settler scholarship provide for" (Dunk, 2017, p. 10). Behrendt, Conor, and Dunk each use the possibilities and limitations of deconstructive theory to recover Aboriginal presence from Settler representations, even if in freeing that presence from the assumption of the text's claim to know, there are other forms of loss.

Having clarified some relevant concerns regarding the relationship between Aboriginal literature and the disciplinary structures in which it is coded, I wish now to discuss the possibilities offered by storywork to Indigenous literary studies in Australia. As recent scholarship surrounding the term has suggested, storywork generally refers to the development and application of Indigenous story for educational purposes, but can be structured around localized and culturally specific protocols for a range of projects and outcomes. The model presented by *Stó:lō* scholar Jo-Ann Archibald Q'um Q'um Xiiem across a range of projects and publications, developed through collaboration and narrative dialogue with her own *Stó:lō* community, perhaps best encapsulates the various forms of engagement that structure storywork:

> Special connections to the land – to "Mother Earth" – help in strengthening our cultural identities. It is important to recognize the spiritual power of particular places and the healing nature (physical and emotional) of the environment. I also learned to appreciate how stories engage us as listeners and learners to think deeply and to reflect on our actions and reactions ... I call this pedagogy *storywork* because the engagement of story, storyteller, and listener created a synergy for making meaning through the story and making one *work* to obtain meaning and understanding. (Archibald, 2001, p. 1)

Eve Tuck and Marcia McKenzie in *Place in Research: Theory, Methodology and Methods* (2014) employ Archibald's development and application of Indigenous storywork methodologies in mapping and place-making exercises, arguing that the immersive and culturally situated values of this configuration make possible the use of Indigenous protocols and principles in research, such as Verna Kirkness and Ray Barnhardt's "Four 'R's" of First Nations and higher education: respect, responsibility, reciprocity, and relationality (Tuck & McKenzie, 2014, p. 131).

Quandamoopah academic Karin L. Martin's doctoral thesis *Please Knock before You Enter: Aboriginal Regulation of Outsiders and the Implications for Researchers* (2008) centralizes a similar model of storywork to guide both her recommendations for outsiders seeking to research her *Noonuccal* community, and her own process developing these protocols. For Martin, storywork is a meta-process of relatedness and immersion, allowing for a range of narratives and teachings to be woven into "the overall research ceremony" (Martin, 2008, p. 21). In this incredibly nuanced study, Martin works with multiple forms, expressions, and treatments of story to develop her research, the most notable of which is the *Quampie* Story and *Quampie* Methodology – a structuring device using the cultural and environmental story of the *quampie* or mud oyster to explore a system of research methods and a framework addressing the challenges faced by Indigenous researchers (Martin, 2008, p. 91).

As Martin's research demonstrates, storywork seeks authority and guidance from ancestors, Elders, land, cultural practices, and protocols. Storywork defies the Cartesian assumptions inherent to conventional Western scholarship, which privilege the idea of the intellectual over the material and spiritual aspects of human and non-human bodies. Storywork draws attention to the reality of capital and the various economies of physical and intellectual labour that govern Indigenous representation and self-presentation. Where theory is useful in certain practices of recovery, as evidenced by the deconstructive work of Behrendt, Conor, and Dunk, the interpretive project of Indigenous literary studies is one that can more appropriately be addressed by the constructive practices of storywork methods. This is not to propose that literary theory and storywork are separate or opposed. In fact, I mean to suggest that we should situate literary theory as a tool of a broader storywork practice, as opposed to storywork being a subset or specific methodology of literary theory. We have seen in the work of Allen, Te Punga Somerville, Justice and Womack that personal and community narratives and positionalities have a central role in the work of Indigenous literary scholars, contextualizing and conceptualizing methods and applications in projects of both recovery and interpretation. In "The Lingering War Captain: Māori Texts, Indigenous Contexts" (2007), Te Punga Somerville uses contemporary Indigenous story to discover spaces of trans-Indigenous solidarity in her reading of Leslie Marmon Silko's *Almanac of the Dead* (1991). The novel's suggestion of the museum as a point of mutual understanding and experience for Indigenous Peoples – an archive of stolen stories and artefacts – offers for Te Punga Somerville a powerful metaphor with which to apprehend and explore ways of reinhabiting colonial space with the object of Indigenous connection. While this reconceptualization does not erase the processes of theft, dispossession, and dehumanization inherent to the museum as an agent of the imperial project, it reinscribes an agency to Indigenous presence within the archive, which has been of great interest to Aboriginal scholars.

Natalie Harkin's work on decoloniality and the archive is perhaps a liminal force in the twin projects of recovery and interpretation, which Allen argues structure much of contemporary Indigenous literary studies. In "The Poetics of (Re) Mapping Archives: Memory in the Blood" (2014), Harkin employs a deconstructive approach in her negotiation of the state's archival records of her family, thematically unifying her theoretical parameters around notions of history and embodiment, blood memory, and archive fever. In presenting her own "critical Aboriginal-sovereign-woman's voice," Harkin positions her-self as both haunting and being haunted by legacies of the archive, demonstrating how theory can be mobilized to disrupt and intervene in Settler inscriptions of Aboriginal presence under broader projects of storywork (Harkin, 2014, p. 3). The "remapping" of this project expands both the narrative and the genealogy of her grandmother's archival records:

> I am in and of the archive, I am my grandmother's granddaughter, her trace is (literally) in my blood, my flesh, my bones, my spirit. But her trace is also written. It is on record. It is a record of many sorts and speaks in multiple ways. I am in the company of others who labour creatively as visual artists, poets, writers, intellectuals, and who labour creatively in the everyday-mundane. We are haunted and we haunt. We write to create, to survive, and to revolutionise; we write to haunt and we ache because we refuse to leave the past alone. (Harkin, 2014, p. 10)

This emphasis on spectropoetics explores and expands the story the archive claims to tell, and gives agency to Aboriginal presence and memory in recovery and interpretation work that goes beyond the act of simply "reading." Harkin extended this work in a 2014 exhibition *Bound and Unbound: Sovereign Acts – Act 1* as part of the *TARNANTHI* Festival of Contemporary Aboriginal and Torres Strait Islander Art by weaving her archival records and her own poetic commentary into baskets. Through cultural practice Harkin works both the inscribed narratives of her colonial otherness and her poetic articulation of her "critical Aboriginal-sovereign-woman's voice" to transform the archive into a material cultural object, recovering far more than simply the redactions of the colonial record. This literal storywork is a far more radical form of historicism than theory alone can provide.

We see from Harkin's practice that storywork more than enables a recovery project; it radically reinhabits the spaces and histories from which these stories are being recovered. Storywork, as Archibald sug-gests, emphasizes the entanglement of story, storyteller, and listener to obtain meaning and understanding. It provides a structure that holds extensive potential for projects of Aboriginal literary interpreta-tion in Australia, although there have been very few projects enacted by the very few Aboriginal literary scholars to fully explore this potential, and there are no clear terms outlining how an Aboriginal literary storywork could improve upon interpretive and pedagogical approaches structured through conventional literary theory. Arrente artist and writer Jennifer Kemarre Martiniello, in her essay discussing the voids and voices of Aboriginal story, uses personal family narratives to circumvent cultural deficit narratives of land and language loss, and reflexively negotiates both the discursive and ontological triangulation of story, body, and dreaming in which she is situated, or rather, inscribed: "I am bark engraved by the continuous cartography of my peoples, their histories – I am Dream. The unsilenced. The ink that runs from the tongues of languages to their inscriptions in print, paper, minds" (Martiniello, 2002, pp. 94–95). It is a beautifully rich entanglement of time and presence, which explores the continuous occupation of spirit and ancestor in all forms and distributions of Aboriginal story, cyclically offering story and questioning its discursive and performative framing:

> In the beginning before everything was made the earth was soft. Fluid. Formless. The Ancestors moved across the land, inscribing the tracks of their journeys in the hills and plains, the mountains, deserts, forests, lakes, the creeks and rivers that they created. When their work was done and they had given the cosmos form and life, they sent their spirits into the rocks, the trees, the waters, the earth herself, the sun and moon and Milky Way. These places are spirit, sacred life, source, being. They are creation and continuum, they are story without end, the earth their living library. Tjukurrpa … Do I speak in italics? Parentheses? To an audience? Or to a black floating space that hovers on its own insubstantiality, an ephemeral gauze spun by a line of mega-lights. The ground of the storyteller is defined by its ambiguity, its resistance to nails, fixation, incarceration by space-time isobars. By the imposition of alien topographic description. Erasure. (Martiniello, 2002, p. 94)

Throughout my work I have argued for Martiniello's use of inscription and her spiritually embodied language of place and narrative as a way of reconceptualizing the boundaries of Aboriginal literature away from Western formal parameters. Here, her articulation of temporality as continuous and multiple is equally pertinent. *Waanyi* author Alexis Wright has written of this interplay of Aboriginal story and temporality, which corroborates Martiniello's world-expanding storywork:

> All times are important to us. No time has ended and all worlds are possible … The world I try to inhabit in my writing is like looking at

the ancestral tracks spanning our traditional country which, if I look at the land, combines all stories, all realities, from the ancient to the new, and it makes ones – like all the strands in a long rope. Our stories are like the music which feeds the soul and the heart, which sometimes flies above the bitterness of pure logic and rational thought. (Wright, 2002, p. 3)

Essays such as Martiniello's and Wright's, which both appeared in *Southerly* journal's 2002 special issue on Aboriginal literature, highlight the unnecessary difficulty in distinguishing between Aboriginal texts that instruct and offer interpretive textual methodologies, and the texts to which those methodologies are to be applied. A strong, poetic articulation of Aboriginal story and temporality can only benefit discourse surrounding Aboriginal literatures. Combined with more direct forms of contextualizing and politicizing the conditions and distributions of Aboriginal representation, these essays present a nuanced and generative potential for such discourse and its pedagogical application.

While not explicitly engaging with the language of storywork, *Wiradjuri* writer and academic Jeanine Leane uses situational, relational, and cultural contexts as a basis for teaching Aboriginal literatures, adapting Bronislaw Malinowski's "context of situation" and "context of culture" to illustrate the relationship between cultural context and cultural representation for students (Leane, 2017, p. 244). Her application of these principles to Archie Weller's *Confessions of a Headhunter* (2009) examines the ways in which Aboriginal culture responds to sociohistorical time and space but continues to centre practices of story sharing and familial gathering, resisting the deficit-charged assumptions of cultural inauthenticity which emerge from less historically and culturally informed readings (Leane, 2017, p. 245). This is not to suggest that the primary function of Aboriginal literature or the teaching of Aboriginal literature is to didactically represent Aboriginal culture, history, and identity for the benefit of a Settler readership. However, Leane is clear in her argument that cultural ignorance restrains the possibility of ethical and generative engagement with Aboriginal literatures and self-presentations, and that the consequences of this ignorance are primarily felt by Aboriginal people (Leane, 2017, pp. 242–244).

Central to this discussion has been the use of storywork as a way of acknowledging and linking various projects that have already been undertaken by Aboriginal scholars to better understand and teach

Aboriginal literatures, but have defied classification under conventional disciplinary and theoretical organizations. The object of Indigenous literary studies is not simply to unsettle colonial literary practices and assumptions, but rather to produce constructive and generative sites of inquiry and interrogation, which can accommodate and encourage new stories, and new ways of understanding and engaging with these stories. Among the many geographically and culturally localized strategies employed by Indigenous literary scholars around the world, storywork is perhaps the most nebulous, but also the most amenable to ethical and culturally guided projects of recovery and interpretation. Storywork appropriately draws attention to the economy of literary representation, reminding us that there is extensive intellectual and cultural labour required of both Aboriginal and non-Aboriginal scholars alike to deconstruct and create space for these more generative discourses and practices. Although storywork's parameters need further development in relation to Indigenous literary studies in Australia, the language and principles of storywork theory and practice provide dynamic and culturally adaptive frameworks with which to progress these studies, and empower communities to guide the terms with which their literatures should be approached. Along with the deconstructions and reconceptualizations of literary practice demonstrated by the recovery and interpretation projects of Indigenous literary scholars Chadwick Allen, Alice Te Punga Somerville, Daniel Heath Justice, and Craig Womack, Aboriginal literary scholars in Australia are increasingly well-equipped to confront the totalizing and erasive strategies of conventional literary theory, and move from voicelessness to representational autonomy in our political, pedagogical, cultural, spiritual, and social treatment of Aboriginal literatures.

References

Allen, C. (2002). *Blood narrative: Indigenous identity in American Indian and Māori literary and activist texts.* Durham, NC: Duke University Press.

Allen, C. (2012). *Trans-Indigenous: methodologies for global Native literary studies.* Minneapolis, MN: University of Minnesota Press.

Araluen, E. (2017). Resisting the institution. *Overland Literary Journal,* 227. Retrieved from https://overland.org.au/previous-issues/issue-227/feature-evelyn-araluen/.

Archibald, J. (2001). Editorial: sharing Aboriginal knowledge and Aboriginal ways of knowing. *Canadian Journal of Native Education* 25(1), 1–5.

Behrendt, L. (2016). *Finding Eliza: power and colonial storytelling.* Brisbane, QLD: University of Queensland Press.

Bentarrak, K., Muecke, S. & Roe, P. (1984). *Reading the country:*

introduction to nomadology. Freemantle, Western Australia: Freemantle Arts Centre Press.

Conor, L. (2016). *Skin deep: Settler impressions of Aboriginal women*. Perth, Western Australia: University of Western Australia Publishing.

de Man, P. (1982). The resistance to theory. *Yale French Studies 63*, 3–20.

Dunk, J. (2017). Reading the tracker: the antinomies of Aboriginal ventriloquism. *JASAL: Journal of the Association for the Study of Australian Literature 17*(1), 1–12.

Eagleton, T. (2008). *Literary theory: an introduction*. (2nd revised ed., anniversary ed.). London, UK: Blackwell.

Grossman, M. (Ed.). (2001). *Blacklines: contemporary critical writing by Indigenous Australians*. Melbourne, VIC: Melbourne University Publishing.

Harkin, N. (2014). The poetics of (re) mapping archives: memory in the blood. *JASAL: Journal of the Association for the Study of Australian Literature 14*(3), 1–14.

Hodge B. & Mishra V. (1991). *Dark side of the dream: Australian literature and the postcolonial mind*. Sydney, NSW: Allen & Unwin.

Justice, D. H. (2018) *Why Indigenous literatures matter*. Waterloo, ON: Wilfred Laurier University Press.

Leane, J. (2017). Aboriginal literature in the classroom. In N. Birns, N. Moore & S. Shieff (Eds.), *Teaching Australian and New Zealand literature* (pp. 237–246). New York: The Modern Language Association of America.

Martin, K. L. (2008). *Please knock before you enter: Aboriginal regulation of outsiders and the implications for*

researchers. Teneriffe, QLD: Post Pressed.

Martiniello, J. (2002). Voids, voices and story without end. *Southerly 62*(2), 91–93.

Said, E. (1978). *Orientalism*. New York: Pantheon.

Silko, L. (1991). *Almanac of the dead*. New York: Simon & Schuster.

Smith, L. T. (1999). *Decolonizing methodologies: research and Indigenous Peoples*. London: Zed Books.

Te Punga Somerville, A. (2007). The lingering war captain: Maori texts, Indigenous contexts. *Journal of New Zealand Literature 24*(2), 20–43.

Te Punga Somerville, A. (2012). *Once were Pacific: Māori connections to Oceania*. Minneapolis, MN: University of Minnesota Press.

Tuck, E. & McKenzie, M. (2014). *Place in research: theory, methodology, and methods*. New York: Routledge.

Tuck, E. & Ree, C. (2013). A glossary of haunting. In S. Holman Jones, T. E. Adams & C. Ellis (Eds.), *Handbook of autoethnography* (pp. 639–658). Walnut Creek, CA: Left Coast Press.

Tuck, E. & Yang, K. W. (2012). Decolonisation is not a metaphor. *Decolonization: Indigeneity, Education & Society 1*(1), 1–40.

Weller, A. (2009). Confessions of a headhunter. In *The window seat and other stories* (pp. 220–240). St Lucia, QLD: University of Queensland Press.

Womack, C. (1999). *Red on red: Native American literary separatism*. Minneapolis, MN: University of Minnesota Press.

Wright, A. (2002). Politics of writing. *Southerly 62*(2), 10–20.

12 | LILYOLOGY AS A TRANSFORMATIVE FRAMEWORK FOR DECOLONIZING ETHICAL SPACES WITHIN THE ACADEMY

Nerida Blair

Introduction

My sense of belonging, connectedness, and relatedness to Country are diverse and shifting, being an Aboriginal woman born in *Wurundjeri* Country, now living in and connecting to *Darkinjung* Country New South Wales, with father and grandmother connecting to *Wakka Wakka* Country in Queensland. Lilyology as a decolonizing framework was birthed from this context and reflects a re-imaged concept of the waterlily. Lilyology metaphorically engages waterlilys,[1] sweet potatoes, spiders, and brick walls, creating a space to reflect on and privilege Indigenous Knowings in the academic context. Lilyology, grounded in Country, reflects the organic and dynamic space that is Indigenous Knowings, the cyclic and holistic patterning of life. It presents a storytelling practice for strategic interventions into operational spaces within academia, which in the model of Lilyology is storyed as a brick wall.

This chapter specifically explores Lilyology as a transformative framework and storytelling practice to decolonize critical ethical spaces for research within academia. This chapter is storyed in the first person, as it engages personal reflections on Lilyology within a Human Research Ethics Committee (HREC) at an academic institution in Australia. These reflections include a specific investigation into the expanding impact of a storyed Acknowledgement of Country within this space and the critical role of an established Indigenous Research Ethics Committee.

Storying: an Acknowledgement of Country

Imagine Sydney Harbour in Australia, 300 years ago, 5,000 years ago. Imagine Cammeraygal and Gadigal mobs. Canoes sailing up and down the harbour. Water colour, reflecting the sky above. Waves moving to calm, still water. Highways of canoes. Small fires lie lit in these canoes; warming, feeding and lighting the way for Gadigal and Cammeraygal mobs. Canoes made by the men, used by the women.

It's August, after the spring rains, and the stringy bark trees are wet, rich with sap and ready for the bark to be stripped off the right trees. The bark is stripped then fired, hardened and fashioned again, concertina-ing until the ends meet. This bark is then fired to harden and season it. Resins from Xanthorrhoea trees are spread over the bark, fashioning the canoes and protecting the bark as it becomes leathery and waterproof.

Imagine canoe traffic in Sydney Harbour 250 years ago, 5,000 years ago: canoes carrying people, fish and light; sustenance, warmth and community. Much like we will be doing today in this Human Research Ethics Committee meeting. We will transport ideas, share new ideas, nourish our souls and light our way as well as that of the researchers who have submitted research applications for us to review.

All of this is guided by the wisdom of those before us, by Country[2] and place. A mix of voices and experiences – the older and the newer, swirling, encased in canoes that exist to transport new ideas and practice to move research practice to higher … no, to more balanced and honest ground; one that encompasses history, that reflects our diversity, celebrating co-existence.

Who would know that this story was the beginning of an HREC meeting at a university in Australia? An Acknowledgement of Country (AoC) always opens the monthly HREC meeting, setting the tone, embracing a story that informs the work done by the Committee. Every member of the Committee is open to creating their own AoC: researching and engaging with their personal connections and relatedness to Country and sharing this with others on the Committee – connecting many diverse elements. The impact of such storying cannot be understated. The storying in this context showcases Lilyology as a transformative framework, decolonizing and crafting a sense of belonging not only to the Country the HREC meets on but belonging to a community of scholars engaging in a practice that is required of such a Committee by law and through policy. A reciprocity is tangibly engaged with.

This chapter specifically explores Lilyology as a transformative framework and storytelling practice to decolonize critical ethical spaces for academic research. This chapter is storyed in the first person, as it engages personal reflections on Lilyology within an HREC at an academic institution in Australia. These reflections include a specific investigation into the expanding impact of a storyed AoC in this space and the critical role of an established Indigenous Human Research Ethics Committee (IREAP).

This chapter will at times ask you, as a reader, to create an image where no images can be provided. I invite you to story using your own imagination, experiences, and contexts. The chapter begins with an understanding of Lilyology; a showcasing of Indigenous Knowings, Western Knowledge, and the space in-between. Lilyology embodies relatedness, connectedness, and a sense of belonging that embraces a co-becoming with Country. The chapter then connects Lilyology to storying, storywork, and the story research process. With an understanding of these concepts and connections the chapter moves into something more embodying of practice, taking a look at how Lilyology has informed and transformed some of the work of an HREC at a university. An AoC as a process at the beginning of HREC meetings, emerging from the space in-between as conceptualized in Lilyology, led to the establishment of an IREAP. The chapter concludes with some reflections.

Lilyology

Lilyology is metaphor and a personal philosophy I created to explore, inform, and permeate my personal understanding of Indigenous Knowings.[3] Lilyology evolved as a means to "proceed through a colonizing world" (Smith, 2012), to "decolonize my mind" (Smith, 2012) in an effort to transform my own and to facilitate others' appreciation of Indigenous Knowings. Lilyology offers a language and process of possibility, a re-imagining and re-articulation of Indigenous Knowings. This chapter storys[4] this philosophy so that you, the reader, have the context for understanding how Lilyology operates beyond where it is cited and commented on but not engaged with, not lived with. It will story how Lilyology has impacted and helped, in a small but effectual way, to transform the practice of a group of diverse people in a university ethics committee to assess research applications across all disciplines.

Lilyology emerged out of the mists of frustration, confusion, and lack of a sense of belonging and relatedness to the academic institutions I worked within. As an Aboriginal woman without knowledge of my traditional language and therefore some of my cultural underlay, I sought a way to understand my own thinking; the disparity between the way I thought and the way I knew the world I lived in. Known to often walk the corridors of a government building (physically and metaphorically) with Texta pens and pulling a whiteboard behind me, known to ask questions no-one else could really connect to, I sought ways to clarify, to make sense of my knowings of the world I functioned in … but the corridors were narrow and tricky to navigate.

Lilyology also emerged from my exploration of Buzan's mind mapping (Buzan, 1997) and time spent and lived in Countrys associated with my PhD research, yarning and storying about what the concept of "research" meant to some Indigenous people. My research colleagues from *Anmatyerre* Country reflected and storyed their understanding of this concept presented as an image. Let me explain this without being able to present the final mage here, other than the one you as a reader are able to conjure.

Imagine being out in desert Country, *Anmatyerre* Country in the Northern Territory, Australia. We are in rich, red dirt, surrounded, though not visibly, by deep but sparse and life-giving water holes, grey green shrubs bearing witchetty grubs deep within the roots, brown snakes and goanna leaving tracks as they move across Country, bright sun bearing down, with lightning in the distance making sounds that awaken and speak to all. It is in this context that my research colleagues[5] and I yarned about and pondered the concept of research in the *Anmatyerra* language.

One morning, some weeks after I had arrived in *Anmatyerre* Country, looking out the window I saw my research colleagues with paints and brushes in hand. The sound of the gate latch being opened indicated something was about to happen. It was time to image an *Anmatyerre* understanding of the word "research." My sister, through the *Anmatyerre* way, whose home I was staying in, went to the cupboard and got a white sheet from it. She laid it over the round dining table. My research colleagues gathered around the table and began their storying of the *Anmatyerre* understanding of "research."

People's hands were covered in paint; the colour dependent on the individual's kinship connection. They laid their painted hands on the cloth and the edge of the table, forming a circle. People's personal totems were drawn a layer in toward the centre and in front of their hand prints. Yellow, green, and grey hand prints connected green bean, brown snake, and dingo paws. Another layer in, we see Countrys people come from: circles within circles. We move further in toward the centre as circles within circles surrounded by half circles are painted: people having come together and sitting down as one, connected, related, yarning, storying the concept "research."

As we switch from our imagination to this storyed text, what emerges from my research colleagues is the concept of research being identified and imaged as people coming together, sitting down, and yarning: people connecting and establishing relatedness and belonging with Country "not as a passive backdrop for human existence" (Bawaka Country et al., 2015, p. 270) and interaction. And not as a passive backdrop to conduct research in. In *Anmatyerre* language my research colleagues agreed that the term "*nyinderrim Inkytuk*" explained the concept "research." This is an important point of difference and one with many layers, though seemingly put very simply. This understanding was a seed which lay dormant in my psyche, my spirit, waiting for moments to play with it in Lilyology's in-between space. The HREC provided such moments.

Returning now to Lilyology we see that it metaphorically images the space in-between, the corridor between Western Knowledge and Indigenous Knowings. Lilyology is the language I chose to represent my understanding of Indigenous Knowings, as well as a model to operate in; one that privileges my sense of Aboriginal Knowings through my connection to Country.

Aboriginal and Torres Strait Islander peoples lived with, co-becoming with Country, for many thousands of years prior to colonization in the 1770s. There were over 500 diverse Aboriginal and Torres Strait Islander Nations[6] and these many clans all had a place and space within the multidimensional world. All were interconnected as active participants in these worlds, these Countrys.[7] Some words from Bawaka et al. (2015) capture this context from *Yolnu* Country ... but we can feel the essence in other Countrys:

> Within a Yolŋu Indigenous ontology, animals, rocks, winds, tides, emotions, spirits, songs and humans speak. They all have language and knowledge and Law. They all send messages; communicate with each other. Country is the Aboriginal English word which encompasses this vibrant and sentient understanding of space/place which becomes bounded through its interconnectivity. Country and everything it encompasses is an active participant in the world, shaping and creating it. It is far from a passive backdrop to human experience, a scene in which humans live their lives, a place in which to embed academics' research. (Bawaka Country et al., 2015 p. 270)

The concept of co-becoming with Country is central to Lilyology and has been best articulated by Martin (2003) and Bawaka et al. (2015) as an intimate relatedness and connectedness between human and non-human entities. Martin (2003, p. 213) states:

> Methods such as storying and exchanging talk are most often used amongst People but methods for interacting with other Entities (e.g. Animals, Weather, Skies) are equally necessary. This requires fieldwork that immerses the researcher in the contexts of the Entities and to watch, listen, wait, learn and repeat these processes as methods for data collection.

Bawaka et al. (2015, p. 277) state:

> All of us, all Country, have a deep responsibility to each other. We have deep ties. We are created together and we live that creation together yesterday, today, tomorrow. We are all part of the Law, we are bound together by the Law and as that Law continues, the stories and the songs and our communication continue.

Co-becoming with Country storys diverse communication and multiple languages, all intertwined into a tapestry of the cycle of life and death, of being in this world.

Lilyology images waterlilys, sweet potatoes, spiders, and brick walls. Lilyology exists with three major elements all storyed within their own frames of reference … but all are interwoven and interconnected. Each and all of the images embody Archibald's storywork elements (Archibald, 2008, p. ix). Respect for Indigenous Knowings is foundational, as is reverence through the privileging of Indigenous Knowings at a deep level of understanding. Holism, synergy, and interrelatedness are showcased in Lilyology as each and all of the elements function and interact, impacting on each other and impacting holistically. Lilyology embeds the concept of co-becoming with Country. All elements, human and non-human entities, speak to each other, are connected and share a belonging. At this point I invite you again to use your imagination to explain, to story this without an image, other than the one you as a reader are able to conjure.

Imagine a drawing of a flat square, a frame with different images inside it: a waterlily, a brick wall, an icon symbolizing a bush potato and an image of lightning. A waterlily is sitting in a freshwater pond, or lake. It doesn't matter what colour the petals are but they are open, with a yellow stamen rising from the centre of the flower holding the petals together. The stem from the flower goes down to some flat, green, broad leaves, which float on top of the water. Below we can't see but we know there is a bulb with rhizomes connecting and weaving their way through the water to other lilys, to other entities within this space, and skimming the top of the water. The waterlily sits inside the square, the frame diagonally across from the image of a brick wall. Now imagine a wall made of bricks: bricks staggered by a half course above and below in a one over two pattern, a running bond I believe it is called. Bricks laid lengthwise one after the other and one on top of the other. Each brick is named using a philosophy or methodology: rhizomatics, feminism, critical race theory – academic frames of reference. In between there are two iconographic images, representing strikes of lightning and a bush potato. The bush potato is represented by circles within circles, which form the centre of the image, with single leaves radiating out, tapering from the centre. Finally, imagine a beautiful, translucent spider web overlaying and connecting all of the images in the large square.

Seeing and feeling this connection of images, let's come to an understanding of what Lilyology is. Lilyology is grounded in Country; water and soil Country, through rhizomes that explore, delving deep in a subterranean world, further exploring where the light transits from dark to bright along the surface of the water. The rhizomes are rich sources of carbohydrates providing and storing energy for future growth, nourishing future growth. When you look closer and attend deeply you will notice new roots that cascade from the rhizomes in web-like arrangements and complexities. Rhizomes metaphorically represent Spirit Knowings embedded in different Countrys; the different waterways that waterlilys exist within. The rhizomes hold the Spirit Knowings, the nutrients (Blair, 2015b, p. 194).

Emerging from the Spirit Knowings, the rhizomes, is the strong and slender stem of the waterlily – the height and width dependent on the Country one is embedded within. The waterlily floats upon wide, flat leaves, which in this story represent the many voices that are Indigenous Knowings: human, spirit, emotion, skies, and animal. In order to hear these voices we must travel up the waterlily stem to find the fruit pod which houses the seeds. These seeds become the flowers, which represent storying[8] through the many different genres; there are many different waterlily flowers; as many different colours, shapes, and textures as there are genres to story our Knowings. These flowers have petals, which are not homogenous and which overlap with each other in a spiral arrangement like the many layers to our storying, the bundle of possibilities storyed. The petals are what are most visible; the different expressions of Indigenous Knowings. The petals, held together by the stigma with stamens pollenating and reproducing through interaction with bees, insects, and others, make visible the different expressions of Indigenous Knowings. Here, life is regenerated, stories are reinvigorated and revived, and possibilities are bundled. Every element of the waterlily is connected and dependent on every other for growth and sustenance, for generation. Every element is connected to Country in its broadest sense: the ecological environment, comprising water, land, soil, air, sun, light, dark, atmosphere … If we all stop in our imaging and listen, we can almost hear the different languages being spoken by all of these elements to each other. We can feel the communication being expressed by all to see the outcome in the form of the waterlily flower. The principles of storywork are operating through each and all of the elements.

There are other characters that have a major role to play in Lilyology; sweet potatoes and spiders, for example, which further the connectedness and dependency through many diverse elements. Spiders, which weave fine, strong, transparent webs, connect across the spaces in-between to allow life's vibrations to be felt from one end to the other. Spiders' survival is dependent on knowing how the different vibrations feel. These webs pattern and connect, showcasing a further element of co-becoming with Country/s.

Sweet potatoes in this story are imaged through the rhizomes that pattern and connect Spirit Knowings both above and below the water line. Sweet potatoes represent Spirit Knowings grounded in water Country, radiating out from a central nourishing core; one that sustains, energizes, and provides the nourishment necessary for growth.

Lilyology storyed, showcases a second element – that of the brick wall. The brick wall represents academia, Western Knowledges. Imagine a brick wall with layers of bricks one upon the other, in rows connected and held together by cement or some other substance. The bricks in the wall are often made from clay that comes from the earth and often comprises a blend of different pigments – Western philosophies, disciplines. The bricks are laid in lines, existing as separate units, compartments, disciplines of knowledge. The boundaries between disciplines in The Academy are in some minds blurred by what we as academics refer to as inter-disciplinarity or multi-disciplinarity. In reality the boundaries are more pronounced. The bricks are laid on top of the earth, forcibly dug into the earth. They are laid with hierarchy in mind; some disciplines have more validity than others. The bricks are held together with mortar: Western Knowledge. The final result is the wall: The Academy. In life a brick wall often blocks things, enforces boundaries. As an Indigenous person working within The Academy I often say I feel like I am hitting my head up against a brick wall; an expression of frustration and stagnation. In The Academy an HREC is often considered by research academics to be a brick wall within the brick wall; something that is perceived by many researchers to block their progress.

Colonization within Australia was contextualized through *terra nullius*. The colonizers believed that Aboriginal people had no boundaries/territory because we did not put up fences/brick walls. The colonizers assumed we did not exist. The imaging of the brick wall in this story is therefore multidimensional in meaning and context.

The final element of Lilyology is the space in-between; the space in-between Indigenous Knowings and Western Knowledge. The space where no single Knowing or Knowledge is more powerful or superior to the other; a space where both co-exist. Engaging with the in-between space is both challenging and exciting. It is a reminder that though Indigenous Knowings are different to Western Knowledge the differences exist in their own right. Through co-existence they can create powerful and dynamic dialogue and discourse leading to transformational learnings, teachings, and knowings.

This chapter storys the experiences associated with the practice of an Australian university's HREC using Lilyology as the framework. This HREC practices a methodology of attending (Bawaka Country et al., 2015. p. 272), where Lilyology was embraced as a relational framework of understanding. This can also be seen as story research practice, a storywork project. By embracing story, specifically story associated with Country through an AoC at the beginning of every meeting, the scene was set for the HREC to critically analyse ethics applications, otherwise a very traditional brick wall research practice, through a different lens. This applied to all human research ethics applications, not just those pertaining to research engaging with Indigenous Peoples and issues.

Reflection around Lilyology led me to clarify conceptual differences such as those of "Country" and "country" and "storys" and "stories" between Indigenous Knowings and Western Knowledge. There are differences associated with the concept of story; the process of storying, the expressions of storys, and how we as listeners engage with the storying process are important. I share these differences not to highlight a dichotomy between Indigenous Knowings and Western Knowledge but to showcase how looking and thinking through different philosophical lenses can lead to mis-reading and/or mis-communicating understandings. Through Lilyology, understanding the differences helps us toward the creation of powerful and dynamic dialogue and discourse leading to transformational practice and celebration through co-existence.

Archibald (2008) helped me to develop practice around Lilyology through her conceptualization of "storywork" and through her seven identified principles relating to First Nations storying. Lilyology as a concept and framework embodies all seven of these elements. As a practice, Lilyology demands that all seven principles are engaged with. It is now important as a part of this chapter's storying to identify the conceptual differences in understanding and associated practices with story, storys, storying, and stories.

Story/storying

Thomas King, a Native American Professor of Literature, states that stories are "all that we are" (King, 2003, p. 2). Storys are "the vehicles that transmit Indigenous Knowings: the flower of the waterlilys. Storys have many dimensions and perspectives; the petals on the different lilys" (Blair, 2016, p. 109). Kwaymullina (2014) powerfully captures this essence:

> I come from generations of storytellers who told tales in words, painted them in art, and sang and danced them in rhythm with the seasons and the sun and the stars. The people were one with the [storys] and the [storys] one with the people, and every tale both embodied and sustained the whole. The Indigenous peoples of the globe have always understood the universe to be a continually enfolding and unfolding place where everything holds everything else. We had no fractured [storys], until the colonisers arrived, bringing with them tales that divided people from people and people from the earth. Indigenous peoples learned to navigate these [storys] too; we had to if we wanted to survive. (Kwaymullina, 2014)

If we look at the work of HRECs, what they do is critically analyse and reflect on the different stories presented by research academics. These stories exist entirely within the brick wall. We see stories/applications bereft of connection and relatedness to Country. Once we embrace Lilyology as a framework, however, we see the stories – the applications as a part of the fractured storys Kwaymullina identifies above, especially where the applications being assessed refer to Indigenous Peoples and issues.

Hokari identifies in *Gurindji* storying what I have found to be a fundamental difference in the conception and processing of story:

> Maintaining the knowledge did not mean finding a "right" story but widening the possibilities of storys. Information of different variations is preferred, pooled and maintained as a bundle of possibilities without judgement. Different storys which contradict each other, do not conflict, but simply co-exist. (Hokari, 2003, pp. 8–9)

Western Knowledge is focused around finding a right story in response to a question. This impacts how we interact with our world, our Knowings, and our expressions of them. When we engage with oral cultures and oral Knowings we need different skills and different energies to effectively connect to cultures that engage more with written, linear text.

Learning the existing oral legacy involves intimate and endless listening to storys and dialogue with Elders and parents. This process takes time and patience. It is iterative rather than linear. The storys are told in a circular or spiral theme, with each thematic repetition or spiral adding a little. This can be contrasted with the step-by-step, linear progression of an Aristotelian argument (Youngblood Henderson, 2000, p. 266).

Engaging with Indigenous story/storying is different too in that "it takes a thousand voices to tell a story" (Wilshire, 2006, p. 160). If then there is "no right story" and people individually contribute their voices, their perspectives, ideas, and experiences as a part of this process, Indigenous storys are not simplistic. They have structure in which this array of voices harmonizes through different movements. "Storys have layers; layers that a few people may Know and more layers that everyone Knows" (Blair, 2016, p. 109).

The role of the storyteller may also be different to that in Western Knowledge and Western understandings of story. "The storyteller is often the listener at the same time as being the story teller. The story teller is often the one being spoken to" (Armstrong as cited in King, 2003, p. 2).

People often associate their own concept of and elements of stories and storytelling with Indigenous story/storying. They understand story through their different lens and for example refer to Indigenous stories as "dreamtime stories" which are fable-like – myths associated with a moral and which are purely oral. They are considered nice stories but stories that have been fabricated for one's entertainment. It is therefore critical that as a part of engaging with Lilyology we let go of the recipe we have for telling and hearing Indigenous storys and develop a new set of skills to listen respectfully in ways that engage all of our senses, those senses that we may need to truly appreciate the full effect of the "dramatic performance" stories elicit (Unaipon as cited in Bell, 1998, p. 394). We must actively engage storywork as a part of the practice associated with Lilyology. Where Lilyology embeds different metaphorical images, its practice embraces storying associated with and privileged through Indigenous Knowings. It does this in the "space in-between." This practice arguably sits within the more recently articulated discourse associated with the Indigenous research paradigm.

The Human Research Ethics Committee

Emerging from what Lilyology storys as the brick wall are various statements and policies associated with human research ethics, including the National Statement on Ethical Conduct in Human Research; the Australian Code for the Responsible Conduct of Research; and major funding agencies such as the National Health and Medical Research Council and the Australian Research Council. Engaging with research that involves Australian Aboriginal and Torres Strait Islander peoples, the AIATSIS (Australian and Torres Strait Islander Studies) (2012) ethical guidelines for conducting research in Indigenous Studies exist more specifically and emerge in association with the brick wall. These guidelines and codes of practice frame the work of HRECs in Australian universities. Though such guidelines have been designed to a certain extent to "protect" Indigenous people's engagement with and experience of research, storys such as those below highlights the need to go beyond these in terms of HRECs' practices.

As so often stated by Indigenous Peoples, we have been "researched to death" (Blair, 2015a). In an ARC-funded research project I yarned with Indigenous Peoples from one state and from one territory in Australia. People's voices from these yarns made the need for such statements, policies, and codes of practice essential to an authentic research experience that engaged Indigenous Australians and Indigenous issues.

One person said "if you want to make something dead, research it" (Blair, 2015a, p. 465). Further:

> Every time research is done a piece of my culture is ... erased. (Transcript from a yarn with an Indigenous woman in community #3. Blair, 2015a, p. 463)
>
> When I hear the word "research" my solar plexus contracts, that's my immediate physiological response. (Transcript from a yarn with an Indigenous woman in community #4. Blair, 2015a, p. 465)
>
> They want something from me, ... what do I have to give up, ... part of me feels my soul is being given away, ... it is my experience ... it is like an emotional photograph. (Transcript from a yarn with an Indigenous woman in community #4. Blair, 2015a, p. 465)

Ethics and the role of HRECs are more than principles, guidelines, and compliance. They should engage with practice that respects the voices of those above, ensuring such experiences never happen again.

I now story the practices of the HREC at the Australian University using Lilyology as a frame of reference for such practice, as a way of understanding the praxis of Lilyology. Three practices emerged from the university HREC, which embody Lilyology. First, I was initially appointed as a member of the HREC and then became the co-deputy chair, heralding Indigenous engagement in the Committee's practices. Second, an AoC became a celebrating ritual before the HREC meeting, held each month. Finally, a sub-committee of the HREC, known as the IREAP, was convened to look at all applications that engaged Indigenous Peoples and, where appropriate, Indigenous issues.

The HREC comprises a mixture of academics and external volunteers, from many different backgrounds and disciplines including law, teacher education, health, business, and religious ministry. They all bring their own unique perspectives to the Committee.

Genuine engagement of Indigenous Peoples in the institutional ethics process

The National Statement on Ethical Conduct in Human Research 2007 requires that an HREC include in its membership at "least one person who performs a pastoral care role in a community, e.g. an Aboriginal elder or minister of religion." This minimum requirement clearly sits within the brick wall of The Academy, of the framework of Western Knowledge.

In employing Lilyology as a practice this HREC has gone beyond this position and endeavoured to engage Indigenous voices in a variety of ways that impact on the space in-between. These ways include nourishing overall dialogue at HREC meetings, informing each individual member and the collective; nourishing dialogue with people in the management of HREC at the university; and of course with the researchers submitting applications for assessment.

Indigenous engagement began, as stated earlier, with my appointment to the HREC as a member. This in itself was a bold move that allowed me to learn about the requirements of human research ethics from the position of the brick wall rather than as an Aboriginal person who has been researched, and who has personally experienced all that is evil and hurtful about research practice. As my knowledge from within the brick wall grew, I developed confidence and skill, which led to my appointment as co-deputy chair of the HREC. In this in-between space, a space that is by its very nature messy and often unsettling and uncomfortable, one experience stands out. In my position in the School of Education I was charged with developing some curriculum for a specialist strand on Indigenous leadership in a Master of Education Leadership programme. A small internal funding grant enabled me to engage some Indigenous Peoples from a variety of states, settings, and professions in a project entitled "Collaborative Community Curriculum Development: Indigenous Leadership in Education." Two face-to-face yarning sessions took place, with online engagement in between the meetings. I had envisaged that we could publish key elements of the yarns as well as them forming the curriculum structure and content.

In the face-to-face yarning sessions that ensued, most of the time was spent discussing the ethics, specifically the informed consent process. Signing the existing consent form was problematic for some people. As a result, people asked the HREC to modify the consent form so that it would "acknowledge and respect the principles of shared and common partnership as a measure of reciprocity and in recognition of and respect for Aboriginal and Torres Strait Islander Knowledge systems, self-determination and accountability" (Notes: Indigenous Leadership Yarn, 2015). The HREC accepted this request and found it a useful consideration that otherwise would not have been thought of. Dialogue was nourished. The establishment of the university's IREAP was the next step and will be storyed later in this chapter.

Acknowledgement of Country

I acknowledge Country of the Cammeraygal Clan, Kurringai Nation
The spirits of the ancestors of the Country
Elders
Contemporary Custodians – this is all of us that connect and
    contact with this Country
I do this not as an act of political correctness
But as an act of connection and connecting
As an act of relatedness
Connection and relatedness to Country, to each other
Connection and relatedness through story.

As a means of connecting with you,
I share some of my story
My father was a Wakka Wakka man from south-east Queensland
His mother's father was from Camboon station in northern
    Queensland
My mother a non-Aboriginal woman from Gippsland in Victoria
I am a woman born in the Kulin nation living in Darkinjung country
    and working on Cammeraygal Country

Connecting and relating through story ...
For as Thomas King, a Native American novelist asserts, "story,
    story is all that we are"
Story not as words grouped together in lines across a page
Story as dance, performance, drawing –
All in many different mediums reflecting relatedness to Country
Drawing on rocks in Darkinjung Country north of the Hawkesbury
    River, in Cadigal Country
Drawing in sand in desert Countrys,
Drawing on bodies with ochres deep from within the earth

The Cammeraygal Country I write and speak from today has
    thousands of years of storys embedded within it
We actively contribute storys today and in the days to come
Replenishing and re-nourishing the Country with new storys whilst
Remembering old storys

An AoC such as the one in the box, expressed at the beginning of each HREC meeting, was initially done as a part of the university's protocol and as a part of my personal and cultural commitment. The AoC grew to include the story told in the preface to this chapter and it was told while people could look out the window at Sydney Harbour and ... imagine. The AoC soon became an important practice from the space in-between as embodied through Lilyology. In order to appreciate this I need to share an understanding of an AoC in an Australian context. Read the AoC above and the story told at the beginning of this chapter, which became integrated as one AoC. What is the purpose of this AoC and how is it an element of the space in-between?

This AoC acknowledges local Country and place by storying connections to Countrys that participants have associations with, by storying connections to the "memories of age-old ceremonies of celebration, initiation, and renewal practised for thousands of generations by Aboriginal people" (McKenna, 2014, p. 480). This AoC is not a traditional practice so much as a way of connecting and "joining the people of the oldest living culture in the world with others who have come from all over the globe and who continue to come" (House-Williams, 2008). It is, as Lambert-Pennington (cited in Merlan, 2014) states, a new avenue for Aboriginal representation and a "wake up" call to the possibility of new kinds of relationships forming with Indigenous Peoples and organizations (Merlan, 2014, p. 303). It is in this vein that I feel the AoC, in the context of the HREC meeting, is an element swirling around in the space in-between. It was messy; people were uncertain and even fearful, but with time and with more experience they engaged, from the heart and soul, showing respect for Indigenous Knowings, finding interrelatedness and ultimately a synergy between the AoC and the business of critically analysing human research ethics applications. Members of the HREC were able, through storying associated with the AoC, to connect and relate these storys to the process associated with assessing research ethics applications, being mindful that such storying embraced connectedness and relatedness to the self, the personal.

The AoC set the scene; it set the tone for the HREC meeting ahead. It went beyond being the "politically correct" thing to do. It privileged Indigenous Knowings – the waterlily – and though the HREC sits strongly within the brick wall, the AoC in its own way brings together Western Knowledge and Indigenous Knowings, allowing them to play and enrich each other – to nourish each other in that space where elements interact without judgement. There is synergy, one of the fundamental principles of storywork (Archibald, 2008, p. 33), where there are critical interactive relationships between the storyteller, their storying in whatever format, and the listeners – between the storyteller, the listeners, and the text of HREC applications to be reviewed. This process demonstrates respect – a further principle of storywork where members of the Committee are engaging respectfully by connecting themselves to Country, connecting their colleagues as active listeners to Country, and by contextualizing the business of the day. The storywork principle of reciprocity is also evidenced here as identified by Archibald: "I first need to understand the teachings/values of the 'old philosophies,' then apply them to my learning in the new environment of Indigenous story research, and then share this learning with others" (Archibald, 2008, p. 48).

Members of the HREC individually and collectively researched and searched for information through an AoC about an understanding of the "old philosophies" and they use these understandings to apply the learned information in the new environment of an HREC meeting: a brick wall construct. Individual members of HREC volunteered each month to research and deliver an AoC – one that had heart and spirit, and was meaningful and genuine, as Rhoda Roberts, an Aboriginal Arts advocate, believes is so important (McKenna, 2014, pp. 486–487). People storied Country where they were born and grew up; where they lived currently; and areas of interest to them personally, such as Aboriginal insights into weather, arts, plants, and astronomy. They crafted an AoC that demonstrated connection to themselves on a personal basis as well as to the business of the day (reviewing human research ethics applications). Committee members, through their AoC, connected to other members of the Committee in ways that shared new knowledge and new understandings of Indigenous Knowings in a context that engaged everyone and placed everyone in a different space and place within an understanding of Australian cultures and histories. The impact of the AoC cannot be underestimated even though this may appear to be a small step; it was one that acknowledged Indigenous Knowings authentically and genuinely.

The Indigenous Research Ethics Advisory Panel

The HREC established the IREAP. All research conducted by the university's staff or students that involves Indigenous people is referred to the IREAP for consideration. IREAP was convened by me and the Panel members – experienced external Indigenous researchers who cover a breadth of research disciplines relevant to the university – and the University's Research Ethics Manager. When researchers indicate on the online ethics form that their research involves Indigenous participants, they are asked to attach an additional document to their application. This document gives researchers the opportunity to explain how they have ensured that their research is culturally appropriate, and how they have addressed the following issues:

community approval/access (where appropriate);

reciprocity and feedback to participants/community;

awareness of local issues;

additional local ethics/other approval requirements (if required);

consent;

archiving material (where appropriate);

and Indigenous Cultural and Intellectual Property Rights.

The application, including this supporting material, is referred to IREAP to either make a recommendation to the university's HREC for approval, with or without amendments, or refer the application back to the researcher for more information or to request changes. Researchers wishing to conduct research with Indigenous participants and communities are expected to demonstrate their respect and care through familiarity with a variety of policy and protocol documents that have been made available on the HREC/IREAP website. Researchers are advised to allow sufficient time to build respectful relationships with communities and individuals, so as to enable proper engagement and obtain necessary approvals and consent.

IREAP had its first face-to-face meeting a year after its inception. The intent was to review how the practice was working and what other things could be done to effectively engage researchers in appropriately conducted research. IREAP members also attended the HREC meeting. These engagements were from a deeper place within Lilyology's space in-between. They would not have been possible without the scaffolding associated with plunging into the space in-between. Storywork practice was Lilyology's tool for connection and relatedness.

IREAP grew out of the acceptance by members of HREC of the AoC and of a greater understanding of the "old philosophies" and of a connection to these by members. Storywork research practice is evolving in the practices operating within a renewed research environment. Each of the experiences described could be seen by some as good practice in an HREC context. This is true, though it is an evolving and organic practice. Through praxis associated with Lilyology, Indigenous voices are being heard. Indigenous practice as opposed to practice that happens to be Indigenous is evolving in the space in-between two very different Knowledge and Knowing systems.

A work in progress: reflections

I began this chapter with an AoC that spoke of a mix of older and newer voices and experiences swirling in a "space in-between," transporting new ideas and practices to move research practice to more balanced and honest ground. By actively engaging different Aboriginal people in HREC practices and members of HREC in genuinely storying an AoC at the beginning of every meeting, new ideas impacted new practice. A safe space was created through the HREC to envisage and try new practices that have tried to foreground more ancient wisdom and understanding. A space was created where members and associated professional staff could begin to decolonize our minds and our practices as researchers through an engagement with storywork. The work of the HREC at this university is a work in progress, a swirling in the in-between space articulated through Lilyology. This work embodies storywork as a process central to the privileging of Indigenous Knowings, the waterlily. In Lilyology's space in-between, the storywork principles of respect, reciprocity, interrelatedness, and synergy are centrally employed.

Future storying will possibly showcase how members of HREC have taken practice associated with Lilyology in the research ethics space and used it in their own research practice. I have been able to take the philosophy crafted in Lilyology and see it bloom in practice through HREC; in practice that has made a difference and embraces co-becoming across each and all of the metaphoric elements storyed in Lilyology. This has been transformative and all associated have found their own ways to decolonize current thinking and practices as members of HREC in ways that nourish and sustain research practice.

Notes

1 Waterlilys is spelt this way throughout the chapter to embody a re-imaged concept.

2 Country refers to lands, and waters, ecosystems of both and the world of the skies above us. Country/Country's is the term I have chosen to use to describe Aboriginal Countrys, spaces, and places. It is capitalized and pluralized to give respect to our diversity. The term Country embodies ecological systems so much a part of Indigenous Knowings; it is not just limited to geographical space and place. I have chosen to spell the plural differently to embrace distinctness of concept (Blair, 2015b, p. xvii).

3 I have used the term Indigenous Knowings throughout this text to identity Indigenous knowledge as something different and distinct to Western knowledge. The word Knowing is capitalized and pluralized to reflect and respect diversity across Indigenous Countrys (Blair, 2015b, p. xv).

4 I have chosen to spell story/storys to reflect and show respect for Indigenous diversity and Indigenous Knowing of the concept of story as opposed to a Western concept of story/stories.

5 I use the term "research colleagues" referring to what academia would normally refer to as research participants. The term "research colleagues" conveys the connecting and relatedness between myself, my colleagues, and Country.

6 I choose to use the term "nations" instead of tribes to more accurately reflect the structure and complexity of our people/mobs.

7 I choose to pluralize Countrys and to spell it this way to reflect the difference in the context of Indigenous Knowings and Western knowledge.

8 I have chosen to use the term Story/Storys to reflect and show respect for Indigenous diversity and Knowing of the concept of Story. The spelling of the plural – Storys – reflects cultural distinctness of the concept (Blair, 2015b, p. xv). Storying is used here as a verb and embodies Indigenous storytelling from an Indigenous context and centre.

References

AIATSIS (2012). *Guidelines for ethical research in Australian Indigenous Studies.* Canberra, Australia. Retrieved from http://aiatsis.gov.au/sites/default/files/docs/research-and-guides/ethics/GERAIS.pdf.

Archibald, J. (2008). *Indigenous storywork: educating the heart, mind, body and spirit.* Vancouver, BC: UBC Press.

Bawaka Country, Wright, S., Suchet-Pearson, S., Lloyd, K., Burarrwanga, L., Ganambarr, R., Ganambarr-Stubbs, M. & Maymuru, D. (2015). Working with and learning from Country: decentring human author-ity. *Cultural Geographies* 22(2), 269–283.

Bell, D. (1998). *Ngarrindjeri Wurruwarrin: a world that is, was, and will be.* North Melbourne, VIC: Spinifex Press.

Blair, N. (2015a). Researched to death: Indigenous Peoples talkin' up our experiences of research. *International Review of Qualitative Research 8*(4), Winter, 463–478. doi: 10.1525/irqr.2015.8.4.463.

Blair, N. (2015b). *Privileging Australian Indigenous knowledge: sweet potatoes, spiders, waterlilys and brick walls.* Champaign, IL: Common Ground Press.

Blair, N. (2016). Australian Aboriginal knowledges and service learning. In Bartleet, B.-L., Bennett, D., Power, A. & Sunderland, N. (Eds.). (2015). *Engaging First Peoples in arts-based service learning: towards respectful and mutually beneficial educational practices* (pp. 99–117). Cham: Springer.

Buzan, T. (1997). *The mind map book.* London: Ebury Press.

Hokari, M. (2003). History happening in/between body and place: journey to the Aboriginal way of historical practice. In *Proceedings of the Habitus: A Sense of Place – Proceedings of the 2000 conference* (p. 2). Perth, WA: Curtin University of Technology, Western Australia, September, 2000. http://www.hokariminoru.org/pdfs/HistoryHappening.pdf.

House-Williams, M. (2008). *Welcome to Country: opening of the 42nd Australian Parliament.* Retrieved from http://parlinfo.aph.gov.au/parlInfo/search/display/display.w3p;query=Id%3A%22media%2Ftvprog%2FRLPP6%22.

King, T. (2003). *The truth about stories: a Native narrative.* Minneapolis, MN: University of Minnesota Press.

Kwaymullina, A. (2014). *Walking many worlds: storytelling and writing for the young.* June 30 in Diversity. Melbourne, VIC: Wheeler Centre. Retrieved from www.wheelercentre.com/notes/e221876968a8/.

McKenna, M. (2014). Tokenism or belated recognition? Welcome to Country and the emergence of Indigenous protocol in Australia, 1991–2014. *Journal of Australian Studies 38*(4), 476–489. doi: 10.1080/14443058.2014.952765.

Martin, K. (2003). Ways of knowing, ways of being and ways of doing: a theoretical framework and methods for Indigenous research and Indigenist research. *Journal of Australian Studies 27*(76), 203–214.

Merlan, F. (2014). Recent rituals of Indigenous recognition in Australia: welcome to Country. *American Anthropologist 116*(2), 296–309.

Notes: Indigenous Leadership Yarn (2015). Unpublished.

Smith, L. T. (2012). *Decolonizing methodologies: research and Indigenous Peoples.* [Kindle version]. Retrieved from www.amazon.com.

Wilshire, B. (2006). On the very idea of "a worldview" and of alternative worldviews. In F. A. Jacobs (Ed.), *Unlearning the language of conquest: scholars expose anti-Indianism in America* (pp. 160–272). Austin, TX: University of Texas Press.

Youngblood Henderson, J. (2000). Ayukpachi: empowering Aboriginal thought. In M. Battiste (Ed.), *Reclaiming Indigenous voice and vision* (pp. 248–278). Vancouver, BC: UBC Press.

13 | PUTTING THE PEOPLE BACK INTO THE COUNTRY

Victor Steffensen

Introduction

The Indigenous knowledge system is the oldest developed source of understanding humans have of the earth and its resources. Today many Aboriginal communities in Australia are attempting to revive this knowledge, following its decline from the effects of colonization. It is the old people's wish to pass their culture on to the youth, to restore wellbeing back into the people and the landscape. The urgency was seen by Indigenous Elders long before the alarm bells of climate change and the threats to the environment we know today. I share a lived story that follows a cultural grassroots initiative, which has succeeded in re-implementing this traditional knowledge in the changing world of today.

The practitioners

From a young age I grew up knowing very little about my Aboriginal heritage on my mother's side. Every time I asked her questions about it she would tell me that my grandmother never liked to talk about it. This was because of the Australian Aboriginal Protection Act that the government had enforced in earlier days. Like many people, my grandmother's family were separated and sent away to missions or placed as servants on cattle stations. All of those colonial deeds from those days led to a dramatic loss of culture and connection for many clan groups in Australia. We know all too well of the great losses from the horrific colonial history of Indigenous Peoples worldwide.

Because of this, it became my ambition to search for my culture and to learn as much as I could. From a young age the search led me to visit other clan groups in my region, connecting with Elders and communities from near and far. Two very special old men in particular were my teachers for a good period in my life. They were the late George Musgrave and Tommy George. These brothers were of the *Awu-Laya* clan from Cape York, North Queensland. I would like to acknowledge these old men as important mentors in my own working contribution to reviving culture and country.

The praction

Learning cultural knowledge is always best done when it is practised traditionally, out on the country. Living the knowledge every day happens by going out on the land, hunting, learning about the plants and animals, while caring for all the special places. I remember walking with the old people out on the land on many occasions. You had to watch the Elders doing the activities, seeing the process happen before your eyes – following them as they took the lead in nurturing their land and culture. It was the best way to learn; to live it as much as possible.

One memorable day was when my teacher unexpectedly came and tapped me on the shoulder. When I turned around he asked me if I wanted to go for a walk with him through the bush. He didn't ask anyone else in the community to go, he was intending it to be just the two of us. I instantly got prepared with our hunting gear and started to follow the old man. He was already walking towards the bush and he didn't look back once to see if I was following. I wasn't sure where we were going or what we were looking for, but I was keen to see what he had in store.

As the old man walked, he didn't say anything but gave some hand signals now and then to indicate his observations along the way. Most of the time he would be reading animal tracks in hopes of finding a wild pig or some other tasty encounter. Other times he would point out plants and different types of country that had special knowledge attached to it. Every step we took was a learning experience in how to be one with the country.

We walked and walked, and walked all day long. Over rivers and through scrub lands, we wove through the rugged landscape. I followed the old man until I could see the sun setting to mark the end of the day. It was then he finally sat down on a big old log for a small rest. I was all too happy to sit down and take a break too as it had been a very long day. I sat on the log wondering what the old man was thinking and why we were at this place.

There was a moment of silence as we sat there regathering ourselves for a moment. I began to wonder how we were going to get home in time before dark. It took all day for us to get to where we were.

Then the old man spoke, "We better go home aye." I gave a quick yes in reply but the old man stayed seated on the log silently peering through trees. He eventually said, "You go first, I'll follow you." When I heard him say those words I just froze. I didn't know the way home at all and I couldn't tell him which way either. So I took my bearings as best as I could and slowly started walking in the direction I thought to be home.

Step after step, I nervously walked. I got about ten metres when I looked around and saw the old man walking off in a different direction. I was instantly embarrassed as I watched my teacher walk off once again without looking back. I quickly gathered my pride and hurried off to follow after him. I was just starting to settle in for the long walk home when I looked up and saw something that stopped me in my tracks. Peering through the trees I could see that the town was only a few hundred metres away. He had walked me all over the country to a point where we were not far from home at all.

Once again I felt a little embarrassed but I knew that it was all part of learning from the old people and the land. On the bright side it was good that we didn't have far to go home. But I was mainly in awe of the cleverness of the old man and what he had just done for me. "You need to take notice," he said. "You need to take notice of everything." He went on to tell me how to navigate better next time, which was one of many great things he taught me that day. "You have to praction," he added. What he was telling me was to practise what he was teaching me. I didn't dare correct him for the incorrect term of praction instead of practice. Besides, I like praction better than practice because it has the action in the praction. I loved how the old people used the English language on their own terms. It was always beautiful to hear them speak their own versions of words so confidently and true.

Over the years I heard the old man say praction to me many times. Every time I heard him say that word I liked it more and more. Over time I eventually realized that it did have a meaning after all. It was the word for teaching and applying traditional practical knowledge to everything in the natural and cultural world. It was the doing of applying responsibility to our everyday activities of living with culture, people, and country. This was how the Aboriginal traditional knowledge system was refined, through learning by doing the action and the praction.

Recording the knowledge

One day, I had the opportunity to get a video camera as a way to document the traditional knowledge. It was just a basic handycam that recorded on tape; there was no tripod or microphone. It was the first time we had our hands on such technology. Even mobile phones were not around at the time. In the beginning the idea was all too new to the Elders; they didn't know what the camera was capable of. But it didn't take long before we had an amazing little traditional knowledge recording team. Rolling live in the bush, ancient wisdom, combined with modern technology.

From the earlier years of learning from these old men, I could see the video camera as being the best way to document traditional knowledge. Writing it down in the form of Western documentation was not clear enough for the complex knowledge systems. Written documentation would only make room for error, and it didn't make sense when the old people couldn't read or write themselves. With film, there was no misinterpretation from anyone else's perspective; the record came from the source itself. The Elders could view the video to see if they had got everything down right, or see if they had missed anything.

We recorded whole processes of bush craft with plants and animals from start to finish. We demonstrated the lore relating to the land, water, fire, plants, animals, and significant places. We made sure that we prepared and completed the whole process of each activity. I found that there were three vital components to the completion of applying knowledge. It came to me to present it as the knowledge triangle: a simple guide to the complete process of practical knowledge transfer. Side one is knowing what it is. Side two is knowing what it does. Side three is knowing how to do it.

Following the knowledge triangle would ensure that the activity was completed and the entire intention of the process was recorded. It is the fruits of these cultural activities that give people the ability to become a living sustainable culture. The three sides of the triangle can also align with other natural elements, like the process of creating life. For fire, it's oxygen, heat, and fuel. For people, it's oxygen, food, and water. For our entire existence it is people, earth, and spirit. If you take away one of the triangle sides, the process of creating life cannot happen. When we apply our knowledge and recording processes this way, it also becomes a living process. This is why Indigenous teaching methods are practical and are based on learning as we apply by doing the activity. Maintaining this quality of learning within our modern world is the key to reviving culture and country through Indigenous-led praction.

The knowledge map of lore

When we look at the sky, the sea, the land, and all its resources, every single living thing contains its own categories of knowledge. Within that there are many qualities that practically interconnect us to those resources in more ways than any of us can understand. The old people have a lore that says every living thing is to be respected and considered to be as important as any other. Everything has a special role and useful purpose that creates one living system. When all of the categories of knowledge are laid out into their fields, they create the form of a knowledge map.

It is through the knowledge map that all our responsibilities and relationships with the natural world and each other are made visible. I found that comparing it with cultural practices such as the use of fire showed a clear benefit for every category on the knowledge map. This ancient cultural practice has been used for thousands of years as a way to care for the country. The trees were protected, more plants grew for the animals, and our human actions were an integral part of the country's wellbeing.

In most cases of traditional tree uses, the tree does not die and is used again and again. Our actions to sustain ourselves must be connected to sustaining every other living thing we share our planet with. This shows how Indigenous people have sustainably been in tune with the whole natural system for thousands of years.

When an example of modern practice from Western society, such as mining, is compared to the knowledge map, it clearly does not benefit any of the categories except for the wellbeing of the people who owned the mine. No other category benefits but instead experiences a threat, which obviously means that a practice such as mining is not a sustainable action. Comparing human actions to the knowledge map is a simple way to see whether a modern practice is in line with natural lore.

The system of natural lore that shaped our ancestors' connection to the land is still relevant today. This lore comes from the land and unlike Western law it never changes. In fact, all of our environmental problems are caused by Western law overriding natural lore. This is why it is a real danger when law becomes more powerful than lore. It is also a clear sign that people are becoming disconnected from the land. "Law is created by man, Lore is created by Mother Earth." Reconnecting people to the system of lore is essential to the revival of cultural and environmental wellbeing.

Technology is a tool

The experience of applying the traditional transfer of knowledge in today's world has also shaped the way we use modern technology. For example, the camera was not just there to record, but more importantly to encourage the actual living praction to happen. To bring the knowledge back to its living form is the main aim of using technology. Having the knowledge restored closest to its traditional form is crucial to ensuring we are applying lore to the process of cultural revival. Knowledge was passed down and stories were kept for thousands of years without the use of modern technology. Having knowledge recorded by technology is a good thing, but having the knowledge living will always be far greater.

However, that doesn't take away the need to build on the power of film to help with the process to get the praction happening. Film can be used in multiple ways to meet the many challenges in applying traditional practices to a modern environment. Much of this work has been done by re-implementing Indigenous fire practices in many parts of Australia. The main aspiration of the Elders was to make the country and the culture healthy again by re-introducing cultural fire. But the dominance of modern governments has made it almost impossible for many clan groups to do any form of cultural land management.

This is where the camera became useful for producing films about people conducting assessments and demonstrations on the land. These case studies involve documenting the process of assessing the land and then the ongoing benefits from applying traditional fire management. Film provides an opportunity to bring the country into the meeting room and help the broader community understand a different way of managing the environment through Indigenous knowledge. Non-Indigenous people could finally begin to see the country through the eyes of the old people. They were starting to see the connection between culture and country. Furthermore, they were seeing the younger people taking the lead role and talking for country. This has made it easier to get ongoing projects and outcomes happening for the community.

Getting the young people on camera has proven to be an effective way to engage them with culture. To engage the youth has always been the aspiration of every Elder I've ever known. To achieve this I tried asking an Elder to stand behind the camera and then put a young person in front of the camera. Giving the Elder the directing role off camera suddenly gave the young people the opportunity to lead with supervision. The camera was suddenly helping the Elder to teach the younger ones the knowledge practices and information. Transformations in the young people happened before my eyes time and time again. Handing the young people cultural knowledge and responsibility was giving them an amazing energy of strength and motivation. It was helping the Elders to teach their knowledge much more easily, due to the challenges of applying their culture in the twenty-first century.

The camera, combined with living knowledge, becomes a powerful education source that helps connect the people with each other and the environment. It was always important to try to keep in mind that technology is more of a tool than a way of life. Using the tools of technology in this case is purely to inspire people to get out onto the land and practise their culture again. Ultimately, having the knowledge living again inside people results in less need to depend on technology.

It is crucial that future generations are more influenced by practical cultural practice than by technology itself. A dear elderly lady friend of mine once commented to me about this subject and said, "You can shoot for the stars, but never forget where you come from." Meaning that we could use the modern tools and technology but keep everything connected to the lore of culture and country. We do not know what effect technology may have on our children in the future.

The language of the land

The most important component that guides people through the process of lore is the land. Just as the old man said, you must take notice of the country. The country is where the knowledge comes from. The old man would look at an ecosystem and read all the indicators to determine its health. He would point out the cultural indicators that showed what the country was useful for and how it was managed. This was a language coming from the country that only trained eyes could see. Applying fire and other practices to the landscape is done by the land communicating with the custodian. Aboriginal people have perfected this technique in synergy with the environment, sustainably, for thousands of years. Traditions and culture developed with the guidance of the natural lore of the land.

Showing other Indigenous people how to read shared indicators in their own country is what really empowered the process. Sharing these principles was helping them rebuild their knowledge of their own country. It was also helping many communities see traditional fire happen on their land for the first time. They were finally experiencing the final side of the knowledge triangle that most people are having trouble with today: knowing how to do it. This was proving invaluable to the communities that had already lost much of their knowledge and Elders. It was showing that not all the knowledge was lost, but hidden away in the landscape.

The key to adapting knowledge principles from one place to another was in the trees, the soils, and the grasses. There are similarities and relationships in natural resources that can be identified all over Australia. For example you can find a Gum Tree in Northern Australia and you can find a Gum Tree in Southern Australia. They both may be different species but they are still Gum Trees. There are even more similarities within the Gum Tree communities such as similar grasses, animals, soils, and even cultural uses. This allows the principles of reading country to be transferred from one related place to another.

There are similarities within different nations or clans of people as well. Clan groups are connected from place to place, making up the special kinship system. Even though they may seem very different to each other, the foundation of natural principles and connections to the land are similar. A whole realm of shared knowledge can be activated throughout the country to help in the healing of people, culture, and the environment. If there are similarities within different people and cultures, then there will be similarities within the landscapes. What makes this possible is that all Indigenous people have evolved their knowledge from the land.

The realm of shared knowledge

When people talk about Indigenous knowledge they immediately turn their thoughts towards sensitive or sacred knowledge. But people don't seem to realize the realm of shared knowledge. This realm of knowledge comes from everyday cultural practices that are aligned with keeping the land and people healthy. They are the practices that we all have in common and are considered more as general information.

Fire strongly demonstrated the sharing of knowledge because every clan group had similar cultural aspirations when it came to reviving their traditional burning practices. To share the knowledge indicators appropriately, it needed to be done by the people themselves. Community mentoring community became the most important part of reviving cultural practices. As clan groups started to regain knowledge, they also started to become teachers. Grassroots mentorship is crucial if Indigenous projects are going to be led by Indigenous people. This strengthens and reconnects the kinship system and allows people to build cultural relationships and encourage each other. Fire becomes a contributor to strengthen the kinship between the communities culturally.

There is a fine line when you are working with communities on the subject of traditional knowledge. There are cultural protocols and lores that need to be considered that come from the people and the landscape. Even in contemporary times these traditional lores and protocols must always be the foundation for progress. It is important to understand that natural lore never changes, unlike Western law, which changes all the time.

One example is the courtesy of being invited by traditional owners to come to their country. This is the first step for dealing with the right people for the subject and place. The process of working with Indigenous people happens on their own country and is based on their own aspirations. This falls around an important protocol that only the people from that country speak for that country and for their own people.

The same lore applies for the country, which also plays a respectful part of the process. Protocol demands that we only talk about managing a certain country by standing at the actual place. This approach means that all of the workshops, assessments, and even meetings are done on the land and the place that is involved with the project. The old people always made accurate decisions based on managing a landscape culturally by reading the country. The country is the major contributor to making decisions.

In modern times shared knowledge is at risk of being exploited or colonized by non-Indigenous people. One fact from Indigenous knowledge on the subject of fire is: "When we apply the fire the right way we improve the health of animals and plants." Science will take these ancient facts from Indigenous people and make it new news. A professor will publish our knowledge and become the expert on this new exciting finding. This appropriation of knowledge has been happening to Aboriginal people since the first Settlers landed in Australia.

Scientists habitually take our knowledge and in return tell the Aboriginal people that they are trying to help them. They then patent our knowledge of fire by giving it different names, creating separate confused meanings. Taking our knowledge of fire and then calling it burning for biodiversity, or taking no notice of the land by calling it fire hazard reduction. They then come up with a name for Aboriginal fire by calling it cultural burning. The truth of the matter is that there is only one fire and that is the right fire for the country. Each fire is named after the country it comes from, like Gum Tree fire is performed on Gum Tree country. Aboriginal people burnt country for biodiversity, to protect the landscape, and for cultural reasons, all in one.

Sometimes Western scientists dispose of our knowledge, then they publish it and become the experts. Calling it another name such as burning for biodiversity allows them to continue the work without involving Aboriginal people. It is now burning for biodiversity and not cultural burning, so now it is science. Next, the scientists and their chosen institution apply for large sums of funding to further exploit their new findings. They take charge of the process and run the programmes the way they want to run them. They usually involve Aboriginal people under their own terms, which colonizes the whole process. This problem is escalating today and the worst part is that people are colonizing without even realizing that they are doing so.

The main ingredients for colonization are dispossession, dependency, and oppression, which in the old days was enforced in a very cruel and obvious way. Today it is just as dangerous but enacted in a more subtle way that affects all people from a community level. This form of colonization is happening to our knowledge today, which continues to be dispossessed, separated, and made dependent on Western management and leadership. The good will of Aboriginal people trying to repair their knowledge and country through shared knowledge is violated. It is not only Aboriginal people who need to decolonize but non-Aboriginal people as well. Non-Indigenous people will never learn from Indigenous knowledge systems and landscapes if they do not decolonize from control and conquer.

However, this can't stop Aboriginal people from continuing the important task of reviving their knowledge and country. If we do stop, it makes it easier for Western institutions to continue to take, separate, and control. This is why the shared knowledge is important to continue to mentor community after community. To ensure that everybody moves together from a grassroots approach.

The land is the boss when it comes to the wellbeing of its resources and the people. It is the land and spirit that we work for, and it is the land that tells us what to do. When this praction is conducted properly it puts everyone on the same page in understanding what needs to be done. This is where not only positive changes occurred in the Indigenous community, but significant changes within the non-Indigenous community as well. The outcome was people were culturally evolving and moving towards one knowledge system.

The power of lore

From the earlier days of just working with Indigenous people on fire, we now have the broader community attending Aboriginal fire workshops. But it wasn't easy. When we were getting our first fires happening, we faced a lot of resistance. Many of the government agencies and land holders ignored Indigenous land management and outlawed fire. Now we are seeing many sectors, from pastoralists to government agencies and private land holders getting involved.

After 20 years of Indigenous-led fire programmes many of the non-Indigenous communities were finally listening and some were getting involved to help. More workshops started to happen all over the country, all delivered the same way. That's when the magic happened, where big changes in people occurred in a single day out in the bush. The experience of reading country put everyone from different backgrounds and opinions onto the same level of understanding.

When the land was interpreted the right way through the right people, no one could argue the facts. But the most amazing thing is that most had never looked at the land from an Indigenous perspective before. Most people have only seen the land through their livelihoods or managed through a government management plan. Seeing burns demonstrated on the landscape instantly gave people an appreciation for Indigenous culture and the country. They were also finding answers on how to best manage country and that gave them a stronger connection as well.

The workshops revealed that many non-Indigenous people had a common goal to that of the Indigenous communities. Everyone wanted to see the country healthy for their future children. This shared goal provided the opportunity for people to work together, while mending strained relationships within the whole community. It was also showing government land agencies the right way to work with Indigenous people and their cultural protocols. More workshops and burns keep on happening from this flow, with Indigenous communities leading the way. Many are continuing their fire management programmes in their areas and some are servicing partnerships and contracts. The process of taking our lead from the country has proved to heal and excite everybody. Everyone was decolonizing together and it is creating incredible outcomes.

Once again it all comes back to ensuring that all the categories of the knowledge map benefit from our praction. When we heal the land, we heal ourselves. I remember one day when the old man told me how the land and people go together. If the people of the land die, the land dies with them. That is a basic but powerful indicator to oversee our overall health. When I measured this from my experiences in visiting many communities I found that it was very accurate.

Everything today is about healing

Most people don't realize that in many parts of Australia the land is very sick. There are weeds, damage from wildfires, land clearing, animals are declining, and in some places even grass is becoming scarce. When we look at the functioning community in these places, they too are not at their fullest potential. Division within the community, racism, social issues, youth problems are just a few of the problems they face. The one thing that they all have in common is that people in these places are disconnected from their land and from practising their culture. People are not looking after the country anymore and in return the country reflects the people. If people start looking after the land again there will certainly be a shift in a positive direction.

What the Indigenous fire work has demonstrated is that healing people and culture goes hand in hand with healing the landscape. The broader community and government agencies need to understand that this initiative is crucial for land and culture to survive. The broader community are part of the cycle and need to connect to the country in sync with the Indigenous communities. If they don't, then there may be less chance of a healthy country and culture for the future generations. Eventually people will have to listen to the voice of the country and start working with it together as one system.

When the first Settlers came to Australia, they saw Aboriginal people for the first time as primitive people. They didn't see any value in them, only the profits from the land. Little did they know that they were encountering people with extremely advanced knowledge systems in sync with natural lore. Since then colonization has systematically destroyed an invaluable knowledge system that has developed over thousands of years. The Indigenous knowledge system is a treasure that holds the answers to many of the social and environmental problems we all face today. It is a crucial platform with the potential to securely guide modern society for possibly thousands of years more.

Re-activating the traditional connection between people and country again will take a lot of work. When people see the scale of the problems within our environment just on fire management, many seem overwhelmed by the mammoth task. If you were to elevate yourself 100 metres from where you stand, you will see that the country stretches on for as far as the eye can see. I always say that it all starts with the work we are already doing, we have already started. Now in the year 2018, there are over 50 communities from six different states activated by Indigenous fire knowledge. There are many more communities all over Australia that are also being active within their own projects. There is so much work to do and there is enough room for everyone to get involved.

It has taken over 200 years for much of the country and culture to be destroyed. It will be even longer before we see the long-term signs of a healthier world. It took 200 years to destroy a landscape and will take double the time to replace a 400-year-old tree. The good news is that if people were to take on healing these values then greater opportunities will arise. The task of healing the landscape alone will take generations, which could help shape thousands of jobs into the future. Understanding the land more deeply can only trigger new ideas and strengthen our current practices.

The important thing about this is that looking after the country never stops. Managing the country with fire, for one, has to go on forever. Once the country is healthy, then we need to maintain it otherwise we end up back in our current circumstances. That is why Indigenous management projects need to be constantly supported; not just by government, but also by the goodwill and cultural responsibility of the communities. Supporting Aboriginal people to deliver this process to the broader community would be an important contributor to evolving a healthier social culture nationally.

It all starts with going back to step on the stepping stones that have been missed in the past. That is why the focus is on strengthening the community, for them to burn their own fires, manage their own country. It is as important for non-Indigenous people as it is for Aboriginal people to get this connection active again. Community education is also a major part of helping with today's knowledge transfer.

The Living Knowledge Place

I remember the days when I used to help the old people teach cultural and language classes at the local school. We would go to the school and walk the students through the bush, teach them craft, sing songs, and do traditional dancing. Bringing Indigenous knowledge to the children was one of the biggest priorities for Elders from just about everywhere. Education has always been a natural attraction because it has been the transition of knowledge since the beginning of time. The application of the knowledge map is based on the core of Indigenous teaching methods.

Technology could help once again to integrate Indigenous learning principals into modern educational outcomes. The idea came to create the Living Knowledge Place (www.livingknowledgeplace.com. au), an online education site structured around the mechanics of the knowledge map. The site is a shared platform intended for the people to lead cultural demonstrations and strengthen community education. Most computerized education programmes encourage the user to become deeply involved with technology and the virtual world. The Living Knowledge Place is intended to do the opposite, by encouraging the user the get off the computer and into the more traditional practical world.

The rules were to manage appropriate shared content according to the values of cultural lore. Learning always involved many teachers within traditional society, which created strong social relationships. Having community as the content delivered through modern technologies can involve hundreds of people participating as cultural leaders. This proudly motivated many practitioners, knowing that the work they were doing for their country was educating the rest of the world.

This is all part of strengthening the cultural environment for Indigenous people to continue to fulfil ambitions such as the use of fire. Applying a practice like fire needs to be supported by activating other traditional practices. A fire that does not activate other cultural perspectives and connections to the land is not the right fire. For example, burning country to grow a healthy crop of weaving grass for the women also attracted many kangaroos for hunting. Other examples have inspired the artwork of artists painting the fire knowledge into their creations. One cultural practice needs to relate and inspire another practice. Understanding how we complement each other culturally is a crucial part of activating ourselves to be in sync with the natural world.

When I look at all the projects today, I think we are slowly starting to achieve a process of re-aligning people back with the country. It is a time to reconnect people with culture to tackle the massive challenges that have been caused by its absence. Right now it is all about upskilling the younger people to learn to read country and continue the knowledge transfer into the future. If we are not doing the practices then we are not practising culture. If we are not practising culture then we are not connecting to the country. The longer we ignore these indicators the harder it will become to revive a relationship with the land that our ancestors took thousands of years to master.

We have come to an overdue point in time; we need to act now. The country is calling for the people to come back and listen to it once again. It is a time of realizing we need to act before we lose the many things we take for granted for good. As the old man said, "You have to take notice of the country, otherwise you will get lost." When we look at our reflection within the landscape today, lost we are indeed. There is a lot of work to do to overcome the impossible, but what this fire-related work shows us is that it is all possible. For community to mentor community, to help each other by putting the country first instead of ourselves. Once you have that, everything can start to move together.

14 | THE EMERGENCE OF *YARNBAR JARNGKURR* FROM INDIGENOUS HOMELANDS: A CREATIVE INDIGENOUS METHODOLOGY

Jason De Santolo

Introduction and context

Whitefella got that piece of paper – might be lease or something like that – but Yanyuwa and Garrwa mob they got to have kujika. When whitefella ask them kids how you know this country belongs to you, they can say we got the kujika. Kujika, you know, like that piece of paper. (Elder Dinny McDinny 2012)

This one is about you know we still got our languages really strong and to keep the land strong, that the land is there for us, keep it strong and for our young children future when they growing up. We teach them and when we go they hold the land strongly. And we talk and tell story. Two word for talk~story, Yarnbar Jarngkurr. (Nancy McDinny 2017)

This paper reflects upon a creative doctoral journey into the transformative power of ancient song renewal. Driven by Indigenous video practices, the creative doctorate sparked renewal of the ancient *Ngabaya walaba* (Spirit Being public songline) and mapped the re-emergence of the *Darrbarrwarra* (good warriors fighting for the land). These ancient song traditions are bound within the eternal guardianship role held by *Garrwa* over our homelands through original laws and practices.[1] Sourced in the *Yigan* (the dreaming creation), passed down through ancestors, Elders, family, clan – these vibrant cultural powers are intergenerational. They guide the enactment of our original laws and practices, they ground us as we mobilize. These songs transcend the dominion of the colonial project, but are still threatened by the ideologies and extractive systems that underpin it.

The creative doctorate reveals *Yarnbar Jarngkurr* as a resonating story continuum across the generations. In this chapter I reflect upon *Yarnbar Jarngkurr* as a journey of emergence that orientates *Garrwa* video practice into greater resonance with the Indigenous storywork principle of interrelatedness where there is a "synergistic interaction between storyteller, listener, and story" (Archibald, 2008, p. 32). The *Yarnbar Jarngkurr* study offers up a creative Indigenous methodology for community researchers, creatives, activists, and water protectors operating in complex Indigenous knowledge spaces (De Santolo, 2018).

In the quote above the late Dinny McDinny hints at the profound nature of song renewal. He was one of three visionary brothers who held strong to the cultural ways of being connected to the land, through sacred song, through the *kujika* (sacred songlines). He passed this knowledge on through the family, through ceremony, through dream – so that today we see these cultural powers driving the *Garrwa* peoples' homeland movement. In the quote above, his daughter, Elder Nancy McDinny (my kinship mother) reflects on *Yarnbar Jarngkurr* as key to conceptualizing meaning-making in a research agenda, emphasizing the importance of revitalizing language for protecting land.

Garrwa people are subject to the disastrous ongoing impacts of mining and this lived experience was a key driver for the framing of the study. The Northern Territory (NT) is rich in minerals and other resources. Of all the mining developments in NT, fracking has been the most contentious. Despite clear evidence of the dangers of fracking the NT Labor Government lifted a moratorium in April 2018. This action was met with widespread outrage and mass mobilizations that condemned Chief Minister Gunner. The division within his own party gave weight to the demands for clean water and a ban on all fracking (Robson, 2018). Ongoing threats to the region are overwhelming as multinational interests in gas (fracking), zinc, uranium, and other extractives heightens into a frenzied level of neoliberal activity.

Impacts from mining reached a new height in April 2018 when Water Contamination notices were delivered to *Garrwa* families. This was only days after the lifting of the fracking moratorium. The NT Health Department letters to residents of *Garrwa* Town Camps in Borroloola essentially confirmed the poisoning of *Garrwa* and *Yanyuwa* children and families (Hoosan, 2018). As a *Garrwa* leader and a father living in these Town Camps, Gadrian Hoosan is demanding answers: what happens when our relational integrity is fractured, when water is no longer life, when water is death?

Yarnbar Jarngkurr evokes storytelling strategies for shielding people and homelands from the poisonous impacts of mining. Due to the sacred and political aspect of the doctoral investigation, the study revealed deep decolonizing knowledge-sharing protocols as enhanced research video practices. I propose that Indigenous story research strategically engages with, renews, and communicates *Garrwa* cultural powers as interrelational enactments of self-determination and homeland autonomy. By enacting *Yarnbar Jarngkurr* the study expands understandings of these cultural powers, asserting that songs have a shielding force against the ongoing encroachment of the colonial project. The *Ngabaya* and *Darrbarrwarra* videos are framed as visual and aural sovereign expressions that exist both within and outside Western legal paradigms (Raheja, 2010; Koch, 2013). Despite the limitations of the academic context, *Yarnbar Jarngkurr* emerges as a family-driven decolonizing methodology with principles and working protocols for community research, creative, activist, and water protector contexts.

Conceptualization

The scope of the study was strengthened through a deep consultation with *Garrwa* and *Yanyuwa* community members. This included Elders, senior knowledge guardians, the Sandridge Band members, community and youth leaders, and extended family (De Santolo, 2015). Visiting Elders is an essential part of the story research; it is part of the renewal process for maintaining relationships. Working in my tribal homelands and community has given the project huge energy and meaning for me personally and for all of my other family and children. Our language is used with the highest respect as this is part of my own decolonizing knowledge journey.

Garrwa is not a written language yet. It has been studied in specific linguistic texts (Mushin, 2012) and other community resources that are not as widely published.[2] I entered into this study knowing that there are still many ways to write and spell as *Garrwa* potentially unfolds into more of a written language. For this reason, the textual component has ambiguities in spelling and in the use of terms that span language groups. A good example is the *Ngabaya* song tradition, which Elders attribute to being *Garrwa* but has been touched up in *Yanyuwa* and also spans a number of clan areas. *Garrwa* voices have been privileged and everyday terms have been used as much as possible, despite some inconsistencies identified in some previous research. In maintaining protocol, the Elders guide revitalizing strategies and processes.

Indigenous stories are often about collective thinking and survival. Some ancient song traditions hold profound lessons for maintaining a balance and harmony with the natural order. Many of the research stories emerging now are also about survival, but in different realms and systems that were not present before colonization. These stories often have a more sharpened, liberational intent – a self-determination that is in line with our own cultural understandings and political aspirations. In the absence of a treaty or autonomy framework, the United Nations Declaration on the Rights of Indigenous Peoples is a good baseline for self-determination in Australia.

The *Darrbarrwarra* song is also significant as a study of consultative and compositional processes that are regionally inspired. The *Darrbarrwarra* dancers, for example, are *Garrwa* and *Yanyuwa* predominantly, but all four tribes are represented in the videos through family ties and kinship links. The dances were inspired not only by the *Ngabaya* dance but also by the oral resistance histories and fighting strategies and shielding practices of our ancestors. There is almost a prophetic moment in the emergence of the shielding song. This year has heightened the genocidal threats to *Garrwa* society through the contaminated water crisis in *Borroloola* Town Camps. These threats involve all peoples in the Gulf – our fates are intertwined with those of the water and our homelands.

The layers of intent behind song renewal

Garrwa Elders have chosen to renew the *Ngabaya* songline at a crucial time in the history of *Garrwa*. There is multilayered intent behind the strategy to reveal these teachings now. Reconnecting with the beauty and power of these ancient discourses is one of the exciting outcomes of this story research process. The doctoral journey has helped to shape principles and protocols for compositional and design processes involved in the renewal of these songs and the sharing of these through Indigenous video practice. I use the term "story research process" as it emphasizes story as a core aspect of the research process and acknowledges the scholarly vision of Indigenous story-work (Archibald, 2008). Paradoxically, the sharing of these songs has powerful shielding capabilities for sacred sites and homelands. The study explored deeper understanding of these transformative shielding powers as strategies to revitalize language and protect homelands. Elders and senior cultural leaders have acted as guardians of culture and land. They are both collaborators and mentors in this story research process. Elders have steered the process of story research and continue to determine when knowledge is ready to be shared and determined as meaningful (Sherwood, 2010, pp. 137–138). For *Garrwa* Elders shielding is also about communicating sustainable autonomy as an overt challenge to extractive industries in the Northern Territory, where exploration licences cover 84.9 per cent of the entire landmass (Kerins, 2017a, 2017b).

The *Ngabaya* is one of the oldest and most powerful of our song traditions. As a public songline, with many cycles, it carries stories of creation and important teachings about how to conduct ourselves and live in harmony with all living beings. The songlines still hold cultural powers that can be harnessed to protect and shield homelands. In most cases there is little real-world context provided in the performance or sharing of ancient Indigenous stories of country or through media. This means that they are often celebrated without an understanding of the genuine threats posed to the very places where these songlines travel.

Yarnbar Jarngkurr is an appropriate praxis for the story research process. It emerges as part of a creatively framed decolonizing methodology that is deeply relational (Archibald, 2008; Smith, 2015; Wilson, 2008). It creatively engages Indigenous participatory video through a trajectory of film collaboration and the place-based decolonizing lens of *Yarnbar Jarngkurr* (Salazar & Córdova, 2008). There is more to the framing of a story methodology that is grounded in the everyday practices of talking and storytelling. In seeking to harmonize creative practices with Indigenous knowledge systems the emergent methodology shifts perceptions of the extraordinary laws, protocols, and beliefs held within vibrant, interconnected *Garrwa* storyworlds.

Living with two laws

Garrwa people have long recognized the duality of law and the often conflicting paradigms imposed on us through the colonial project in Australia. The story of colonialism is often masked to hide away the ongoing violence and oppression of Indigenous Peoples in Australia (Wright, 2016). The experience of living with two laws was powerfully enacted in the landmark documentary *Two Laws*, which was filmed over a number of years and released in 1981. *Two Laws* shared the story of historical injustice in the South West Gulf through a "proper way" that still resonates with the *Borroloola* community today (Cavadini & Strachlan, 1981; De Santolo, 2008, 2014). *Two Laws* strived towards

Elder-controlled production processes as co-producers, effectively creating a paradigm shift in documentary making (Ginsburg, 2008). The very premise of *Two Laws* is key to understanding the framing of the video studies as an exploration of Indigenous jurisprudence and legal pluralism. This experience set a benchmark for some *Garrwa* Elders, who now approach knowledge-sharing collaborations with caution, especially if they do not feel in control or respected in the process.

The doctoral journey asserted that renewal reimagines songline logic; a logic that taps into the creational and cultural powers of song as ancient interrelational jurisprudence. As such it also aligns with other ancient story ways and specifically with Jo-ann Archibald's foundational theory of methodology and pedagogy – Indigenous storywork. Indigenous storywork embodies seven principles: respect, responsibility, reciprocity, reverence, holism, interrelatedness, and synergy (Archibald, 2008, p. 140). Indigenous storytelling is at the heart of the creative doctorate as it navigates story research principles as interrelational dimensions of video (Archibald, 2008, p. 111). The moving image enacts interrelationality in significant ways today. It is clear to the Elders that music and video are very popular aspects of youth culture today. With youth so engaged with Facebook and YouTube it is important that revitalizing strategies also reach them in new meaning-making spaces.[3] Songlines on Screen is the strongest broadcast reflection of this as a collaboration between National Indigenous TV and Screen Australia Indigenous Unit. In this collaboration, eight songline film projects were funded and aired from remote regions of the continent (National Indigenous TV, 2016). If we all strive to see and hear the story in context with the storyteller, then there is much potential to explore in terms of the role of video in intergenerational transmission of knowledge.

A decolonizing journey

If our truths are held within the land and through our languages, then our collaborations must hold true to the modalities that bring that to light. Indigeneity in the academic world is about interconnectedness and the liberation of our own semiotic resources that have been tied down and rendered powerless through a colonizing lens (Rigney, 1997). In response, Indigenous theories are emerging as liberational strategies to survive the policies and impacts of colonial governments and neoliberal economic systems (Pihama, 2015).

This scholarly activism has been driven in part by the decolonizing research movement and in particular by the enactment of decolonizing methodologies (Hemming et al., 2016; Pihama, 2015; Sherwood, 2010; Smith, 1999). Indigenous research is still finding recognition in academic circles, yet there are huge implications from its fluid and organic growth as the work in this area often has no disciplinary bounds. Rather, Indigenous renaissance is tied to a global movement that reclaims our narratives, authority, and autonomy from within an Indigenous self-determination framework (Behrendt, 2016; Moreton-Robinson, 2015). To simplify the theory, one might describe it as a way of understanding a phenomenon, or relationships between two concepts/things (Maxwell, 2005, p. 49). This study emerged from this transdisciplinary context and sits within a broader Indigenous research paradigm (Pihama, 2015; Wilson, 2008) of Indigenous storywork (Archibald, 2008, p. 153; Lee, 2015).

At the same time, we are witnessing a renaissance in storytelling and teaching that is vibrant, relational, and deeply connected to the land (Archibald, 2008; Lee, 2015). It is not just about revitalizing Indigenous languages through a reinvigorated understanding our own epistemologies and ontologies. Decolonizing journeys are also fundamentally about action and striving for self-determination and autonomy in a constantly renewing interrelational context. This is also evoked through a deep self-reflection and analytical struggle to maintain disciplinary relevance. There is a question here – do we as "native thinkers" have a role in the translation of our own experiences in the world as cultural artefacts (Salmond, 2013)? There are multiple reasons why we do and should – but one clear strategy is the need for a decolonizing framework to map research processes as a journeyed experience into meaning-making.

This is an age of new writing, in which the recognition of inequalities of communication, power, and perspective are understood as part of a more conscious movement for change and social justice. Talking in our own languages is a political act in Australia, where the educational policies in the Northern Territory outlawed bilingual models in the mid-1990s (De Santolo, 2008). The idea that different cultures find meaning in different ways is not in question. Rather, to interrogate unequal power relations within the colonial project we need to shift the way we analyse and conceptualize meaning as it exists in dominant communication paradigms (van Leeuwen, 1999). This is proving to be a difficult task, especially in light of the constantly shifting media landscapes and the hierarchical bureaucracies that drive those media. These landscapes are now highly pervasive and influential through social media.

Our Elders still hold our languages and our laws are still enacted, mediated, and celebrated. Appointed cultural leaders still hold the *kujika* (our sacred songlines) and these stay alive through ceremonies and the embodied memories of the guardians of these lands. These resonating stories are best described using super vital language (Bradley, 2010, p. 251) – that is the *kujika* and the myriad of relationships, emanations, and enactments around which our songs of creation come into being.

To reflect on this means to understand the meaning-making potential of enactments in context of country and as an outwards story practice, with or without specific intent. This study is unique in that the Elders and the Sandridge Band have a clear, courageous intention to revitalize language and protect the land from mining and development. This *Garrwa* worldmaking prowess is birthed from before time, of the land and sky. Our worldmaking prowess derives from deeply interrelational stories that are highly sophisticated yet organic and enacted through ceremony, story, and now beyond known realms and into the media matrix. Extending these notions into video allows for a new positioning of these ancient songs as expressions of visual and aural sovereignty and as maximum-autonomy pathways to self-determination.

Like other *Garrwa* cultural leaders before him, Gadrian Hoosan describes the *Yigan* as the source of all life for *Garrwa* and the other clans of the Gulf country (De Santolo, 2018). As a *Garrwa* leader and activist, Gadrian Hoosan explains the importance of keeping culture alive as a foundational aim of *Garrwa* self-determination:

> When the white people came to this country, we had our own autonomy. We had our own laws and our leaders. Our ancestors went through so much, a history of being treated cruelly, or shot. But our ancestors have kept this culture alive, and now our elders they pass it on to our kids. If we lose that, we are nothing. (De Santolo, 2018)

As one of the Sandridge Band leaders, his work with Elders (alongside Bruce King, Scott McDinny, and Conrad Rory) has forged a whole new body of work that is deeply inspired by culture and language.

There are strong *Garrwa* epistemological and ontological insights at play here. At one level, the idea of creating music videos is one that explores the implications of presenting ancient songlines of the land within Western formatted spaces. At another level it is about the representation of *Garrwa* society within the music video domain that is dominated by pop trends and cults of celebrity. All too often we have witnessed the recontextualization of our knowledge systems and worldviews into storied myths or legends, often by racist Eurocentric modalities. Yet according to these renewal processes our ancient teachings and cultural practices will always survive the trends of the West.

Our own languages, story practices, and laws are critical in the fluid and organic expression of our political aspirations. Romaine Moreton has poetically inspired us as emerging scholars to "believe in the Dreaming, not as a past concept, but a current, ongoing, unstoppable force" (Moreton, 2006, p. 42). A deep relational sophistication is at the heart of these aspirations, a profound relationality that has grown with the land over many thousands of years and been kept alive through stories, songs, dances, painting, and ceremony. *Garrwa Yarnbar Jarngkurr* is the voices and stories that shape renewal of the relational world through song, dance, ceremony, and ancient practices of the land. It is offered as a central motif in exploring the transformative potential of storying Indigenous resurgence in our homelands and the shielding of *Garrwa* homelands, waters, and sacred sites against extractive industries and interventionist policies (such as the racist NT Intervention) through actions, strategic alliances, and the revitalization of languages and cultural practices. The NT Intervention is an extreme example of overarching racist government policy that oppresses Aboriginal people in NT and makes it very difficult to enjoy basic citizenship rights and land and resources that were returned through land rights.

This study continues this legacy by opening up space for *Yarnbar Jarngkurr* to emerge as a creative Indigenous methodology grounded in *Garrwa* concepts, thinking, actions, and story practices. *Yarnbar Jarngkurr* is also about the everyday practices of talking and telling stories. There are many ways to share and access stories these days and many of us also choose a creative practice (such as video) as a secondary source (Archibald, 2008, p. 111). In the process of returning to my family homelands I have contributed to the making of short videos about our resistance histories; about our movement to protect our homelands; and about the revitalization of our languages and traditions. The *Ngabaya* and *Darrbarrwarra* videos extend this body of work at a deeper level of song renewal and through this story research are able to offer unique insights into filmmaking processes, techniques, and video technologies.

Video plays a big part in today's technologically mediated world; it is one of the communication keys for reconnecting and sharing values, experiences, and teachings for generations to come. Younger generations are experiencing many aspects of life mediated through story platforms and technologies. These platforms shape the way we relate to certain things and add layers of meaning that I am sure were not contemplated pre-invasion. These powerful new meaning-making ecologies present new challenges to Indigenous families and societies as they often impose hierarchical values and Western worldviews.

Māori scholar and activist Leonie Pihama asserts *Kaupapa Māori* theory is derived from organic *Māori* movements (such as *kōhanga reo* and language revitalization), and the organic nature of the theory determines that it can be articulated in many ways and is therefore not singular in nature (Pihama, 2015, p. 13). This can be expressed more profoundly as a key aspect in the essence of seeking life, resonance, and a relational reality for all Indigenous Peoples (Cayete, 1994). If the logic behind theorizing is driven by an eternal need to create a model or map of why the world is the way it is (Maxwell, 2005), then Indigenous theories must reflect the local worldviews and knowledge practices of the people within that world. Aileen Moreton-Robinson offers powerful insights into the unique epistemological aspects of Indigenous sovereignty in the Australian context (Moreton-Robinson, 2004, p. 5). So it made sense in this study to use theory derived from the original sources of life, knowledge, and meaning-making for *Garrwa*.

Indigenous scholars and practitioners have historically struggled to operate in universities with predominantly Eurocentric value systems at their core. I know I certainly have struggled. In this journey I was very fortunate to meet in person, collaborate, and discover the synergy with Jo-ann Archibald's visionary "Indigenous storywork" and Jenny Lee-Morgan's *pūrākau* – Māori storytelling. Their deeply generous and groundbreaking research offered a theoretical framing and storied experience of the challenges involved in renewing ancient song traditions. Meeting and working on this book collaboration with Jo-ann and Jenny gave strength and clarity to the study, for which I am very grateful. Archibald masterfully weaves "the design of a *Stó:lō* and Coast *Salish* storytelling basket based on the storywork teachings of respect, responsibility, reciprocity, reverence, holism, interrelatedness, and synergy" (Archibald, 2008). Jenny's groundbreaking work illuminates a pathway in understanding *pūrākau* (Māori storytelling) as pedagogy, allowing for an emergent space that "re-presenting *pūrākau* as peda-gogy, re-portraying *pūrākau*, re-creating *pūrākau* as political, re-telling *pūrākau* as provocation, re-storing *pūrākau* as powerful" (Lee, 2015).

In many ways the conceptualization, composition, design, and edit-ing of the videos is like storywork weaving, especially on entering the writing phase of a creative doctorate. Indigenous storywork offers an important allied framework for story research process and in the emer-gence of *Yarnbar Jarngkurr* principles. Many of us in the Indigenous world believe story is integral to survival. Story is recognized as part of the fluidity of our ways of engaging knowledge and story (Archibald, 2008). Pihama also equates navigational expertise with a range of com-plex sciences, asserting that "ancestors have always theorised about our world" (Pihama, 2015, p. 6). This study is an act of survivance and an expression of the vitality that is expressed through song and dance.

In conceptualizing the Doctorate of Creative Arts project within the community, there was significant emphasis on the importance of song and music as a uniting force for the clans of the regional home-lands. Relationality is a fundamental essence of talking and storying and what is communicated through the practice of enacting these song traditions. Some of the analytical aspects of the study were real-ized through dialogue with this important notion as it interacts with *Yarnbar Jarngkurr*. In Australia each tribe or clan generally holds sig-nificant, discrete, interwoven expressions of knowledge, language, law, and practice. Speaking from a *Garrwa* position, we hold ancient laws and ceremonies, and with that a profound connection and authority within our world through the *kujika* and the continual enactment of what we could term a songline logic. *Kujika* are like scriptures, they hold immense creation powers as ecological depositories and profound mapping of the land through the super vital language of the songlines (Bradley, 2010, p. 251). This is a very old way of understanding and theorizing the world; a world that has been under immense threat since the violent colonization of *Garrwa* territories around 200 years ago (Roberts, 2005).

As I grew to learn, trust and draw upon my own *Garrwa* teachings in language and law, unique *Yarnbar Jarngkurr* principles of enactment emerged. The top level principles formed the basis for the theoretical innovation in my study. As an emerging framework of creative research principles, *Yarnbar Jarngkurr* offers transformative potential for enacting *Garrwa* Elders' aims to revitalize language and protect homelands. This doctoral journey grounded Indigenous theorizing firmly within an Indigenous research paradigm and also extended into the creative music video domain through the lens of *Yarnbar Jarngkurr*. In this study I dedicated significant effort to being grounded and in tune with the Elders as senior *jungkayi* and knowledge holders; it is part of the learning and enactment of our law to offer this respect. Going deeper into the knowledge journey has been very humbling, especially in the process of learning more of my language and law through yarning (yarning circles), *Dardirri* (deep listening) (Atkinson, 2002), painting, and being on country (co-becoming).[4]

If revitalization is a key reason for sharing knowledge, then it must have a strong emphasis on effective intergenerational transmission of knowledge. What role and form should video take in revitalizing language as a creative research practice? There are clear pedagogical implications for this work in terms of understanding renewal in its broadest sense (Lee, 2015). The story research study shed light on the transdisciplinary nature of Indigenous research and the potential of relational collaboration by unpacking the importance of meaning-making and truth modalities as analytical elements of a decolonizing framework. Moving beyond outdated understandings of the way we form meaning helps to reveal and unlock the transformational power of revitalizing Indigenous languages.

A decolonizing methodology

The process of creating two meaningful videos required significant time with Elders and the Sandridge Band members, on country and in story research spaces where we talked, listened, and shared (Archibald, 2008). Each music video has interrelated contexts to explore in terms of conceptualization, design, composition, performance, and production (van Leeuwen, 2011). Storying, knowing, mapping, and protecting the land is at the heart of the *Ngabaya* and *Darrbarrwarra* stories.

In revealing layers of meaning, *Yarnbar Jarngkurr* perceives meaning-making as a spiralling process, as reflected in Elders' ways of teaching through story and action (Bradley, 2010; Archibald, 2008, p. 1; Sherwood, 2010, p. 143). Story research involves important processes for respecting existing localized Indigenous research principles and video protocols. The interactive and reflexive process shifted my own creative research practice and also informed the development of story and knowledge-sharing principles and protocols unique to the study.

With the *Garrwa* language in danger of extinction, key methodological principles and communicative protocols have aligned with the revitalization of language through assertion of our original laws and as an enactment of resurgent cultural powers to shield homelands from mining. These principles have strong alignments with Indigenous storywork principles (Archibald, 2008), decolonizing methodologies (Pihama, 2015; Smith, 1999), and broad Indigenous video practice principles and protocols (Janke, 2009; Langton, 1993). This study acknowledges the influence of this foundational work and extends this revitalization work into a specific *Garrwa Yarnbar Jarngkurr* context of renewal.

These principles are informed by deeper conceptualizations of *Garrwa* story and Elders' aims to revitalize culture and shield and protect homelands. In conversation with Elders and band members we decided that one way to understand and share this way of renewal is through the naming of the process, and so it was named *Yarnbar Jarngkurr*. As a communicative protocol it also acts as a practice-driven guide to the creation of the videos while shaping meaning-making processes within the story research journey. Embedded within *Yarnbar Jarngkurr* is a story research methodology with three key interrelated foundational principles: *Darrbarrwarra, Karja Murku*, and *Ngirakar*.

Story research principles

Story research principles emerged as cultural, relational, and liberational principles for this study. The working elements involve action and the weaving of meanings together through the story research process of *Yarnbar Jarngkurr*. These fluid concepts connect the story with a research process led by *Garrwa*-protocol Indigenous video. *Darrbarrwarra* is a term that has been used in a number of yarns and actions that focus on the warriors who fight for the land. As a *Garrwa* term it encapsulates all generations and is not gender specific. It therefore aligns somewhat with certain parts of the *Ngabaya* song tradition where men and women dance together. At a higher level it evokes the *Darrbarrwarra* journey as one of eternal guardianship. This role is embodied in the role of *jungkayi*, as holders and enforcers of law, the lawyers or managers for the *ngimirringki*, or owners of the land. The phrase *Garrwa Jungkayi Ngarra Ngarra Darrbarrwarra* used by Elders has been abbreviated here to poetically express the key principle of the eternal good warrior or *Darrbarrwarra* as Warriors Eternal.

Karja Murku emerged at the height of the protests and rallies taking place in 2014–2016. To start with it was a respectful and excited term that named all of the people who came together for a specific liberational purpose. The biggest mob of people came together in September 2015 for the Our Land Is Life protest in Darwin, the capital city of the Northern Territory. The anti-fracking protest, led by Frack Free NT, was groundbreaking in the way it brought traditional owners from 15 different communities together with pastoralists, tourism operators, and environmental and Indigenous activists. The video used for the protest features *Ngabaya* and other footage from Sandridge outstation and the protests in *Borroloola*.

A huge contingent of *Garrwa* and other *Borroloola* mobs came to this and showed great strength and leadership on horseback and at the front line of the protests in front of Parliament House. Allies and accomplices also came from as far away as Sydney and Palmerston North in Aotearoa New Zealand. The Elders termed this *Karja Murku* when referring to countrymen or our relations from across NT. The Elders referred to *Murnkiji* – our skin name relations.[5] From there the phrase *Murnkiji Murku Karja Murku* emerged – for all of our relations in the struggle to protect the land and keep culture strong (Tuiono & De Santolo, 2018).

Ngirakar has been used in different contexts to mean power, energy, or powerful. Throughout this study there were quiet moments of reflection and storytelling over cups of tea. This often involved long sessions where Elders painted and discussed stories and shared teachings. Many of the paintings involved resistance histories or warriors fighting for the land. Characters are often depicted using traditional war strategies and weaponry. The shielding of lands was something that emerged from discussions around the use of *ngarri*, an old battle strategy, and other cultural powers afforded to songs and weapons. *Ngirakar Bununu* emerged both as a metaphoric expression of the shielding force of cultural practices and a historical honouring of the ancestors and warriors who fought so hard to protect the land. It is now a new dance that emerged from the *Darrbarrwarra* music video storyworld. These moments of reflection and storying were vital in the spiralling of meaning that takes place as Elders share stories and knowledge and celebrate victorious histories. In a way this reflects a cyclical praxis that leads towards greater consciousness of the story in various contexts.

Working elements of relational collaboration

Yarnbar Jarngkurr emerges from these deeply grounded principles and contexts and as such holds a theoretical fluidity that suits the specific terrain (Smith, 2015, p. 26). If *Yarnbar Jarngkurr* is to remain responsive to the everyday practices of talk/story, it must also have the potential to merge with other specific projects or relational collaboration frameworks and protocols. As a creative Indigenous methodology, *Yarnbar Jarngkurr* strategically aligns with *Garrwa* principles, laws, and ancient practices of autonomous sustainability and has vast potential within relational collaboration and international rights-driven contexts (Tuiono & De Santolo, 2018). There are also clear synergies with transdisciplinary work and thinking that poetically inspire a (trans) forming of being (Gibbs, 2017, pp. 54–55). These frameworks can be thematically broken down into working elements for story research collaboration, beginning with conceptualization, and followed by intent, orientation, relationality, and enactment. As working elements, they describe and map methodological processes and creative actions that weave *Yarnbar Jarngkurr* principles together. As critical elements for consideration they activate and realize the transformative potential of *Darrbarrwarra, Karja Murku,* and *Ngirakar* principles. In practice these elements are explored alongside ethical frameworks and creative protocols that seek to enhance project processes and outcomes for Indigenous Peoples.

Weaving together action and meaning-making

In the study I reflected upon the importance of meaning-making as a contextual extension of songline logic. This illustrates the dialectical relationship between theory and practice and informed a blended analytical framework and praxis throughout the study (Smith, 2015). *Yarnbar Jarngkurr* principles and working elements are at the core of this study yet it also demanded robust analysis of multimodal texts and jurisprudential discourses. In light of this challenge I drew significantly upon multimodal discourse analysis through the critical lens of social semiotic theory (van Leeuwen, 2016). This was done in the understanding that analysis of the song tradition involves methods to reveal aesthetic and production choices that are or are not available according to socialization and binding *Garrwa* laws and protocols. As an example, there are clear rules around who to consult for different aspects of design, and there are strong boundaries around who performs, where it is filmed, who is present, what can be in the shot, what frame is appropriate and what colouring and references are necessary to convey certain aspects of the song.

This interplay offers a rhythmic key to understanding how *Garrwa* Elders mediate authority and enact original laws within holistic kinship ecologies that span across the Gulf country region and beyond. In seeking greater understanding of this rhythmic key through song renewal I also explored van Leeuwen's proposition that sound unifies. How do these knowledge systems connect and how does merged meaning occur in a robust dialogue that extends beyond Indigenous knowledge paradigms and into social semiotic multimodal theory (van Leeuwen, 1999, p. 196)? Van Leeuwen suggests that analysing rhythm:

> provides the framework with which the signs of other semiotic modes are aligned and rhythm is also the physical substratum, the sine qua non of all human action. Everything we do has to be rhythmical and in all our interactions we synchronise with others as finely as musical instruments in an orchestra. (van Leeuwen, 2011, p. 677)

Rhythm also reaches across distance as we listen, dance, and move to the same music, but at times, in different spatial configurations. The different time scales also reflect rhythms and relationship ecologies on grander scales, such as those reflected in the seasons. The act of making music or listening to it has a rhythmic interplay that by nature is "a form of social interaction, and the relations of power and solidarity that are created by musical interaction are a primary source of musical meaning" (van Leeuwen, 2012, p. 322). According to van Leeuwen there are "cross-modal rhythmic relationships" in film (van Leeuwen, 2011, p. 173) and it is this rhythm that plays a key role in creating cohesion and meaningful structure (van Leeuwen, 2012). It is this deeper approach to speech, music and sound, and the courageous work of calling out racist discourses that led me to incorporate aspects of multimodal analysis into the analytical framework.

Enactment and song as ancient jurisprudence

We are witnessing an unprecedented resurgence of Indigenous movements around the world. Idle No More, Standing Rock, and *Mauna Kea* have all grown from the desire to protect sacred sites and homeland territories through the assertion of original laws and cultural rights as framed in an Indigenous jurisprudential paradigm. These understandings are sourced in ceremony and held within the sacred nature of many of our songs and practices. *Darrbarrwarra* is a relational collaboration with *Yuin* producer Nooky, who created the beats. This was an intentional expression of respect from *Garrwa* on the understanding that this song, and its production, performance/distribution through this project potentially lies to the east, away from our territories. By showing that respect we have built strong connections that resonate across our territories through the songs' rhythm and the story research process. The study explored the resonant jurisprudence of Indigenous song and the design and production choices as they align with Indigenous worldviews on communicating authority and visual and aural sovereignty. In moving into the Indigenous jurisprudence realm we reveal *Garrwa* ways of communicating relationships to the land as a means to inform self-determining frameworks of legal plurality (Behrendt, 2003; Te Kotahi Research Institute, 2017) and the aspirations of an unstoppable sustainable homeland autonomy movement as expressed in the *Ngabaya* and *Darrbarrwarra* videos. *Yarnbar Jarngkurr* takes up the challenge of innovating Indigenous self-determination discourses by creating expression media as enactments of visual and aural sovereignty.

Conclusion

Yarnbar Jarngkurr was a momentous personal and political journey of emergence that documented *Garrwa* resurgence and renewal. It has orientated *Garrwa* video practice into greater resonance with the Indigenous storywork principle of interrelatedness (Archibald, 2008, p. 32). As a creative Indigenous methodology *Yarnbar Jarngkurr* emerges with potential applications for community researchers, creatives, activists, and water protectors operating in complex Indigenous knowledge spaces. For *Garrwa* it is a strategic enactment of our ancient laws and role as guardians and it is our eternal story. In this moment, as our children and families are being poisoned by contaminated water, it proudly reflects a story of *Garrwa* resurgence that seeks life and shields homelands, for

When water is poison we rise.
When water is poison we unite.
When water is poison we fight or die. (Hoosan, 2018)

Notes

1 *Garrwa* homelands are in the South West Gulf country of what is now known as the Northern Territory (NT) of Australia.

2 For example, the Gulf Country Songbook is a musicology project that includes text, audio, and video of songs from *Yanyuwa, Garrwa, Marra*, and *Gudanji* (Reiderer, 2015).

3 Popular music can now only be fully experienced alongside a music video and sites like YouTube harness huge audiences; for example, Luis Fonsi's "Despacito" ft. Daddy Yankee, launched in January 2017, is the most viewed video to date, reaching 4.3 billion views by November 2017, www.youtube.com/watch?v=kJQP7kiw5Fk. Facebook also plays a significant role, reflected in the term "sacred FB" coined by Aunty Pua Case in her keynote address at He Manawa Whenua 2017, where she asserted that music will play a key role in the rise of Indigenous resurgence movements around the world, www.youtube.com/watch?v=A-BVnkE9lcM.

4 Yarning circles are a commonly used method for talking and listening and honouring many voices in the discussion and exploration of Indigenous experiences and ways of doing things. Deep listening is also an important aspect of dialogue for Indigenous people and *darrdirri* is a well-documented way of doing this (Atkinson, 2002). There are emerging fields and discourses which talk about co-becoming and post-human contexts; even though this is of relevance the scope of the study limited further exploration of these bodies of work.

5 Bradley and MacKinlay (2000) did significant research into *Yanyuwa* and *Garrwa* song traditions and elaborated on the profound relational concept of *Ngalki*, which has layers of meaning including tune and essence and "presents the Yanyuwa way of making sense of complex relationship between the people who make music, the process of music-making and the sound which music makes." Elders have referred to this as a word for skin as part of the broader skin name relationship concept.

References

Archibald, J. (2008). *Indigenous storywork: educating the heart, mind and body and spirit*. Vancouver, BC: UBC Press.

Atkinson, J. (2002). *Trauma trails, recreating songlines: the transgenerational effects of trauma in Indigenous Australia*. Melbourne, VIC: Spinifex Press.

Behrendt, L. (2003). *Achieving social justice: Indigenous rights and Australia's future*. Sydney, NSW: Federation Press.

Behrendt, L. (2016). *Finding Eliza: power and colonial storytelling*. Brisbane, QLD: University of Queensland Press.

Bradley, J. (2010). *Singing saltwater country: journey to the songlines of*

Carpentaria. Sydney, NSW: Allen & Unwin.

Bradley, J. & MacKinlay, E. (2000). Songs from a plastic water rat: an introduction to the musical traditions of the Yanyuwa community of the southwest Gulf of Carpentaria. *Ngulaig 17*, 43–45.

Cavadini, A. & Strachlan, C. (1981). *Two Laws*. Sydney, NSW: Smart Street Films.

Cayete, G. (1994). *Look to the mountain*. Durango, CO: Kivaki Press.

De Santolo, J. (2008). *Two laws: notes on resonance*. Kanymarda Yuwa/Two Laws – Special DVD Dossier. *Studies in Documentary Film 2*(2), 185–189.

De Santolo, J. (Director/Producer). (2014). *West to east*. Documentary, NITV. Retrieved from https://vimeo.com/104358468.

De Santolo, J. (2015). *Conceptualising research and consultation within a creative doctorate*. International Indigenous Development Research Conference 2014, Conference Proceedings, Auckland, Aotearoa/NZ. Nga Pae o Te Maramatanga, University of Auckland.

De Santolo, J. (2018). *Towards understanding the renewal of ancient song traditions through Garrwa video: an Indigenous story research study*. Exegesis submitted in partial fulfillment of requirements for award of the degree Doctor of Creative Arts. Sydney, NSW: Faculty of Arts and Social Sciences, University of Technology Sydney. Retreived from http://hdl.handle.net/10453/127979.

Gibbs, P. (2017). Transdisciplinary thinking: pedagogy for complexity. In P. Gibbs (Ed.), *Transdisciplinary higher education: a theoretical basis revealed in practice*. Cham: Springer International.

Ginsburg, F. (2008). *Breaking the law with Two Laws: reflections on a paradigm shift*. Kanymarda Yuwa/Two Laws – Special DVD Dossier. *Studies in Documentary Film 2*(2), 169–174.

Hemming, S. J et al. (2016). Speaking as Country: a Ngarrindjeri methodology of transformative engagement. *Ngiya: Talk the Law 5*, 22–46.

Hoosan, G. (2014). The land is the most important thing for Indigenous people. *The Guardian* (Australia). Retrieved from www.theguardian.com/commentisfree/2014/oct/10/gadrian-hoosan-the-land-is-the-most-important-thing-for-indigenous-people.

Hoosan, G. (2018). *When water is death*. Indigenous X Australia. Retrieved from https://indigenousx.com.au/gadrian-hoosan-when-water-is-death/.

Janke, T. (2009). *Pathways and protocols*. Screen Australia. Retrieved from www.screenaustralia.gov.au/getmedia/16e5ade3-bbca-4db2-a433-94bcd4c45434/Pathways-and-Protocols.

Kerins, S. (2017a). *We never ceded our countries*. Poster for an exhibition by Jacky Green, Therese Ritchie and Sean Kerins, Northern Centre for Contemporary Art, 5–28 August 2017, Darwin.

Kerins, S. (2017b), *Open cut: life on an Australian frontier 150*. Melbourne: Arena Magazine.

Koch, G. (2013). *We have the song, so we have the land: song and ceremony as proof of ownership in Aboriginal and Torres Strait Islander land claims*. AIATSIS Research Discussion Paper No. 33, Canberra, AIATSIS.

Langton, M. (1993). *"Well, I heard it on the radio and I saw it on the television": an essay for the Australian Film and Television Commission on the politics and aesthetics of filmmaking by and about Aboriginal persons and things.* Sydney: Australian Film Commission.

Lee, J. (2015). *Ako: pūrākau as pedagogy.* Tuia te Ako Conference Te Kete Ika, 9 July, Canterbury, Lincoln University.

Maxwell, J. A. (2005). *Qualitative research design: an interactive approach* (2nd ed.). Thousand Oaks, CA: Sage.

Moreton, R. (2006). *The right to dream.* PHD thesis. Sydney: University of Western Sydney.

Moreton-Robinson, A. (2004). The possessive logic of patriarchal white sovereignty: the High Court and the Yorta Yorta decision. *Borderlands* e-journal, University of NSW, Sydney.

Moreton-Robinson, A. (2015). *The white possessive: property, power and Indigenous sovereignty.* Minneapolis, MN: University of Minnesota Press.

Mushin, Ilana. (2012). *A grammar of (Western) Garrwa.* Boston, MA: De Gruyter Mouton.

National Indigenous TV. (2016). *Songlines on screen: learn Indigenous Australian creation stories – "Songlines on Screen" multimedia features.* NITV/Screen Australia.

Pihama, L. (2015). *Kaupapa Māori theory: transforming theory in Aotearoa.* Hamilton, New Zealand: Te Kotahi Reader, University of Waikato.

Raheja, M. (2010). *Reservation reelism: redfacing, visual sovereignty, and representations of Native Americans in film.* Lincoln, NE: University of Nebraska Press.

Reiderer, K. (2015). *Gulf country songbook,* (Yanyuwa, Marra Garrwa, and Gudanji families). Borroloola, NT: Waralungku Arts.

Rigney, L. (1997). Internationalisation of an Indigenous anti-colonial cultural critique of research methodologies: a guide to Indigenist research methodology and its principles in the *Journal for Native American Studies. WICAZO Review 14*(2), Fall edition, 109–121.

Roberts, T. (2005). *Frontier justice: a history of the Gulf country to 1900.* Brisbane, QLD: University of Queensland Press.

Robson, P. (2018), Communities protest NT government's betrayal on fracking. *Green Left Weekly,* Sydney. Retrieved from www. greenleft.org.au/node/65828.

Salazar, J. & Córdova, A. (2008). Imperfect media and the poetics of Indigenous video in Latin America. in P. Wilson and M. Stewart (Eds.), *Global Indigenous media: cultures, poetics, and politics* (pp. 39–57). Durham, NC: Duke University Press.

Salmond, A. (2013). Transforming translations (part 1). *HAU: Journal of Ethnographic Theory 3*(3), 1–32.

Sherwood, J. (2010). *Do no harm: decolonising Aboriginal health research.* PhD Thesis. University of New South Wales.

Smith, G. H. (2015). *The dialectic relation of theory and practice in the development of Kaupapa Māori praxis.* Hamilton, New Zealand: Te Kotahi Research Institute, University of Waikato.

Smith, L. (1999). *Decolonizing methodologies: research and Indigenous Peoples.* London: Zed Books.

Te Kotahi Research Institute. (2017). *Moana Jackson Keynote: He Manawa Whenua Te Kotahi Research Institute, University of Waikato* [Video File]. Retrieved from www.youtube.com/ watch?v=zV2PoRbBQsM.

Tuiono, T. & De Santolo, J. (2018, forthcoming). *Relational*

collaboration. Joint Paper at He
Manawa Whenua Conference 2017,
Hamilton, New Zealand, Te Kotahi
Research Institute, University of
Waikato.

Van Leeuwen, T. (1999). *Speech, music,
sound*. London: Palgrave Macmillan.

Van Leeuwen, T. (2011). Multimodality.
In J. Simpson (Ed.). *The Routledge
Handbook of Applied Linguistics*
(pp. 668–682). Abingdon: Routledge.

Van Leeuwen, T. (2012), Multimodality and
rhythm. In C. A. Chapelle (Ed.), *The

Encyclopedia of Applied Linguistics*.
Oxford: John Wiley and Sons.

Van Leeuwen, T. (2016). A social semiotic
theory of synesthesia? A discussion
paper. *Hermes: Journal of Language
and Communication in Business 55*,
105–120.

Wilson, S. (2008). *Research is ceremony:
Indigenous research methods*. Black
Point, NS: Fernwood Publishing.

Wright, A. (2016). What happens when
you tell somebody else's story?
Meanjin 75(4), 58–75.

AUTHOR BIOGRAPHIES

Jo-ann Archibald
Q'um Q'um Xiiem
Jo-ann is from the *Stó:lō* and *St'at'imc* First Nations in British Columbia, Canada. She is a Professor Emeritus in the Department of Educational Studies at the Faculty of Education, University of British Columbia. She was the former Associate Dean Indigenous Education and the director of NITEP (Indigenous Education Program). She received a Bachelor of Education (BEd) degree from the University of British Columbia, a Master of Education (MEd) degree and Doctor of Philosophy (PhD) degree from Simon Fraser University. Jo-ann's scholarship relates to Indigenous knowledge systems, storywork/oral tradition, transformative education at all levels, Indigenous educational history, teacher and graduate education, and Indigenous methodologies. Over a 45-year educational career, Jo-ann has been a school teacher, a curriculum developer, a university administrator, and professor. She is also a very proud mother, grandmother, and auntie.

Larissa Behrendt
Distinguished Professor Larissa Behrendt is a *Eualayai/Gamillaroi* woman who holds the Chair of Indigenous Research at the Jumbunna Institute of Indigenous Education and Research at the University of Technology, Sydney. She is a graduate of the University of New South Wales and Harvard Law School. She has published numerous textbooks on Indigenous legal issues. She is an award-winning novelist and filmmaker. Her most recent book is *Finding Eliza: Power and Colonial Storytelling* (2016).

Nerida Blair
Nerida was born in the *Kulin* Nation, lives in *Darkinjung* Country on the Central Coast of New South Wales and until recently worked in *Kuringai* Country at the Australian Catholic University. Nerida Blair Consultants is the new gateway for engaging Nerida's passions. Nerida has spent three decades working in universities in New South Wales and Victoria and over one decade in the Public Service Canberra; Department of Education, Department of Foreign Affairs and with the Human Rights and Equal

Opportunity Commission in Sydney. Education is her passion, believing education is the most powerful tool that Indigenous Peoples have to fully engage in a safe and fulfilling lifestyle; education that is participatory, imagined, creative, holistic, sensual, and story-based.

Donna Campbell

Ngā Puhi, Ngāti Ruanui
Donna is an artist, lecturer and researcher in Māori Creative Practice at the Faculty of Māori and Indigenous Studies at the University of Waikato. She is a passionate practitioner in the field of *raranga* (weaving), creating sculptural garments for the body. Donna has worked on many community projects and continues to align with projects that interweave artists, practitioners, and researchers. She is a passionate advocate of the fibre arts as pathways to well-being and continues to extend the current discourse of Māori fibre arts practice in Aotearoa.

Hayley Marama Cavino

Ngāti Whitikaupeka, Ngāti Pūkenga, Pākehā
Hayley is of Māori and *Pākehā* (English) descent. She holds a PhD (Sociology of Education) and CAS (Women's and Gender Studies) from Syracuse University (Syracuse, NY), Master's and Bachelor's degrees in Psychology from the University of Waikato (New Zealand). Hayley is a previous recipient of the New Zealand Psychological Society James Ritchie Fellowship for Contributions to the Development of Bi-Cultural Research, Syracuse University School of Education Creative Research Grant, New Zealand Health Research Council Postgraduate Fellowship (facilitated through Te Atawhai o Te Ao Independent Research Unit for Environment & Health – He Kokonga Whare program), and the Ithaca College Dissertation Diversity Fellowship in Women's and Gender Studies. She is currently an adjunct professor in Women's and Gender Studies and Native American and Indigenous Studies at Syracuse University where she is especially grateful to teach, mentor, learn from, and hold space with *Haudenosaunee* and other Indigenous students. When not at home in Aotearoa she lives on occupied Onondaga Territory with her partner and three boys.

Dorothy Christian

Dorothy Christian *Cucw-la7* is a visual storyteller, writer, and editor who is from the *Secwepemc* and *Syilx* Nations of British Columbia. Dr Christian completed her PhD in early 2017 at the Department of Educational Studies, University of British Columbia. Her dissertation "Gathering Knowledge:

Visual Storytellers and Indigenous Storywork" links land, story, and cultural protocols. Her MA thesis, "A 'Cinema of Sovereignty': Working in the Cultural Interface to Create a Model for Fourth World Film and Pre-production and Aesthetics" was completed in 2010. Her graduate work examines the role of culture in Indigenous film production practices. Her publications include: co-editor of *Downstream: Reimagining Water* (2017); co-author of the chapter "Unmapping Watershed Mind" in *Thinking with Water* (2013); the chapter "Reconciling with the People and the Land" in *Cultivating Canada: Reconciliation through the Lens of Cultural Diversity* (2011); and co-author of the chapter "History of a Friendship" in *Alliances: Re/Envisioning Indigenous and Non-Indigenous Relationships* (2010).

Evelyn Araluen Corr

Evelyn Araluen Corr was born and raised in *Dharug* country and community with ancestral and language roots to the *Bundjalung* Nation. She is a poet, educator, and PhD candidate working with Indigenous literatures at the University of Sydney. Her research is concerned with anticolonial and decolonial literary practices, contemporary Aboriginal women's literature, and the relationship between Aboriginal literature and colonial archives. In 2017 she was awarded the Nakata Brophy Prize for Young Indigenous Writers, and in 2018 she was awarded the Judith Wright Poetry Prize. She is a co-coordinator of Black Rhymes Aboriginal Poetry Nights in Redfern.

Sara Florence Davidson

Sara Florence Davidson is a *Haida* educator and Assistant Professor in the Teacher Education Department at the University of the Fraser Valley in British Columbia. She has a PhD in Language and Literacy Education from the University of British Columbia, and her research interests include Indigenous education and storytelling; literacy education; culturally responsive teaching and research practices, with a focus on Indigenous and qualitative methodologies; and narrative writing and research. For nearly a decade, Sara worked in the K-12 system with upper intermediate and high school students in rural British Columbia and the Yukon as well as adult learners wishing to upgrade their education.

Jason De Santolo

Garrwa, Barunggum

Jason is a researcher, creative producer, and father committed to striving for Indigenous self-determination and liberation. Born in *Larrakia* homelands, Darwin, he moved to Aotearoa New Zealand at an early age, growing up to eventually study treaty and international environmental law. On graduation he trained as a researcher at the International Research Institute for Māori and Indigenous Education at the University of Auckland. His unique research practice integrates video, creative practice, and story shielding through a *Garrwa*-driven paradigm of liberation. In 2018 he completed a creative doctorate exploring the renewal of ancient song traditions through video. Jason is currently Associate Professor of Design in the School of Design, University of Technology Sydney (UTS) and was previously Senior Researcher at Jumbunna Institute for Indigenous Education and Research UTS.

Hineitimoana Greensill

Tainui, Ngāti Koata, Ngāti Porou
Hineitimoana is a Senior Lecturer in Te Pua Wānanga ki te Ao, Faculty of Māori and Indigenous Studies at the University of Waikato. She researches and teaches at the intersections of Māori language, *mātauranga* Māori, Māori and Indigenous studies, and *mana wahine*, or Māori feminist discourses. Hineitimoana was also a part of the *Tiakina Te Pā Harakeke* project, which looked at the ways in which culturally grounded knowledge, values, and practices can be better employed to enhance the well-being of Māori children and *whānau*.

Carwyn Jones

Ngāti Kahungunu
Carwyn Jones is a Senior Lecturer in the Faculty of Law at Victoria University of Wellington. His primary research interests relate to the Treaty of Waitangi and Indigenous legal traditions. Carwyn has previously worked in a number of different roles at the Waitangi Tribunal, Māori Land Court, and the Office of Treaty Settlements. He is the author of *New Treaty, New Tradition: Reconciling New Zealand and Māori Law* (2016), co-editor of the *Māori Law Review* and an associate director of the New Zealand Centre for Public Law.

Jenny Bol Jun Lee-Morgan

Waikato-Tainui, Ngāti Mahuta
Dr Lee-Morgan is Professor of Māori Research, Te Wānanga o Wairaka, Unitec. Her Māori tribal affiliations are to *Waikato-Tainui*. Her doctoral study "Ako: *Pūrākau* of Māori Teachers' Work in Secondary Schools" (2008)

was seminal in the methodological development of *pūrākau* as narrative inquiry. Formerly a Māori secondary school teacher, Dr Lee-Morgan is a senior *Kaupapa Māori* researcher whose work focuses in the areas of Māori education, Māori language, and Māori housing. In 2016, she was awarded the Te Tohu Pae Tāwhiti Award by the New Zealand Association for Research in Education in recognition for her high-quality research and significant contribution to the Māori education sector. Her most recent co-edited book *Decolonisation in Aotearoa: Education, Research and Practice* (2016) presents a broad decolonized agenda for Māori development. She is also a mother of seven, and a grandmother.

Georgina Martin

Georgina Martin is an Indigenous scholar and community member that is committed to honouring her community and ancestors. She is *Secwepemc* (*Shuswap*) and a member of the Lake Babine Nation (*Carrier*). Dr Martin grew up alongside her grandparents in the *T'exelc* community in British Columbia, Canada. Her approaches centre on Indigenous knowledge in her teaching, methodologies, and research approaches. As a professor in First Nations Studies, she combines her lived-experience, community-based knowledge, and Indigenous ways of knowing while seeking to enhance relations between university and community. Dr Martin's research agenda builds upon her PhD research titled *Drumming My Way Home: An Intergenerational Narrative Inquiry about Secwepemc Identities* that examined the stories of three generations of *Secwepemc* peoples to show how knowing oneself strengthens identities.

Cynthia Nicol

Cynthia Nicol is an Associate Professor in the Department of Curriculum and Pedagogy at the University of British Columbia's Faculty of Education. Of Settler ancestry, living and teaching in British Columbia's Pacific Northwest instilled deep connections between land, community, culture, and mathematics. Her projects keep her connected to the place and people of *Haida Gwaii* where she is working with communities to explore the nature, possibilities, and challenges of living culturally responsive education and research. Her research interests include teacher education, mathematics education, Indigenous education, refugee studies, place-based and community-based education, and culturally responsive teaching, ethics, and research practices.

Leonie Pihama

Te Ātiawa, Ngā Māhanga a Tairi, Ngāti Māhanga
Associate Professor Leonie Pihama is a mother of six and a grandmother of five. Leonie is an Associate Professor and the Director of Te Kotahi Research Institute at the University of Waikato. She is a leading *kaupapa Māori* educator and researcher who has extensive expertise connecting her to a wide range of Māori and international Indigenous communities. Leonie was a recipient of the Hohua Tūtengaehe Post-Doctoral Research Fellowship (Health Research Council), and was a Fulbright Senior Māori Scholar with the University of Washington. In 2015, she was awarded the New Zealand Association for Research in Education (NZARE) 'Te Tohu Pae Tāwhiti Award', for excellence in Māori Educational Research. Te Kotahi Research Institute was awarded the 2017 NZARE Group Research Award and the 2018 'Te Tohu Rapuora – Māori Health Research Leadership, Excellence, and Contribution Award' from the Health Research Council. Leonie is currently the Ngā Pou Senior Māori Health Research Fellow, and is Principal Investigator on a range of national collaborations with Māori communities and organizations.

Joeliee Seed-Pihama

Taranaki, Te Atiawa, Ngāruahine, Waikato
Joeliee is an emerging *Kaupapa Māori* researcher with an interest and passion for Māori ancestral knowledge, storytelling, and language. Joeliee recently completed a PhD in Māori and Indigenous Studies at the University of Waikato in 2017. Joeliee has a broad range of experience across several sectors and specialist areas. Currently, Joeliee leads a project for Te Whāriki Takapou, a *Kaupapa Māori* sexual and reproductive health organization, which seeks to create and implement *Kaupapa Māori* sexuality education for and with total immersion Māori-language schools in Aotearoa. She is also currently employed as a research officer for Te Kotahi Research Institute at the University of Waikato where she is working on a Te Taura Whiri i te Reo Māori funded project looking at the subjective motivations of organizations that use and promote *te reo Māori*.

Victor Steffensen

Victor Steffensen is a *Tagalaka* descendant from Far North Queensland of Australia. His works specialize in the application of traditional knowledge for the wellbeing of cultural and environmental wellbeing. He has developed the practice of influencing traditional teachings with many Elders from related clan groups within his region. With a powerful combination of filmmaking, writing, and musician skills, Victor has succeeded the many challenges of applying traditional knowledge values to a changing world. This has lead to the opportunity of working with many people and cultures in developing their own aspirations all over Australia and other parts of the world. Throughout Australia Victor plays a strong role as an Indigenous fire practitioner and continues to influence Indigenous and non-Indigenous people with his practice. As a motivator and speaker he is driven by a vision to see Indigenous Peoples take their rightful place as land managers and as equal and active participants in future Australian and international programmes.

Jean William

Elder Jean William is the cultural advisor and member of the *Secwepemc* Nation in British Columbia, Canada. She was born in the *T'exelc* community in BC, and she was raised by her grandparents. Through listening to the stories of the Elders in her community, she was inspired by their teachings and she became knowledgeable about the traditional practices. Jean is committed to preserving, protecting, and sharing her traditional knowledge with future generations. Jean taught in the Williams Lake School District in British Columbia for 17 years. She later returned to university and graduated in 2003 with her Bachelor of General Studies from Simon Fraser University. Since then, she has proactively provided guidance through her role as cultural advisor in her community for several treaty and resource-based projects. Her support includes researching, collecting, and recording the Elders' stories to identify place names. She is a fluent speaker of the language and teaches *Secwepemcstin* for the Little Chiefs Day Care in her community.

Joanne Yovanovich

Joanne Yovanovich was born and raised in the *Ts'aahl* Eagle Clan of Skidegate on *Haida Gwaii*, British Columbia, Canada. Her *Haida* name is *Taanud Jaad*. She has worked with School District #50 in *Haida Gwaii* since 1995. Joanne began working as the Full Day Kindergarten teacher and Vice-Principal, then she became the Principal of Sk'aadgaa Naay Elementary School. Currently she has the position of Principal of Aboriginal Education. She is rooted in her community and the place of *Haida Gwaii*. Joanne strives to connect the worlds of cultural and school knowledge. She is deeply committed to make a difference in student success rates on *Haida Gwaii.* Joanne believes that culturally responsive education is a key to student success. Culturally responsive education can be transformative, inspiring, and validating for students and staff that embrace and practise the philosophy.

INDEX

Note: page numbers followed by *n* indicate an endnote with relevant number.